W9-CBH-847

No Regrets

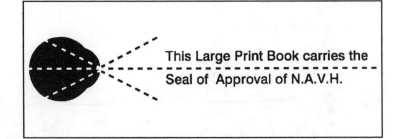

This Large Print Book carries the
Seal of Approval of N.A.V.H.

NO REGRETS

And Other True Cases

ANN RULE'S CRIME FILES: VOL. 11

ANN RULE

THORNDIKE PRESS

An imprint of Thomson Gale, a part of The Thomson Corporation

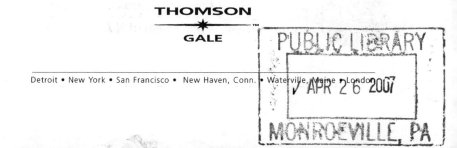

THOMSON

GALE ™

Detroit • New York • San Francisco • New Haven, Conn. • Waterville, Maine • London

THOMSON

✷ ™

GALE

Library of Congress Control Number: 2006935803

ISBN 10: 0-7862-9067-6
ISBN 13: 978-0-7862-9067-3

Published in 2007 in arrangement with Pocket Books,
a division of Simon & Schuster, Inc.

Printed in the United States of America on permanent paper
10 9 8 7 6 5 4 3 2 1

*To the Puget Sound Pilots'
Association, which has provided
safe passage through Northwest
waterways for ships, their
passengers, and their crews
since 1935. They take care of
their own — never more so than
in their long search for the old
man who was a pilot on the
Sound for more than forty years.
He guided hundreds
of ships safely into port; when
he himself was lost, the Puget
Sound pilots were the first to
sound the alarm.*

ACKNOWLEDGMENTS

Readers and other writers often ask me how and where I research the details for my true-crime books. I must admit that I start each book with the sure knowledge that I will never discover enough to reveal all the facets of the cases I choose. But I have learned to plunge in, semisecure that I will find the public records I need, and that those who were involved in the investigation and prosecution of suspects and witnesses will talk with me. I go to the places where the often-shocking events took place, take photographs (the blurriest photos in the picture section are almost always mine), and talk to the people who lived through the cases.

In the end — at least so far — I find I do have a book, after all. And I sincerely thank those who have shared their memories with me, memories that many would choose not to access again. So many people went out of their way to help me in this book. I hope they know how much their input has meant to me!

Six different cases make up *No Regrets*. The names that follow begin with "The Sea Captain" and continue in the order of the half dozen cases.

Thank you to: San Juan County Deputy Sheriff (retired) Ray Clever, Barbara Clever, San Juan County Deputy Sheriff (retired) Joe Caputo, San Juan County Prosecuting Attorney (Criminal) Charlie Silverman, Washington State Supreme Court Judge Greg Canova, Dr. Robert Keppel, Superior Court Clerks Mary Jean Cahail, Connie Burns, and Karen King, San Juan Historical Society, Jan Fleming, Kris DayVincent, authors Al Cummings, John Saul, Michael Sack, Gordon Keith, Captain Richard Mc-Curdy, President, Puget Sound Pilots' Association, Blood Pattern Expert Rod Englert, juror number one, Lisa Boyd, Frances Bacon, the *San Juan Journal,* the *Seattle Weekly,* the *Seattle Times,* the *Seattle Post-Intelligencer.*

"It (Ain't) Hard Out There for the Pimps." During my days as a Seattle police officer, I worked beside the Crimes Against Persons Unit's detectives. They relived this remarkable investigation for me: Joyce Johnson, Noreen Skagen, Beryl Thompson, Pat Lamphere, John Nordlund, Larry Gordon, and Danny Melton. As an author, I rode shotgun with the Seattle Fire Department's Medic One paramedics for forty-eight hours. I learned how they can make the difference between life and death — as they did in this case!

"The Runaway and the Soldier." Thanks to the Bellevue Police Department, this case that began with scattered human remains was solved. The investigators went over the case with me: Chief of Police Don Van Blaricom and Detectives Roy Gleason, Gary Trent, Marv Skeen, and Patrol Officer Bob Littlejohn.

"The Tragic Ending of a Bank Robber's Fantasy." The Seattle Police Department's Homicide Unit worked around the clock to find a killer who was escaping to paradise. My gratitude to George Marberg, Al Gerdes, Gary Fowler, Nat Crawford, John Gray, Bob Holter, Al "Beans" Lima, Jerry Yates, John Nordlund, Mike Tando, John Boatman, and Don Cameron.

"A Very Bad Christmas." This story comes from the Multnomah County Sheriff's Office in Portland, Oregon. Detective Orlando "Blackie" Yazzolino of the Homicide Division related it to me, and Robert Pinnick and Bob Zion of the Scientific Investigation

9

Unit told me about how they preserved the physical evidence that helped to identify both the victims and the killer.

"To Save Their Souls." My appreciation goes to Detective Archie Pittman of the Pasco Police Department for his trial testimony, and to the late Dorothy Allison of Nutley, New Jersey, whose psychic visions were stunningly accurate.

". . . Or We'll Kill You." My appreciation goes to "Kari," who had the courage to tell me the story of her terrifying brush with death as the victim of a kidnapping and sexual attack.

In this, the eleventh edition of my Crime Files, I continue my fortunate association with the team that helps me get the words from my computer into a real live book: my publisher, who believes in me, Louise Burke; my editor Mitchell Ivers, who edits so gently and diplomatically, but effectively, that my writer's pride emerges unscathed; Josh Martino, perhaps the most efficient and dependable editorial assistant in publishing; Felice Javit, the patient attorney who "has my back" on legal issues; my publicist Melissa Gramstad; production editor Stephen Llano; and art director Lisa Litwack.

I depend on Gerry Brittingham Hay, my

"first reader," who grabs my manuscript while it is still smoking from the printer, reads it immediately, and tells me unflinchingly whether it holds her interest — or not. She has packed hundreds of pages to take on her vacations, to the beauty parlor, and to read by flashlight. Thanks, Gerry!

To the only literary agents I've ever had. All on a handshake, we began a completely symbiotic relationship. I appreciate them more with every book: Joan and Joe Foley.

I've been very lucky to have the support of my children throughout the writing years: Laura, Leslie, Andy, Mike, and Bruce. The younger generation is growing. Beyond Rebecca, Matthew, Olivia, and Tyra, we have two new additions: Logan and Miya Dawn.

While I have been hunched over my computer, my garden and house have been saved from falling apart by Kevin Wagner, Matt Parker, Justin Robison, and Perry Wilson. And, last, I must acknowledge a whole new support group, which appeared almost magically on the guestbook of my website pages at www.annrules.com. The ARFs (who came up with their own name for "Ann Rule Fans") are an extremely lively group who welcome newcomers. They are also Ann Rule *Friends!* Please come and visit.

CONTENTS

PREFACE

Most of us have made decisions that we wish we could go back and change. Sometimes it is for something we have done and then again, we may regret something we should have done and didn't. "Conscience doth make cowards of us all," Shakespeare once wrote, and like scores of the Bard's quotes that have stood the test of time, this is as true today as it was hundreds of years ago. Even if we are the only ones who know our secrets, that little voice inside reminds us. That nagging voice brings back memories that are painful to people who have empathy for others' feelings and who do have consciences. But not everyone does. For some, yesterday is gone and entirely forgettable, the slate is wiped clean, and they never look back. Some of the most horrifying crimes I have ever chronicled were committed by people for whom another's life is no more important than that of a flea or a crushed rose.

In *No Regrets,* I write about a number of murderers who didn't feel at all sorry for what they did to further their own purposes, but I also tell some heart-wrenching stories of people who had profound regret. They could technically be called killers, although I believe they suffered more than their "victims." There are even a few cases here where one might say the so-called victims reaped grim rewards they deserved. Over the many years I have written about actual criminal cases, I have learned that there is nothing about any homicide that can be taken for granted. Just as human behavior is unpredictable, so are the many views of each murder. Like snowflakes, no two cases are just alike, and some are shockingly unique.

I have written more than a thousand articles and twenty-six books about murder. I have never forgotten any of them, although I must admit that sometimes names escape me. This is Volume 11 of my Crime Files series. Only those stories that have stood the test of time make the cut when I'm selecting cases.

That is true for "The Sea Captain," the book-length case that comes first, and for all the shorter cases that follow:

"It (Ain't) Hard Out There for the Pimps," "The Runaway and the Soldier," "The

16

Tragic Ending of a Bank Robber's Fantasy," "A Very Bad Christmas," "To Save Their Souls," and ". . . Or We'll Kill You."

A few of these cases reduced me to tears, and, frankly, some frightened me. Even though a number of years have passed since I first heard their details played out in courtrooms, it hasn't been easy to live through them again. My own emotional reactions came tumbling back as I visited them once more, surprising me with their intensity. There are other cases here that I knew of, but had never before researched or written. And one came to me through an email after I had already started writing this book.

In the end, there were myriad motivations that sparked murder: greed, lust, jealousy, naked masochism, fulfillment of fantasy, insanity, and — strangely — even love.

THE SEA CAPTAIN

Sometimes it takes a hundred years or more for a true story to be told and retold so often that it is eventually tinged with enough rumors and unsubstantiated "facts" to make it barely distinguishable from fiction. Long-ago murder cases have been transformed into ghost stories, and real homicides become folk tales, both categories so often repeated that it's hard to know what to believe. A very few move rapidly into the folklore category. The case that follows is one of those. It isn't that old in years, but the bizarre circumstances of the case made it prime material for half-truth/half-fiction: the identities of the victim and the purported killer, the isolated location of the crime, the modus operandi, and the lingering mystery that continues to this day.

Although there is nothing vaguely humorous about the disappearance of eighty-year-old ship's marine pilot Captain Rolf Neslund, his vanishing into the mists of Washington State's Lopez Island in the Strait of Juan de Fuca is the stuff of urban legend. Some people found this story comical, while others were sickened by the rumors of what might have happened.

Rolf Neslund made headlines several times in his long life, and he had more close friends than most men. He appeared to be utterly indestructible: a man who would go on forever — the kind of guy who would surely appear one day in his local newspaper blowing out a hundred candles on a birthday cake. But if Captain Rolf is blowing out enough candles to start a fire, he isn't doing it on Lopez Island.

For all of his life, Rolf Neslund had been extraordinarily lucky, escaping death or serious injury any number of times. It would seem that he had paid his dues in life and certainly deserved the quiet pastoral life he enjoyed in his eighth decade.

No one knows for sure where Rolf is, although a court of law has ruled that he is, indeed, dead. And well he may be, possibly from homicidal violence.

ONE

Even his actual birthdate has a sense of mystery about it. However, most people agree that Rolf Neslund was born at the turn of the twentieth century on November 3, 1900, in Konigsborg, Norway, far away from Lopez Island. His family's business was in shipping, and Rolf was one of three sons: Harald, Erling, and Rolf. There was a single sister — Eugenie. Any formal schooling for him was abbreviated, taking a backseat to his craving for adventure. Rolf, a strong, handsome kid who appeared older than he was, ran away to sea at the age of fourteen.

He soon found a job on a brigantine trader named *Staatsraad Ericksen.* He stayed for six months — until the ocean began to feel more like work than a place for excitement. The young teen ran away again, leaving the *Staatsraad Ericksen* behind. Although he was devoted to his family, he felt that he should go to America if he was ever to make his fortune. He had an aunt living on Long Island, and figured he could live with her until he saved enough to support himself.

Rolf stowed away on a passenger ship full of Norwegian immigrants and managed to lose himself in the crowd. But immigration authorities on Ellis Island spotted the boy with no papers, and sent him right back to Norway on the next boat.

Rolf was far from giving up, and he had learned a lot from his ill-fated first trip to the United States. The next time, he was able to hide his presence more effectively. His second journey was on the Scandinavian America Line: the *Frederick VIII*. He was old enough and clever enough to convince the immigration officers that he would be a benefit to America and dependent on no one. And he was right: Rolf applied for a job so dangerous that there weren't a lot of applicants. He was hired as a painter to work on the steel beams of a skyscraper being built on Forty-second Street and Madison Avenue in New York City, a looming edifice that still stands today. Young Neslund walked the beams hundreds of feet above the bustling streets, balancing with ease and unafraid of falling. The fair Norwegian teenager was one of a very few Scandinavians who worked up there in the clouds beside the more traditional steelworkers, who were mostly Italian immigrants and Native Americans.

The money was good, and few could argue that the job wasn't exciting, but still Rolf wasn't content. Having had a taste of life on the ocean, he longed to smell the salt spray once more and ride the pitching deck in a storm where the giant waves tossed ships like toys. Rolf was still very young — only seventeen. With World War I looming in Europe since 1913, going to sea wasn't the safest option, but Rolf had never put safety first. He took the advice of a Swedish sea captain who told him to register with the Norwegian Consulate in New York and to take that opportunity to add a few years to his age. He did that, and gave his birthdate as July 7, 1897. Overnight he was twenty years old, old enough to go to sea. He went down to the docks of New York City, willing to sail on any ship that had a job he could fill. He was soon hired on as a mess boy for the British merchant ship *Ganges.* In June 1917, he found the shipping line where he would remain for the next twenty-six years: the Luckenbach Steamship Company.

Rolf's miraculous luck began to reveal itself a year later as he worked as a quartermaster/helmsman on the *Harry Luckenbach.*

Although his ship was torpedoed by a silent, deadly German submarine, and at least eight of his shipmates perished, Rolf survived and somehow made his way to France.

By the time he was really in his early twenties he was exceptionally strong. Soon, he was working on another ship in the Luckenbach line. He continued his steady progress up the ladder, through all the on-deck ranks and, by 1926, to his first command. Rolf Neslund became master of the *Robin Goodfellow.*

One of the diciest jobs on ships is that of pilot. It requires great skill and natural instinct to guide mammoth vessels from the oceans through narrow waterways leading to city ports where they are loaded and unloaded. Being a ship's pilot is one of the most prestigious jobs in the shipping industry. After commanding a number of Luckenbach ships on intercoastal routes for ten years, Rolf became a pilot. He was in particular demand to direct vessels in and out of the intricate harbors of Puget Sound.

In 1935, the Puget Sound Pilots' Association was established, a brotherhood of skilled seamen who shared a special camaraderie. Most of them were, like Rolf Neslund, once captains of their own ships. Rolf was one of their earliest members. The association exists today, licensed by the State of Washington and the U.S. Coast Guard with very strict codes of training, experience, skill, and conduct to protect both citizens and natural resources.

Although he was a good-looking man, a fine example of his Norwegian background, it isn't surprising that Rolf married later in life than most men. He had dropped into many ports and been consumed with his duties, and that left him far too busy to think of marriage, but not too busy to think of women.

He was thirty-four when he married his first wife, Margot,[*] in 1934. With that marriage, Rolf Neslund began a most complicated round-robin of romantic entanglements. Margot was also a native of Norway, the country where Rolf felt most at home. In 1935, he met her baby sister, Elinor, who was only eleven years old at the time. He scarcely noticed her, but Elinor found him very handsome, a hero larger than life, and she never forgot him. Rolf, of course, was old enough to be her father.

Elinor didn't see Rolf again for twenty-one years. When they met once more, it was in

[*]Some names have been changed. The first time such names appear, they are marked with an asterisk.

Seattle in 1956. She was thirty-two, a single mother of two young girls, and he was nearing his middle fifties.

Rolf had had many adventures during the two decades since he'd last seen Elinor. If possible, he was even more heroic and attractive to her.

But he was married to her sister.

Margot and Rolf had never had children. That wasn't surprising. Initially, he was scarcely around often enough to impregnate his wife. After three years as an independent pilot, Rolf Neslund had again decided that he missed the open sea. The 1940s was not an era in which most men would have chosen to be at sea. There was, of course, a new world war going on, and submarines prowled, silent as sharks, beneath the ocean's surface. Rolf wasn't worried; he had been on a ship sunk by a submarine before and emerged safely.

In 1943 he walked up the gangplank as master of the *Walter A. Luckenbach*. Later that year, Rolf commanded a huge freighter — the *Andrea F. Luckenbach* — as it traversed the Atlantic Ocean headed out of New York City and bound for Liverpool, England. Upon its arrival in the city that would one day be most famous as the home of the Beatles, Rolf's ship was called into service as part of the Merchant Marine fleet. The *Andrea Luckenbach* was ordered to rendezvous with other vessels during the invasion of North Africa.

But that was not to be. The massive ship never made the invasion. Rolf Neslund would have the dubious record for most times torpedoed. The *Andrea F. Luckenbach* took a hit from a submarine and sank, taking twenty-one of his men to their deaths far below. Although many people were unaware of it, those serving in the Merchant Marine had a higher mortality rate than those in any of the armed forces, losing one out of every twenty men to enemy attacks. But not Rolf Neslund. Once again, he survived unscathed.

Undeterred, Rolf moved to another Luckenbach ship and commanded it and others anywhere he was needed. On one trip from South Africa to Brazil, he and his men saved the entire crew of a company boat that was sunk seventy miles off the Cape of Good Hope.

By the time the war ended in 1945, Rolf was in his mid-forties, still a long way from retirement. He had finally had enough of life on the ocean, however, and became a Puget Sound pilot again. When he finally retired from the Puget Sound Pilots' Association thirty-four years later he would do so as the oldest — and, arguably, most beloved — member in their history.

Blond and ruddy, Rolf Neslund was a ladies' man — at least when he was in port long enough to meet women. He looked a great deal like a movie star of the forties: Paul Henreid, the actor most remembered for lighting two cigarettes at once in a three-handkerchief movie entitled *Now Voyager*. Henreid's character handed one smoldering cigarette to sloe-eyed Bette Davis in a movie scene considered one of the most romantic of all time. It was the kind of gesture Rolf was capable of, too.

When Rolf wore his captain's uniform with four gold stripes on his left sleeve, his cap loaded with more gold braid and insignia, he was handsome enough to rival any screen hero. This was the man who had dazzled eleven-year-old Elinor and who fascinated her again as an attractive grown woman.

Rolf Neslund was a man full of the lust for life, one with scores of friends, and he took the time and trouble to keep his friendships alive. For many years, he sent out 550 Christmas cards, painstakingly addressing them himself. He also made sure that elderly friends and relatives had birthday cards each year. Everyone liked him.

■ ■ ■ ■

Margot Neslund became chronically ill, and Rolf persuaded Elinor to move in with them in their home north of Seattle. Margot needed someone to care for her, and who better than her own sister? Elinor had grown up to become a willowy blonde, quite pretty in a quiet way.

Rolf was a virile man and the forced celibacy that came about because of his wife's long illness was proving difficult for him. He was in his fifties when Elinor moved into the Neslund home. Rolf was not blind to Elinor's attractiveness and he saw that she watched him when she didn't think he was aware of it.

It was probably inevitable that Rolf and Elinor would become intimate, living so close together, each of them longing for passion and sexual fulfillment. Whether Rolf's wife was aware in the beginning that her sister and her husband were having an affair is questionable. She probably knew and chose to look away. But Elinor took good care of Margot, and the first Mrs. Neslund may have made up her mind to leave things alone and pretend not to see. At least for a time.

By the time Margot Neslund finally realized the affair wasn't going to end and filed for divorce, Elinor was pregnant, an obvious condition that made it impossible for Margot to rationalize her suspicions away.

While the Neslund divorce was in the works, Elinor held her head up, ignoring the buzz of local gossips. She and Rolf were married in Finland that year — 1958 — and she gave birth to a son, and named him after his father: Rolf. Two years later, she was pregnant with a second son, Erik. At sixty, Rolf Neslund was the father of two young boys.

Elinor was living temporarily in Norway, and Rolf was often working as a ship's pilot in one faraway port or another. What Elinor didn't know — nor, perhaps, did Rolf — was that she and Rolf were not legally married. At the time of their Finnish wedding ceremony, Rolf's divorce from Margot was not yet final.

Elinor had high hopes for their marriage when Rolf sent for her and little Rolf to come to Vancouver, British Columbia, Canada. She was happy that their second baby would be born there with his father close by.

Rolf bought plane tickets to bring the pregnant Elinor and their little boy to Vancouver, the Canadian city about 140 miles north of Seattle. Many people hoping to emigrate to America go first to Canada because it's easier to cross its borders.

Elinor was shocked, almost speechless, when Rolf admitted to her that he had learned they weren't really married. But he quickly explained that he was now divorced from her older sister and he wanted to marry her legally. He had even obtained a Canadian marriage license.

It should have been a rather romantic happy ending — except for the fact that Rolf had yet another woman in his life, someone he had met in Seattle while Elinor was in Norway. Her name was Nettie Ruth Myers, and, like Elinor, she was a generation younger than Rolf.

Outside of her immediate family, she seldom answered to "Nettie," and preferred to be called "Ruth." Ruth had a very strong personality and a native cunning that made her much more talented in getting what she wanted than Elinor was.

And what Ruth wanted was Rolf.

Despite Rolf's denials, Elinor suspected that from the beginning. Ruth was omnipresent in their lives, and when Rolf introduced Ruth to Elinor, he explained that she was a close business associate of his. But Elinor wondered what kind of business that could be, since Rolf cared only about his ships and wasn't in any way a businessman.

Worse, Elinor, heavily pregnant and feeling unattractive and awkward, was suspicious when Rolf said he had hired Ruth to be a kind of "housekeeper" who would help Elinor until after their baby was born. She didn't want Ruth around and she didn't need her, but Ruth moved into their Vancouver house and made herself at home.

Elinor was worried — and she had reason to be. She herself had become intimate with Rolf when she was in his first wife's home, caring for her own sister. If he had cheated with her, how could she be sure he wouldn't cheat on her with another woman? The whole plan was too much like the one Elinor had lived through in Seattle; the only thing that would change would be that now Elinor would be Rolf's wife, and Ruth would be the other woman living in their home. Elinor didn't care for Ruth at all. Ruth wasn't friendly and she seemed to wield more power over Rolf than Elinor herself ever had. Ruth did very little housekeeping and she certainly didn't appear to be doing any business with Rolf. After Elinor gave birth to her second son, Erik, Ruth Myers didn't leave. In fact, Ruth became even more entrenched in their lives. She gave her opinions very freely on what should have been private matters.

"Once," Elinor later recalled, "Ruth suggested that I return to Norway and have the children adopted out! It was a very miserable situation for me."

Elinor wouldn't think of giving up her boys. She loved Rolf and Eric; they were Rolf's natural sons. And Rolf seemed to care for Elinor and the little boys. Still, however outrageous Ruth's remarks were, Rolf never asked Ruth to move out.

It was a stressful time — two women, each of whom wanted to marry the man they shared a house with. It was a standoff, but neither woman gave up.

In 1961, Rolf obtained another Canadian wedding license, and told Elinor that he really did want to marry her. It seemed that Elinor had won her man back. But there was much more than a slight hitch in his plan to marry her. To Elinor's horror, Rolf confessed that he was already married to Ruth Myers, and had been for months.

That didn't mean, he said with truly flawed reasoning, that he couldn't marry Elinor, too!

"I was so suspicious of their relationship all along," Elinor said. "When I found out that they were married, I knew I didn't want to marry him again."

Rolf assured Elinor that he'd had no choice but to marry Ruth. It wasn't that he loved her, but she had threatened to expose him — and told him that Elinor would, too. He wanted to stay in America, his adopted country, but Ruth lied and said that Elinor was threatening to turn him over to immigration authorities for fraud.

"Ruth says you're going to tell them about how I lied about my age way back when I stowed away on the ships from Norway," he told Elinor. "She said they'll deport me for that."

"I wouldn't do that," Elinor breathed. "How could you believe I would betray you?"

But Ruth's psychological manipulation had made Rolf paranoid about what might happen if Elinor ever got angry with him. Ruth had succeeded in convincing Rolf that the only way he could feel secure about staying in America would be for him to marry a native-born U.S. citizen. Ruth was an American citizen, born in the heart of America in Illinois. If Rolf married her, he could not be deported.

And Ruth, of course, was prepared to provide him with that safety net. She herself would marry him.

Ruth convinced Rolf to marry her in a

quiet ceremony on April 24, 1961. He was sixty-two and she was forty-one. And, of course, that legal marriage meant that he could not marry Elinor. Ruth made sure of that.

"Why didn't you ask me about this sooner?" Elinor gasped. "I would never have done that to you." She assured him that Ruth had been lying to him.

But it was too late. Even though Rolf kept proclaiming his love for the Norwegian beauty who was twenty-five years younger than he was, he continually gave in to what Ruth wanted. It was almost as if Ruth had hypnotized him.

Ultimately, Elinor refused to go through with a second sham marriage, and stepped aside, her dreams in ashes. Rolf and Ruth were already married to one another, and there was nothing Elinor could do about that.

Although Ruth scoffed at the idea for years, there is ample evidence that Elinor still loved Rolf and that he cared deeply for her, continuing to visit her and their sons while she remained in Vancouver. It is likely that their forbidden romance continued for decades, but they could never marry. Their route to the altar had met with one blockade after another, the vast majority of them erected by Nettie Ruth Myers.

Rolf wanted to live in America, but he told Ruth he would never cut his ties to Norway and to his brothers and sister there. And he told Elinor he would never forget her or his two sons.

TWO

Rolf and Ruth moved back to Washington State. Now that she was married to him, she didn't want him to have anything to do with Elinor, Rolf Junior, or Erik. She kept tabs on him to be sure he wasn't giving Elinor money to live on. He was giving them money, though, and most of the time Ruth didn't know. When she discovered from time to time that he was helping Elinor out, she was angry. Once she found a greeting card he planned to send to Elinor and it had five hundred in it. Ruth was furious.

How on earth had Rolf Neslund, essentially committed to Elinor Ekenes, become so intimately involved with the woman who was now his wife?

Theirs was a chance meeting, but Ruth had taken it from there. In the late 1950s, Ruth Myers worked for an insurance agency in Seattle. She had planned to have lunch with a man whose offices were in the Smith

Tower, but her lunch date was canceled. Fate then placed her on an elevator in the building just as Rolf Neslund stepped in. She often recalled that she was instantly attracted to him. He had a full head of iron-gray hair and a classic jawline, and carried himself like a much younger man. Before Rolf got off that elevator, Ruth first made sure that she knew his name and that he knew hers and how to get in touch with her. And then she asked him out to lunch, boldly showing her interest in him. Flattered, he accepted.

"She saw Rolf," Deputy Ray Clever of the San Juan County Sheriff's Office said many years later, "and she decided she wanted to have him."

Even though Rolf Neslund was a generation older than the forty-one-year-old Ruth, that didn't daunt her. He was an undeniably handsome man who led an active life. She was even more interested in him when she learned he made good money as a pilot on Puget Sound, and he was not without means. Ruth's hardscrabble background had taught her to appreciate a man who could provide her with a comfortable life. But at first it wasn't money or security on Ruth's mind. She wanted him as a lover.

Ruth could probably have made a fortune

teaching a course on how to enchant a man. Nettie Ruth Myers was not a great beauty, but she had a pleasantly curving figure and she was a lot of fun. She had a full face with a sharp chin, a somewhat bulbous nose, and tightly permed hair and she wore glasses with lenses so wide that her eyes sometimes took on an owlish cast. Even though she was no Lana Turner, Ruth had something more important than sheer physical beauty. She knew how to interest a man and how to please him. She had had to perfect that particular talent to lift herself out of the poverty of her youth. Perhaps, most of all, it was her forte as a consummate actress that helped her get what she wanted. Throughout her life, Ruth was able to be whatever she sensed people wanted her to be — seductive, sweet, cozy and comfy, sharp in business deals, stubborn, controlling, or compliant. And she would always have both her detractors and her supporters, some who declared she was the devil and others who swore she was an angel on earth.

Nettie Ruth Myers started her life in the Midwest. She was born on February 8, 1920, in Beardstown, Illinois, about fifty miles northwest of Springfield, a small town in Cass County with just a few thousand residents. It was hard by the Illinois River and the site of the Lincoln Courthouse and Museum, but it wasn't the kind of town where young people tended to stay. Most of them grew up and moved away to bigger cities where salaries were higher and there was more to do.

Life itself was a challenge for Nettie Ruth. There were ten children in her family — some born in Ohio and some in Illinois: Mamie, Mary, Robert, Walter, Asa, Paula, Carl, Enoch, Paul, and, finally, Nettie Ruth. Some of them remained in the Ohio and Illinois area, but most moved to places as far-flung as Biloxi, Mississippi, Rockaway, Oregon, and Los Angeles, California.

One of Ruth's siblings didn't live to adulthood. Like most families whose children were born in the early part of the twentieth century, the Myerses lost a baby: Enoch. He died at the age of one year. Another brother simply disappeared. Carl Myers walked away from his family home during World War I.

"He left home and never came back," Ruth recalled. "He was just — he just went missing. [They] sent his trunk back and all of his possessions. That was in 1919. We don't know whether he's dead."

Ruth and her brother Paul were the

youngest of the Myers children; she was the youngest girl and he was the last boy to be born. Ruth explained that their positions in the family birth order had made them quite close.

Ruth left the Midwest for Louisiana and moved in with a man named Morris Daniels when she was in her mid-teens. She had her first child a year later: Morris Daniels, Jr. Warren "Butch" Daniels was born when she was twenty. Whether she raised her boys from infancy to maturity isn't known. They were in their twenties by the time Ruth met Rolf in Seattle. It's quite possible that she had left them behind for their father to raise; as grown men, they still lived in Louisiana while their mother was in Washington State. Still, as adults, her sons — particularly Butch — were steadfast in their allegiance to her and she was in close touch with them.

Ruth had relatives all over America. Surprisingly, she managed to keep in touch with many of her siblings. She would often say how much she loved her family, and how — as she grew older — she realized the importance of having a family you could count on.

Unfortunately, when Ruth met Rolf Neslund, her mother was dead. Some members of the Myers family whispered that Ruth was responsible for that.

Even though her mother lived in Illinois and was elderly, Ruth had managed to write a life insurance policy on her through the Seattle company Ruth worked for. Not too long after, her mother became ill. When Ruth learned that her mother had been hospitalized back in her home state, she rushed to her side. Ruth soon managed to convince her mother's doctors that she could take much better care of her at home. As it turned out, she could not — or did not. Some of Ruth's sisters claimed that she deliberately fed their mother the very foods that the doctors had put on her forbidden list. The elderly woman died shortly thereafter.

"Ruth was the beneficiary of our mother's insurance," a relative sniffed in derision. "She collected her money, and when anyone said anything to her about how she gave in to Mom's cravings for sugar and all, Ruth just said, 'Well, she was going to die anyway. . . .'"

Her sisters may only have been jealous; Ruth was already a lot better off financially than most of her siblings were.

Her mother's insurance payoff wasn't much of a windfall, but Ruth was very good with money. At the time she met Rolf, she was buying the small house she lived in in

Everett, Washington, twenty-six miles north of Seattle. She paid five thousand dollars for her little house. This was in an era in Washington State when a newly built three-bedroom house could be purchased for about ten thousand dollars. After Ruth met Rolf, she sold her bungalow for a few thousand more than she paid for it. She also owned a vacant lot near Paine Field. The real estate boom in the area was some years away, and her houses and lots were excellent investments.

With his wanderlust, Rolf had never cared much about owning real estate, and, planning to reunite with Elinor, he had been living in a cheap apartment about ten miles south of Ruth's place when he met her.

Whatever his true feelings were for Elinor Ekenes and the two small boys who were almost certainly his sons, Rolf Neslund was quickly bewitched by Ruth, and seemed to enjoy being married to her. They were not a young couple, but they appeared to get along with each other — once Elinor was essentially out of the picture. Most people who knew them thought it would be fine if they ended up together, living out the rest of their years in a companionable way rather than with a wild sex life. But their age belied the very real attraction that sizzled between them. Ruth wanted Rolf, and he had come to want her — a lot. Initially, there was probably more sexual electricity there than anyone suspected. And they had much in common: Both of them had colorful pasts marked by poverty in their early years, a history of numerous other relationships, extensive travel, and, particularly in Rolf's case, near-death experiences.

Despite her many relatives around the country, Ruth had been basically alone when she met Rolf. But she wasn't a helpless single woman or anyone to be pitied. Although she had very little formal schooling, she was highly intelligent. She was most adept at arithmetic, and kept perfect records, even when she didn't have much to keep records about. It was probably predictable that she sought some permanency in her life. Her ambition was to own a great deal of property, to have something solid that belonged to her, something she could see. She could certainly see Rolf, and he had an air of confidence and stability about him. He didn't dress like a rich man, but she had quickly ferreted out that his pilot's position made him well off. And he planned to work for many more years.

Rolf had been something of a barterer, trading goods for service, and he owned some oil stock that had impressive-looking certificates, but he wasn't nearly as interested as Ruth was in making money. After he ran off to sea, Rolf's family in Norway had built a thriving shipping business. His mother had left her estate to him and his three siblings, and he had about nine thousand (American) dollars in a Norwegian bank. Rolf was quite willing to let Ruth keep the books and look around for property to buy. She called herself a "horse trader," and he was impressed with her business sense.

The Neslunds soon moved off the mainland of Washington State. After looking at property, they settled on Lopez Island, one of four rocky outcroppings that make up the San Juan Islands: San Juan, Orcas, Shaw, and Lopez. Islands adrift in the Strait of Juan de Fuca some eighty-five miles northwest of Seattle, all of them astoundingly beautiful places to live.

Forty-five years ago, there wasn't much going on in the San Juans except for the promise of serenity, more sunshine than the rest of Washington State, and the feeling of being part of a community where people knew and cared about one another. Even twenty years ago, there weren't more than twelve hundred people living on Lopez Island. There was virtually no felony crime, and murders were extremely rare.

But progress, for better or worse, was edging into the San Juans. Tourists were beginning to discover the tranquil forests, gently rolling meadows, and vistas of the sea from countless miles of shoreline. Quaint shops and restaurants attracted visitors, and a number of artists and writers were drawn to the islands.

Bestselling thriller writer John Saul built one of his many homes on the edge of a cliff on Lopez Island, next to where his parents had lived for years. Writer Charlotte Paul lived there. Actor Tom Skerritt and his wife resided on Lopez whenever they could get away from Hollywood, and later on, they opened up a bed-and-breakfast. Richard Bach, author of *Jonathan Livingston Seagull,* took up residence on nearby Orcas Island. A number of familiar faces from Hollywood vacationed there. In the San Juans, they were all just part of the community, and not celebrities to be pointed out or stalked. The area was an oasis from a world that moved too fast.

Lopez was a particularly friendly island. It was the custom there to wave to anyone you passed on the road — friend or stranger.

Unlike the well-known people who moved

to the San Juan Islands, the Neslunds were far from famous or sought after, but like them, enjoyed the serenity and peace. In 1974, they bought a 7.2-acre plot of land with an old house on it on Alec Bay Road, on the south end of Lopez. The next year, the house mysteriously burned to the ground. With the insurance money, Ruth designed and built a five-thousand-square-foot home, one of the largest on Lopez. An almost hidden dirt road led to the backyard of their barn red rambler, while the front windows looked out on Alec Bay. They fenced in meadows on either side to make pastures for sheep and cattle.

Ruth handled it all. She wrote the checks that chipped away at their mortgage with payments of $152.00 each month, only occasionally falling behind. She always managed to catch up on mortgage payments and taxes just in time to keep them from losing their property. She knew it was a canny real estate investment; by 1981, one estimated appraisal of their house and land was an almost unbelievable five hundred thousand dollars. By that time, Ruth had whittled their mortgage down to only sixty-five hundred dollars. She knew all about how compound interest could build a fortune, and she always deliberately waited five years to pay their taxes because she knew she could use that money in ways that brought in more in interest than she lost in penalties.

Early on, the Neslunds established a pattern where Rolf turned his pilot's salary over to Ruth, and she wrote all the checks to pay bills. He preferred to handle cash only.

To be sure he always had spending money, Ruth kept cash on hand in a dresser drawer. Sometimes, it was twenty dollars; sometimes it was fifteen hundred. "Whenever he needed money," she said fondly, "he would tell me and I would go and get him some. I always wanted him to have the cash he needed."

In November 1962, a year and a half after their marriage, Rolf wrote his last will and testament. He left virtually everything to his new bride, with apparently no provision for his sons or their mother. Ruth kept the will in a strongbox in their home.

A few years later, on May 27, 1965, the couple signed a "boilerplate" form Ruth had purchased at a stationery store. It was very simple: They filled in the spaces that showed they agreed that if one of them should die all of their holdings were to be considered community property and go directly to the survivor. They had a notary public validate their signatures, and they filed the agreement at the courthouse the next day.

What belonged to him would be hers, and what belonged to Ruth would be Rolf's. Their signatures each had large, sweeping capital letters at the beginning, although Rolf's writing was a bit more flamboyant than his wife's. A graphologist would probably say that they were both confident — and even dominant — personality types.

Ruth decorated their large home in the style of the 1960s and seventies, buying plush, velvety furniture in shades of brown and gold that blended perfectly against wood-paneled walls. The carpeting was mocha shag piling, with a pattern of darker colors sprinkled across it. Her lamps and knickknacks were much more feminine than anything Rolf would have chosen, the end tables draped with starched and embroidered white linen, the matching lamps with either ivory globes or marble bases. As almost every woman crafter did in that era, Ruth crocheted afghans in the ubiquitous zigzag pattern of orange, brown, and white.

The Neslunds' native stone fireplace with its thick wood mantel held a chiming Seth Thomas clock, and their walls were hung with numerous paintings, some of the ocean, some of flowers, some with big-eyed children.

Ruth collected and resold antiques, but her favorites were the parlor furniture which had once belonged to Rolf's mother in Norway.

"I took it all apart," Ruth recalled. "It came over on a ship and it was pretty well fractured. I restored the wood, braced it, glued it, and reupholstered it. [There's] a little love seat with four parlor chairs. That's not for sale."

Rolf was a man of the sea, his very blood seemingly infused with salt water, and on Lopez the smell and sight of the sea was everywhere. Still, it was nice for him to come home from standing against the icy winds on the bridge and riding the troughs and peaks of storm-tossed waves, pleasant to share his evenings with Ruth.

She tended a big vegetable garden and strawberry patch, and either froze or canned what they didn't eat during growing season. In a good strawberry year, Ruth sometimes had a stall over in Anacortes where she sold berries to people waiting for a ferry. She was a pretty fair cook and joined Rolf in a drink or two before dinner.

Theirs was an idyllic life, or so it seemed to those who knew them.

Northwest islanders are a different breed, content to be far away from city traffic and problems. Their lives revolve around the arrival and departure of the ferries that come and go each day, bringing in supplies and visitors, taking residents off-island when they have business in Seattle or Bellingham or Vancouver, British Columbia. Lopez Island is almost as close to Canada as it is to the mainland of Washington State, a fairly self-sufficient community caught between two countries. The island certainly proved to be the perfect place for Rolf and Ruth.

They made friends on Lopez, and Rolf had a large circle of friends among the other pilots in the Puget Sound Pilots' Association, so the Neslunds had ample opportunity to socialize. The ship pilots were an extremely tight-knit group, as loyal to one another as any military men who have fought wars together. They took care of their own, and Rolf Neslund was definitely one of their own.

As it turned out, Rolf would work as a pilot for eighteen years after their marriage, but Ruth never felt alone; she had neighbors she could count on. Through the early years of their marriage, it seemed that the couple had made a good match. Rolf was gone quite a bit and Ruth had her friends on the island to have coffee with, or to invite in for supper. She had her garden, of course, and she was always looking for antiques or other items she could refurbish or resell.

She continued to look around for reasonably priced pieces of real estate. Rolf didn't care much about real estate investments, but he wasn't against putting his money to work — as long as Ruth took care of all the paperwork, and saw that payments were made.

One drawback, perhaps, to living on an isolated island with a small population was that everyone knew your business; there were very few secrets. If married couples had loud arguments, details of the encounters soon spread. When somebody got drunk in a bar or even at home, people knew. Actually, there were only two public places to drink on Lopez: the Islander-Lopez or the Galley. They were close together, and lots of rumors passed back and forth.

Ruth and Rolf had their share of arguments over the years. What they argued about was not initially obvious, although it would become more so as the years passed: It was almost always about Elinor. Oddly, Ruth would always deny that she knew precisely what Rolf's relationship with Elinor Ekenes had been. She insisted that she and Rolf never really spoke of Elinor, and she was vague and uninterested in talking about the situation. But everyone knew that Ruth frowned whenever she heard Elinor's name.

It was apparent to close observers that she knew more than she would say about Rolf and Elinor. Indeed, she remained terribly jealous of Elinor, and believed that Rolf was still carrying on with her — even after she and Rolf had been married for two decades.

Over the years, Ruth had deftly rearranged the truth to her own satisfaction. She maintained that Rolf had never spoken to her of any affair with his late wife's sister, and he certainly never told her that Rolf and Erik Ekenes were his sons. She said she had never asked him about the boys directly.

She insisted that she knew very little about the boys: They lived in Vancouver, British Columbia — a whole other country, albeit only a short distance by sea from the San Juan Islands. She was lying, of course, but her friends believed she only fibbed to save face.

The truth was that Ruth had met Elinor in Vancouver in 1960 or 1961, and of course she actually lived in the same house with Elinor and Rolf. Ruth knew the facts of the whole situation, but she chose to pretend she didn't.

This was pretty hard for neighbors to believe since Elinor's sons sometimes came to Lopez Island to spend part of their vacations at the Neslund home on Alec Bay. Ruth allowed them to visit at the Neslund home in the summer.

Public records indicate that she had been forced to deal with the facts about Rolf's young sons a year or two after she married him. Elinor had filed a paternity suit in North Vancouver, British Columbia, claiming Rolf was her sons' father, and that he should be supporting them.

Rolf was ordered by the court to support young Rolf and Erik, and he actually did that until 1970, when they became beneficiaries of his Social Security dependents' benefits. Ruth wrote the checks in the family, and it must have been galling for her to see the bank accounts that were so important to her lowered by the needs of the boys, constant reminders of Rolf's affair with Elinor.

Even though Rolf would have had to notify Social Security offices in 1970 and verify that Rolf and Erik were his sons for them to collect from his account, Ruth was still adamant that she didn't know that firsthand. "I don't know anything about it," she said flatly. "I'm pretty sure that he [Rolf] signed every document that their mother put in front of him."

While Ruth denied that she knew anything at all about the boys purported to be her husband's children, the rest of her memory was impeccable. She recalled every single financial deal she had ever been involved in. Her mind was like a big steel filing cabinet, full of details that proved her business acumen.

The Neslunds never had children together, possibly because Ruth was in her forties when they married. But she kept in touch with about a dozen of her nieces and nephews and was very close to her niece Donna, who was a frequent visitor in Ruth and Rolf's home. Ruth was something of a surrogate mother to her. Ruth claimed that Donna didn't like her own mother, Ruth's older sister Mamie, and that she was trying to effect a reconciliation. In the meantime, she welcomed Donna into her home. And so did Rolf.

The first ten years of the Neslunds' marriage passed quietly, and they weren't at all newsworthy. They were simply an older couple living in a very nice home set far back off the road in a sheltered cove of Lopez Island.

But over the next decade, their relationship took an ominously violent turn.

THREE

Financially, the Neslunds had done extremely well as they approached their twentieth wedding anniversary. Rolf had his salary, and Ruth's dabblings in real estate were paying off. She acquired two lots in Port Townsend, and two more in Anacortes, the first city on the mainland where ferries from the islands docked. The Anacortes lots had come about in trade for a high-powered boat engine Rolf owned.

"Rolf did it," she said, proudly. "Sight unseen by both parties."

The early building lots Ruth bought cost no more than $800 originally, and she didn't make a huge profit on them. But by the late seventies, she was much more savvy. On one day in May, she bought two lots for a total of $18,000 and turned them around in two months, selling them for a $4,400 profit. She bought another in Bellingham for $3,000, knowing she could sell it the next day for more than double that. She usually had her buyers lined up before she purchased the properties; she didn't even have to use her own money in the purchases: That came out of her profit.

While she was paying off the mortgage on the Alec Bay house, Ruth began collecting cars and other valuables: a motor home, a Dodge van, a classic 1966 Mustang, a Lincoln Continental, an Oldsmobile convertible, farm trailers and boat trailers, a twenty-eight-foot cabin cruiser, Duncan Phyfe tables and other antiques, a coin collection, silver flatware. She registered the cars illegally in Louisiana, "because it was cheaper there," and used an ambiguous "R. Neslund" as the name of the registered owner, which could have been either Ruth or Rolf.

Ruth acquired horses, buggies, and more houses on Lopez Island itself, and sold them on contract with 12 percent interest coming to her. Without striving to remember, she could tally up every single asset she had, how much she owed, how much was owed her — at what interest — and she never had to glance at notes. She knew how much was in each of many bank accounts.

When Rolf retired, he would receive a pension of $1,800 each month from the Puget Sound Pilots.

They were doing very well indeed.

But that was on the business side of their union.

Over the years, Ruth and Rolf Neslund extended their evening cocktail hours further and further into the night. And when they drank, they fought. Their midmarriage arguments had long since exacerbated to ugly episodes. What had begun as grumbling and sniping at one another soon became angry words and insults. At a certain point, they began to actually exchange physical blows. They scratched, hit, bruised, and even bit one another.

Once, Ruth claimed to San Juan County sheriff's deputies Greg Doss and Joe Caputo, Rolf actually forced her head into the kitchen stove's oven. What he intended to do next was a question. Turning on the gas wouldn't work, and she was far too plump for him to push her all the way in and roast her as the Wicked Witch threatened to do to Hansel and Gretel.

Ruth told Caputo that she had been seeing to a roasting chicken in the oven when Rolf leaned on her shoulders and pushed her arms against the hot grill. She held her arms up quickly and showed him the "burn marks." Caputo wasn't sure if she was really burned, or if the oven racks were dirty, leaving grease marks on her lower arms.

It was just drunken stuff, but disturbing nonetheless.

Usually, the Neslunds had had so much to drink that they couldn't even remember the details of their fights. They would waken in the morning and be shocked by their own reflections in the mirror. Ruth looked haggard, and Rolf often had dried blood on his face, deep scratches, black eyes and bruises, bite marks, bald spots where hair had been pulled out, and other wounds from their violent domestic battles.

Sometimes, Ruth would run away from Rolf and lock herself in the little bunkhouse behind their home while Rolf slept it off. She claimed to have been terrorized, but, in truth, she gave as good as she got. Perhaps even better.

Ruth's plans for gracious entertaining and lovely dinner parties for their friends usually ended disastrously. The facade she tried to present is reminiscent of the character "Hyacinth" on the popular British comedy show, *Keeping Up Appearances.* Hyacinth's "candle-light suppers," meant to be her open door into high society, never quite succeed — and neither did Ruth Neslund's. Both the TV character and the real woman had fine china, floral arrangements, silver, and linens — but the women themselves lacked the charm and civility to carry these social evenings off. Many of the Neslunds' long-time friends began to find excuses to decline Ruth's invitations.

One couple on Lopez Island would recall an evening with the Neslunds. The food was wonderful, and everything went well until the liquor began to flow and one of their hosts took offense at some remark the other made. Soon, the guests were forgotten and the meal was over as Ruth and Rolf battled with each other. Their company watched, stunned, and then tiptoed out.

"Ruth called me the next day," the wife of the guest couple remembered, "and I could tell she felt so bad. She apologized over and over for the way her dinner ended. I could tell she was terribly disappointed — and humiliated, too. She asked us to give her another chance, swearing that it would never happen again."

At length, the guests agreed to return for another meal with the Neslunds. Again, the table setting was perfect and the food was even better. But Ruth and Rolf could not seem to get through an evening without a fight, and the after-dinner "entertainment" was a repeat of what had happened before.

Gossip about the failed dinner parties soon spread around Lopez Island, and those who considered themselves comedians added to it. Dining at the Neslunds' home became a joke, and both career authors and other residents who lived on the island wrote hilarious, long poems or fashioned elaborate stories about them.

In a way, it was sad that a couple who had been together for so long should come to be a laughingstock. In between their arguments, though, the Neslunds appeared to be happy enough. There are couples who seem to enjoy fighting and making up as much as they do making love — who actually use arguments as foreplay. Maybe the Neslunds fell in that category.

They didn't live close enough to their neighbors that their shouting carried through the woods, so no one cared very much. They were peculiar, but there were lots of "peculiars" in the islands and they were all accepted by the natives. The Neslunds had the right to do what they wanted.

Although he was in his eighth decade, Rolf Neslund had no intention of retiring. He was one of the most dependable ships' pilots around.

He was well past his seventy-fifth birthday

when the United States Coast Guard renewed his license on November 3, 1975, for five more years.

TO U.S. MERCHANT MARINE OF-FICER

This is to certify that Rolf Neslund, having been duly examined and found competent by the undersigned, is licensed to serve as Master of Steam or Motor Vessels of any gross tons upon oceans; radar observer; also First Class Pilot of New York Bay and Harbor to Yonkers; Boston Light Vessel to Boston, Via North and Narrows Channels; Nantucket and Vineyard Sounds; Delaware Bay and River to Philadelphia, Pa; Los Angeles Harbor to Wilmington; San Francisco Bay and Return; Columbia River, Astoria, Oregon to Sea and Return; and on Puget Sound and Connecting Inland Waters for the term of five years from this date.

For nearly three more years, Rolf Neslund was considered to be fully capable of maneuvering huge ships from coast to coast and on the Atlantic and Pacific. He had every reason to be proud of his prowess, and, indeed, he was. The young boy who had stowed away in Norway to make his way to America had more than proved himself.

If Rolf had his way, he intended to work until he died at the helm of a ship. And he came close to doing just that. But he would soon have both his reputation and his physical body threatened by a cataclysmic event. Rolf would become, if not "famous," then infamous in the annals of shipping in the Northwest — long after most men would have retired.

On June 11, 1978, Rolf was either seventy-eight or eighty-one — depending on which of his birthdates you believed. He was healthy and he loved his job and the camaraderie he shared with other members of the Puget Sound Pilots' Association. He was an institution, a grand old man who was much admired by far younger members. Everybody liked him, and he was in the midst of life when most men his age were sitting beside their fireplaces, or on a patio in Arizona.

He and Ruth had their fine home that was almost paid for, and, despite their violent domestic issues from time to time, their marriage had survived for seventeen years. Survived, perhaps, but no one could say it was exactly thriving.

Amazingly, Ruth was still jealous of Elinor, and continued to suspect that Rolf was sneaking away to meet with her for who knew what kind of carrying on.

While it was true that Rolf and Elinor had never really lost touch with one another, it's doubtful that at this point there was anything even slightly illicit between them. They were close friends, and Rolf loved the two sons they shared. Over the years, he made many trips to his homeland in Norway, and if Elinor was there when he was, they saw each other. He still sent her money behind Ruth's back from time to time.

In early 1978, Rolf finally decided to put in for his pension. By the end of the summer, he planned to say good-bye to the ships and his piloting duties, and return to Lopez Island for good.

But then something shocking happened that no one who knew Rolf Neslund would ever have predicted. This extremely careful and canny pilot destroyed one of the most important bridges in a city so surrounded by waterways that every bridge is vital to the orderly passage of traffic.

When the first pioneers arrived in what would one day be the great city of Seattle, they settled on Alki Point. Many years hence, the waterfront land they called "New York Alki" (Chinook tribal jargon for "bye and bye") was to become "West Seattle."

Back then on November 13, 1851, the Denny Party, including Arthur A. Denny, Charles Terry, and other famous pioneer families, suffered through a bitter cold and rainy winter with only jerry-rigged shelters. Their wives sobbed with homesickness and their children sickened. No one could ever have convinced those first settlers that West Seattle would one day become a most desirable place to live for the working men and women who commuted to downtown Seattle.

Seattle is landlocked to the north and to the south, with Lake Washington on the east and Puget Sound and Elliot Bay on the west. Its destiny has always been dependent on waterways.

The Duwamish River Waterway separates West Seattle from the main part of the city. This is a comparatively narrow ribbon of water, just wide enough to make it impossible for West Seattle dwellers to reach Seattle without crossing a bridge or taking a ferry. Without a drawbridge, commuters would have to drive south, east, and north again — almost twenty miles out of their way — to get to work, go to the downtown theaters, hospitals, sports events, and other important sites in the heart of Seattle.

In 1978, the West Seattle Bridge was cer-

tainly in need of refurbishing. Back in 1924, the first of two bascule-designed bridges over the Duwamish Waterway was completed — the ultimate in modern construction at that time. An identical span opened in 1930. Forty-eight years later, the old bridge sorely needed replacement. It was barely serviceable enough, though, until bonds in the amount of $150 million were voted in to pay for a new, higher, pivot-wing bridge.

At least it was until the dawn of June 11.

Rolf Neslund was serving as the pilot of the vessel *Chavez*, a forty-ton, 550-foot ship capable of holding twenty thousand tons of gypsum rock. He stood on the ship's bridge as it idled near Duwamish Head. He had successfully guided the *Chavez* to that point from the Pacific Ocean, and then into Elliot Bay, something he had done scores of times.

Everything seemed normal.

It was only ten days from the longest day of the year, and the dawn of day was still just hidden behind the mountains to the east, so it was dark and warm as they headed toward the loading area. A good morning to be at sea. Armed with the confidence born of all he had survived in his tussles with oceans and rivers, Rolf Neslund believed in himself, and in his almost mystical grasp of what it

took to get a ship to do what he wanted. With his wide-planted feet, he felt the *Chavez*'s heart rumbling and beating through the decks, and he knew all the sounds and the smells and the shifts that meant he was right on target.

Two tugboats began to move into their slot so they could help bring the huge ship from the wide waters to the north into the narrow slice that is the Duwamish's West Waterway. Neslund, the old pilot, would call out the commands to keep the *Chavez* straight and true in an almost impossibly tight and shallow river which local industrial waste had turned the color of lead. The West Seattle Bridge's drawspan was up and waiting.

Later, there were those who came forward to say Rolf was getting a little vague and that sometimes he didn't pay as much attention as he should. He knew they were wrong. It was true that he didn't like modern tools like radios and other electronic devices used by the young pilots; he was like an old cowboy who knew how to control a bucking horse or an angry steer. He sensed in his bones what was right, and he would give his orders to the helmsman without using the portable radio.

As the ship's pilot, Rolf Neslund was the top man in navigating the *Chavez* safely into port. From the moment the pilots board the big ships, they instruct everyone from the ship's crew — including the captain — to the longshoremen who man the lines and the tugboat crew on what to do and when. Visibility, storms, ferryboats, and docked ships can all make a pilot's job more difficult. On this night, the tugboats needed to pull the *Chavez* to the left because there was another ship on the right — an ancient freighter waiting to be dismantled and recycled partially blocked the already-tight route.

This was a dicey route, and seconds counted as the *Chavez* moved through the waterway. Men aboard a Coast Guard boat on traffic duty watched the massive ship warily.

The Coast Guard officers called Rolf on the portable radio and got no answer. The reason was simple. Rolf Neslund had turned the damned thing off.

In the hierarchy of the sea, Rolf was in charge. No one else on the ship could countermand his orders, and it was a heady feeling, as it always had been — whether he was the captain or the pilot. He ordered the helmsman to turn to port (left) and they slid by the no-longer-seaworthy freighter.

And, then, for some inexplicable reason, the old man had a spate of forgetfulness, possibly even a small stroke — a TIA (transitory ischemic attack) — something that made him lose precious seconds of awareness. The West Seattle Bridge lay ahead, its red lights blinking to warn drivers that the barricades were coming down. Its alarm bells were harsh in the soft darkness. Cars that looked like toys lined up obediently at the edges of the huge bridge, held back by the safety arms.

For those precious instants, Rolf Neslund apparently forgot that he was the pilot in charge, neglecting to notice that he had not ordered the seaman at the helm to turn back starboard (right) and then to straighten it out.

The *Chavez*'s captain, a citizen of Yugoslavia who had an impeccable safety record, suddenly realizing they were in trouble, raced to the wheelhouse, shouting "Hard-a-starboard!" And then he desperately ordered the man at the wheel to put the huge ship into reverse.

They were headed straight for the West Seattle Bridge's east support piers at a speed of nearly six knots.

At that point, Rolf snapped back to alertness and realized the danger, too. He stumbled toward the wheelhouse to repeat the same order the captain had just given. The

only thing they could possibly do to stop —
or even slow — the *Chavez* was to drop the
anchors. But that maneuver wasn't likely to
work because the ship's path was already
committed. From his long, long experience,
Rolf knew that there were huge cables carrying power and phone lines to homes and
businesses on either side of the bridge span
below. If they dropped the anchors, they
would cut underwater cables which were as
thick as a man is tall.

It was far too late to do anything but stand
on the *Chavez* and wait for what was about
to happen. It only took ten or twenty seconds, seconds when the tugboat captain of
the *Carole Foss* frantically did what he could
to keep his crew from being crushed between the ship and the bridge piers or decapitated by wires, ropes, or knife-like slivers
of shattered steel from the bridge.

And then, inevitably, the *Chavez* sliced into
the bridge as if the span's supports were
made of butter. There was a tremendous
shudder and a sound like an earthquake as
the force of the impact exploded, sending
steel and concrete and wood, and everything
else that made the West Seattle Bridge
strong, into the river and its shores.

It was quite possible now that the whole
structure would fall down upon those who

watched, almost stupefied with shock. Everything was suspended for seconds that seemed hours. The ruined bridge could easily plunge into the sudden abyss: the cars and their drivers and passengers, the bridge tender in his little house, all of it.

Thank God, however, the remnants of the ruined bridge held, and no one died.

That was the good part of it, the almost miraculous part of it. But there was hell to pay, and a long Coast Guard investigation lay ahead. The young Yugoslavian captain lost his job, Rolf Neslund lost his reputation as a peerless captain and pilot, and people who lived in West Seattle or wanted to go to West Seattle had to wait seven years for a new bridge to be built.

Even so, some residents of West Seattle were oddly grateful to Rolf Neslund for doing what they had hoped for for years. One woman, a high school student then, recalls: "Most people don't realize that some of us in West Seattle were almost glad [when] Rolf Neslund finally forced the city, county, and state to do something about the old drawbridge and the awful traffic snarls it caused.

"Our Job's Daughters' group sold T-shirts that summer that said, 'Where were you when the ship hit the span?' and they were a big hit. It couldn't have been easy for Neslund to be the butt of such jokes, but surely he also knew it wasn't all a bad outcome?"

Rolf was allowed to retire without censure, but there were many who thought how much better it might have been if he had chosen to bow out a year or so earlier. And the Coast Guard enacted age regulations for future pilots. It was the end of an era.

Rolf's fellow pilots continued to revere him and welcome him to their meetings, parties, and celebrations. He had had so many, many years of being among the best men on the sea. Nevertheless, Rolf Neslund became a target for jokes — not just on Lopez Island for his domestic fisticuffs — but for being the man who destroyed the West Seattle Bridge.

Everyone who read the newspapers or watched television recognized his name.

Rolf returned to Lopez Island, to his wife and his home on Alec Bay Road. Lesser men might have been humiliated and hidden away, but he wasn't a broken man, not at all. Some people even said that he looked back on the whole incident with a sense of humor, while others said he was simply whistling in the dark.

The former was closest to the truth. He

had survived much devastation in his long life, and Rolf continued to appreciate the twilight of his years. He preferred to listen to those who said he had done West Seattleites a favor. He had only hurried the project along.

Now retired, Rolf returned to Norway for another visit in 1979, joining his siblings in Oslo for the skating championships.

"He was happy and gay," his sister Eugenie recalled. "The last time I saw him was in Oslo and he was just like himself. We had lots of fun."

This was probably the twelfth trip Rolf Neslund made to see his family in Norway, and neither Eugenie nor his brother Harald found him depressed about the debacle surrounding the West Seattle Bridge collapse. He was like he had always been, except perhaps a little more content to stay at home. If he ever needed to talk about what had happened, Harald felt he would know and they would talk about it then.

As things turned out, no one would have much of a chance to ask Rolf exactly how he did feel about the bridge.

No one would have much of a chance to ask Rolf anything.

FOUR

In the seventies, Ray Clever was a cop in Newport Beach, California, a smart young policeman who hoped one day to emulate the older, experienced detectives he watched with something like awe. "They could get suspects to tell them almost anything," he says with a smile. "I used to sit in the interrogation rooms just to watch them work, hoping I could learn from them."

One of Clever's heroes was a detective named Sam "the Shark" Amburgy, whose mastery of interrogation was phenomenal — low key and silent and deadly as his nickname — and who always wore a fedora. A younger officer with a friendly open face, Clever carried out the usual routine duties of patrol, but his ambition was to be a criminal investigator himself one day. He remembered the way the experienced detectives questioned suspects, noting that they often let them ramble on long enough to back themselves into a corner without ever realizing it. What might seem to be only a casual conversation could be, in reality, a delicate game of cat and mouse.

Some of the older detectives were very intense and some seemed laid-back, but Clever found them remarkable in their ability to elicit information that their subjects never expected to reveal.

Clever rose through the ranks in the Orange County department and become a detective there, but his first marriage ended in what he recalls as "a bad divorce," when he was in his midthirties. He didn't have much to distract him from the disappointment of his failed marriage; he was back working patrol rather than investigating baffling murder cases. He wanted to change his life completely and move someplace as unlike Orange County, California, as possible. Clever's brother, Dick, was a reporter for the *Post-Intelligencer,* the morning newspaper in Seattle, Washington, and he made Seattle sound like a good place to live. Ray moved north.

He became a building contractor first. He was always talented in construction and tile and granite work. It wasn't his real ambition — that was law enforcement — but Clever also enjoyed building.

"But then there was a downturn in the economy," he recalls, "and pretty soon I needed a job."

San Juan County was hiring deputies, and Ray Clever had experience. He was hired on in February 1981. He didn't expect a lot of action on any of the four little islands that composed San Juan County. It wasn't the ideal place to commit robberies or burglaries since the felons would have to wait for the next ferry to make their escapes. DWIs (Driving While Intoxicated) and family fights were more likely than homicides, although anywhere human beings live there are sex offenders, disputes between neighbors, and even love triangles. Still, there was little chance that all Clever's studying and observation of master detectives in Orange County was going to pay off in San Juan County, Washington. Nevertheless, Clever liked the region and he was glad to have the job.

He was assigned to Patrol on Lopez Island and told the name of his first partner: Senior Deputy Greg Doss. Clever didn't know the geography of Lopez Island, or anything about its residents. For that matter, he had never even seen Doss before they met on Clever's first day on the job on February 23.

The two deputies had been asked to check

on the welfare of a longtime Lopez resident named Rolf Neslund. Apparently, he hadn't been seen in his usual haunts for some time, and members of the Puget Sound Pilots' Association had become concerned. Gunnar Olsborg, a retired pilot and a Norwegian like Rolf, who had been his friend since 1945, talked to a number of pilots who were used to seeing Rolf often. He found that no one had seen Rolf for months. Gunnar was worried enough to call the sheriff's office. He had also notified Rolf's relatives in Norway. He made sure the Puget Sound pilots all knew that Rolf seemed to be missing.

Ray Clever, of course, had never heard of the allegedly missing man, but then he didn't know anyone on Lopez. This call sounded routine, a familiar task for any police officer anywhere. Adults usually disappeared for their own reasons and most of them came home within a week . . . or eventually.

"Our first dispatch, my first call ever on the San Juan Sheriff's Department," Ray Clever remembers, "was to the Rolf and Ruth Neslund residence on Alec Bay Road."

As they headed toward the Neslunds', Doss gave Clever some background on the couple. They had become very familiar to local deputies. "We've been called out there on a lot of domestic disturbances," Doss said. "It's probably something like that again."

Doss told his new partner that he'd been on a call to the Neslunds on June 15, seven months earlier. At that time, he'd seen obvious signs of a physical fight. "Their place was a mess," he recalled. "There were dishes and the tablecloth on the floor. Rolf had fresh scratches along the side of his face from his ear to his chin."

Ruth, he said, had been hiding in the bedroom, her clothing and hair a mess, her face puffy. She told Doss she was safe there, but if Rolf came in, she was going to shoot him.

In July, Ruth called the sheriff again, complaining that Rolf had "decked" her. She pointed to a rifle and said that he would never do it again.

It had seemed an idle threat at the time.

Ray Clever wondered how a couple whom Doss described as sixty and eighty years old could do much real damage to each other. He fully expected his first assignment as a San Juan County deputy to be quite ordinary. "Domestics" were the most dangerous calls for law enforcement officers, but the Neslunds sounded pretty long in the tooth to be a danger.

He had no idea how wrong he was. Nor did anyone else.

FIVE

It was midafternoon on that blustery February day, but Ray Clever noted the magnificent view as they approached the Neslund home, passing the McKay Harbor Inn, where off-islanders were glad to pay the upscale prices for gourmet meals, and then turning down the lane to the sprawling red house set close to the water. Ruth Neslund welcomed the deputies and invited them in. She was a matronly looking woman with short, dyed hair set in a tightly curled permanent, her eyes magnified behind her glasses. She had carefully applied bright red lipstick. She didn't appear nervous and she was pleasant enough. Her home was warm, clean, and decorated comfortably.

The two deputies explained why they had come — just to check on how her husband was doing. Ruth assured them that Rolf certainly wasn't missing. "He's gone," she said cryptically, "but he's not missing."

She told them calmly that she knew perfectly well where her husband was, and there was no reason for anyone to be concerned.

Sighing, she spoke to the deputies in a confidential tone. She admitted that her marriage was going through a rough patch. By mutual agreement, she and Rolf were technically separated — but only while they worked things out. Clever studied her face as she talked. She anticipated their questions, quickly filling any silences that might be awkward with what seemed to him far too many words. She was quite animated, but something rankled them. Her explanations about her husband's whereabouts were much too detailed. Clever thought that Ruth Neslund was telling them far more than she needed to, as if she was trying too hard to be convincing. He wondered if she might even have planned what she was going to say if anyone asked.

Clever had a lawman's "hinky" feeling about the situation, wondering if it was possible that his very first call on his new job might not involve far more than a marital spat. To be on the safe side, Doss and Clever agreed that Ruth Neslund should be advised of her rights under the Miranda Law.

Clever read each clause, and she shook her head willingly, almost impatiently. She knew she didn't have to talk with them, that she could have an attorney present if she wanted, and if she couldn't afford one, the county would pay to have one appointed.

"Are you willing to talk with us?" Clever asked.

"Of course," she said.

Ruth explained that Rolf had left their home on Monday, August 11, 1980 — a little more than six months earlier. After consulting a calendar, she changed her statement a little.

"You know, it might have been the Thursday after that — the fourteenth," she mused. "I really can't remember which. I recall that he took his clothes, and he wanted some of the furniture. But he never came back to get it."

Ruth said that she had come across Rolf's favorite vehicle — his Lincoln Continental — in the employees parking lot of the ferry dock over on the Anacortes side of the ferry run. But that had occurred by chance some two or three weeks after Rolf walked out on her. She had then arranged to bring the car back to their residence.

Considering that they had been married for almost twenty years, it seemed odd that Ruth was so sanguine about her longtime husband's disappearance, but she continued to discuss the precise details of his leavetaking in a dispassionate way. It was as if he had only stepped out to go to the store for milk and bread, never to return.

Maybe she had grown tired of their relationship; perhaps she had come to accept that he wasn't coming back to her in the six months since he'd left her. Different people face life-changing events in their own way. Clever didn't know Ruth at all; she might just be a stoic woman, long since grown used to disappointment in her life.

Ruth told them that she was pretty sure she knew why Rolf had left her. She had always suspected that he was sneaking around with a woman named Elinor Ekenes, his old girlfriend from way back in 1961. She'd been suspicious of their relationship for as long as she could remember. In fact, she believed that Rolf was currently with Elinor — the two of them flying away together.

"Rolf's gone off to Norway with Elinor," she said firmly. "I did my best. I followed him all the way to Norway. I took Flight 726 on Scandinavian Airways."

"When was that?" Clever asked.

"I think it was on October 10," Ruth said. "I spent two days in Norway looking for him. But I didn't find them."

No, she said she hadn't contacted any of

his family members in his native country because she didn't think they'd know where he was.

Clever jotted the information about her flight to Norway in his notebook. "Fine," he said, smiling. "We can check on that and you'll be on the list of passengers."

As he glanced up, he saw that the lines in Ruth Neslund's face had suddenly rearranged themselves into a mask of shock. "She was really startled," he recalled. "Her face just dropped and her mouth hung open. She hadn't expected anyone to follow up on what she told us. She figured we'd just go away and be satisfied with her version of where her husband was."

A man in his fifties — or even sixties — might be expected to leave his wife and a comfortable home in a midlife crisis and take off with another woman. But eighty? It didn't ring true to either Greg Doss or Ray Clever, and Ruth Neslund noticed their doubt.

Her answers became much more guarded as they questioned her about her flight to catch Rolf with her rival. She wasn't giving nearly as many details, and her hands fluttered nervously in her lap as they continued to ask more specific questions about why Rolf had left — and when.

Doss and Clever spent about half an hour in the Neslunds' home, with the interview growing more stilted as the minutes passed. Ruth had gradually turned toward Greg Doss, whose questions weren't as accusing, dismissing Ray Clever. It was apparent that she didn't care for Clever or his constant note-taking.

When they left, she was far less animated than she had been. As they drove away, Clever remarked to Doss, "I don't know whether she killed him or not, but she did something to him, and she's lying to us."

They were back at the Neslund house the next day. Ray Clever read Ruth her Miranda rights again, and asked if she would be willing to continue their conversation. Ruth seemed somewhat more relaxed than she had been when they left. Again, she said, "Of course."

The investigators proceeded, deliberately giving the impression that they believed that Rolf Neslund might have left of his own accord, but could subsequently have had an accident or even died of a stroke or heart attack. Clever asked Ruth if she had a current photograph of her husband, and she gestured toward several color photos on an end table. They were mostly family pictures, showing Ruth and Rolf together at different stages in their marriage, or with other family members.

It looked as though Ruth might have been feeling sentimental about her marriage because there was a projector set up with a screen in the living room. Several slides of happier days lay near the projector.

She picked out two pictures of Rolf and handed them to Ray Clever. "This looks like him now," she said.

Ruth began another long and rambling monologue on her suspicions of where he might be. It was difficult to break into her opinions, but Clever interrupted her. "Can you give me any information about your husband that would help us identify him — even if he should not be alive now?"

She stared at him, as if it had never occurred to her that Rolf might be dead. "Well, he has some tattoos — old tattoos," she said. "On his right forearm, he has a heart with an arrow through it — and it says 'Muriel' above it. That was some girlfriend he had a long time ago. She's dead now.

"And on his left forearm, he's got something that looks like a Coast Guard insignia, or maybe it's an American flag. And on the middle finger of his right hand, there's an arrow tattooed around that finger."

Ruth remembered myriad details about

85

her missing husband. When Clever asked her if there were dental X-rays available for Rolf, she shook her head. "His teeth are false — both uppers and lowers. Dr. Sam Anderson made them. His office is on Northwest Eighty-fifth in Seattle. And he had prescription glasses from Dr. Heffernan at the Pay-Less Drugstore at Thirty-fifth and Aurora."

According to Ruth, it was also quite possible that Rolf had once had two broken fingers. "I think Elinor broke them once in her lawyer's office in Canada. He never got them treated, as far as I know."

Now Ruth began to talk about Elinor again, going into detail about all the legal problems she had endured because of Elinor and her attorneys. Whether she was questioned about her alleged love rival or not, Ruth was determined to bring Elinor into the conversation.

"Have you had any letters or calls from Elinor or her attorneys recently?" Ray Clever asked her.

"No," she said firmly. "Of course not. That's ridiculous, because I have nothing to do with her." Ruth re-emphasized her lack of communication with Rolf's one-time fiancée.

"Anything else about Rolf that makes him stand out?" Clever asked.

Ruth half-smiled as she told Clever that Rolf was bowlegged. "Too many years of riding decks on the ocean." He also had a split diaphragm, an injury that he sustained when he was a young man and lifted a heavy log.

Ruth Neslund was clearly a woman with a keen memory, and a talent for minutiae. Whatever their differences, she had known her husband well.

She listed his clothing sizes: "Jacket, 41 chest; shirt, 15 1/2 neck, 33 sleeve; pants, 35 waist, 29 inseam. He wore size 9 1/2 shoe, and a 6 7/8 hat."

She suggested that the investigators check Elinor Ekenes's house to see if Rolf had his clothes stored there. She recalled that Rolf had a particular set of cuff links that he always wore with his French cuff shirts. "They were Viking ships. He had other cuff links, too, but I never saw him without the Viking ship ones."

Clever asked if they might look at Rolf's jewelry box — still at the Neslunds' home — to see if he had left anything behind. But Ruth kept talking as if she hadn't heard him. After he'd asked her several more times, she finally agreed to lead the deputies to the box. When Clever glanced in, he saw at once that the Viking ship cuff links that she had just described were among her husband's left-behind jewelry. There was also a very expensive man's watch with a broken metal wristband.

When Doss and Clever found the cuff links that she'd insisted Rolf was never without, Ruth became very nervous. Her voice quavered and her hands shook as she tried to backpedal on her own remarks. She began to talk again about the histories of the cuff links and the watch. She clearly wanted to show that she and Rolf had been very close and that she had been a huge part of his life, at least until their recent arguments.

"Could you tell us a little more about the day that your husband left?" Clever asked her. "What did he say?"

"Well, he said, 'I'm not coming back.' Or he might have said 'I'll be back after the first of the year — if ever!'"

The more she talked, the more she raised the deputies' suspicions. Ruth said she knew there had been gossip on Lopez. She was well aware that a man who lived on Lopez was spreading rumors that Rolf was dead.

"I made him apologize to me once for gossiping about someone I was supposed to be married to before Rolf."

But, oddly, Ruth said she hadn't confronted the man for saying that Rolf was dead. She didn't comment on why she hadn't done so.

Ruth Neslund's conversation skipped along like a stone flung upon the waves.

"Rolf drinks like a European, you know," she said. "That means beer in the morning almost every day, sherry in the afternoon, and several highballs before dinner, and then wine and Aquavit with dinner."

She explained that all that drinking only made Rolf's diabetes worse. "And it made his blood toxic, too," Ruth said firmly. "That's why I tried to make excuses for him when he started hitting me. He never remembered later about fighting with me."

After two visits from Clever and Doss in two days, Ruth Neslund was becoming more agitated and more talkative, but she wasn't giving much information that was helpful about where her husband might be six months after he reportedly stalked out of their home, saying either that he was never coming back, or that he might be back after the first of the year. It was now the end of February. The "first of the year" had come and gone.

Ruth was also angry. "She phoned our undersheriff, Rod Tvrdy," Clever said. "She admitted to him that she might have embroidered some of the things she told us, but she said that was because she didn't like the 'California detective's' questions, so she'd made some things up."

Ruth had singled Clever out as her least-favorite deputy, and she particularly resented what she considered his "arrogant California attitude." What she did not know was she had previously dealt with another investigator from California: Joe Caputo, Greg Doss's former partner.

"Ruth always liked me," Joe Caputo recalled. "She evidently didn't know where I was from . . ."

Joe grew up in Old Town in San Diego, and then in Escondido and San Marcos. He didn't start out wanting to be a cop; he went to school to be a dental technician. Even though he eventually had his own dental lab, he admitted to himself that he'd never been "all that interested" in dental work. A cousin was a reserve officer for the Escondido Police Department and Joe joined, too.

"I realized then," he said, "that that was what I really wanted to do."

He was on several departments' waiting lists for entry-level positions in southern California when he made a trip to Lopez Island to visit his cousin who was working as a San Juan County deputy. Ironically, the cousin went back to work as a dental tech, and in 1978 Joe replaced him. Like Clever,

Caputo was single and didn't mind being either on patrol or on standby for forty-eight-hour shifts as there were only two deputies assigned to Lopez. One was off-duty while the other was on.

"I liked Lopez and the unique people there," Caputo recalled. "I must have had fifteen places where I could count on a cup of coffee or a piece of pie. I enjoyed my time on Lopez. I stopped by Rolf and Ruth's place a number of times for a brief visit or to pick up some flats of strawberries that Ruth was selling."

Caputo liked both Ruth and Rolf, but he and Greg Doss had been called to settle the Neslunds' domestic disputes from time to time. "Rolf was always sitting in his 'Easy Boy' recliner," Caputo recalled. "He sat there bleeding from his head and face, and Ruth didn't show anything in the way of injuries — only those marks that she claimed were burns from her oven."

Joe Caputo felt that Rolf always got the worst of their fights. "I don't think that Rolf would ever have hit a woman. Ruth was bigger than he was — she put on weight over the years — but Rolf had these massive forearms. He always reminded me of Popeye; his arms just bulged out beneath his short-sleeved shirt. Ship pilots had to climb from tugboats up maybe fifty, sixty feet onto ships on these rope ladders, lots of times in bad weather. He had to have arms like that to make it."

When Ruth had been drinking, which was usually the case before the Neslunds' fights, Caputo found her to be "the type that people would be embarrassed to be around — she wasn't the 'kind grandmother type.' Ruth had many good points to her personality, and she certainly could be entertaining at a get-together," Caputo said wryly, "but I'm also sure that Adolf Hitler had some good attributes."

When the Neslunds had one of their fights, it was always Rolf who volunteered to spend the night at the Islander-Lopez Resort's motel/apartments. "By the next day, they'd be back together," Caputo remembered.

Joe Caputo was a quiet and thoughtful man who kept his personal opinions hidden. That may have been why Ruth didn't resent him the way she did Ray Clever.

If Ruth thought that her tattling on them to Sheriff Ray Sheffer would make Doss and Clever back off, she was mistaken. Her indignation only made them more skeptical.

Caught in what were clearly lies, Ruth grew irate at the deputies' persistence. They were snooping into her personal life, pestering a poor woman whose husband had left her alone, acting as if she had done something wrong when they should have been more sympathetic. She was the one who'd been victimized. She was a longtime resident on Lopez Island and she deserved some respect.

Many of her neighbors echoed her feelings. Yes, there were a few Lopezians who liked to perpetuate rumors, but most people who knew Ruth said they couldn't imagine that she was capable of doing real harm. She was kind and friendly, and not that different from other island women in their sixties, familiar — even beloved — by some.

Not everyone was pleased to know that the San Juan County sheriff's deputies were worrying Ruth with their daily visits. A lot of neighborhood women felt sympathy for her. Her health wasn't that good, and still she had tried to keep her garden up, out there in soggy weather planting bulbs and flowers, or inside cooking for friends. No one to help her with chores, or comfort her when it grew dark at four in the afternoon in the wintertime. Ruth had a good business head, sure, but basically she was only an ordinary woman, aging, fighting weight gains, and now deserted by her husband after twenty years of marriage. Ruth had her sixty-first birthday on February 8. She spent it all alone.

"Rolf didn't even send her so much as a birthday card," one woman tsk-tsked. "He always sent cards to everyone, but not to his own wife."

On February 25, for the third day in a row, a sheriff's police cruiser turned into the lane leading to the Neslund house. This time, Undersheriff Rod Tvrdy accompanied Deputy Ray Clever. Ruth knew Rod, at least, and felt he would be nicer to her than Ray Clever.

They found Ruth Neslund still maintaining that Rolf had run away with Elinor Ekenes. She embellished her recall of Elinor's impact on her marriage even more. She believed her marriage would never have fallen apart if she hadn't had to deal with the woman who bore Rolf's sons.

Ruth told the investigators that she remembered more now about the arguments she and Rolf had just prior to his leaving. They had definitely been about Elinor.

"He wanted to give money to her," she said indignantly. "Fifteen thousand dollars! He was putting pressure on me to let him give that woman fifteen thousand dollars of our money. It was my money, too."

94

That had upset her terribly, Ruth said, because she was the one who brought most of the money into their bank accounts. She was the one with the business head who made investments, paid their bills, took care of everything so that Rolf didn't have to worry about it. All he had to do was ask her for whatever cash he wanted. It was always there in the dresser drawer for him. But not to give to Elinor.

Tvrdy and Clever nodded sympathetically as she talked. After her first unexpected encounter with Clever, Ruth had regrouped and seemed quite confident that he believed what she said. She didn't know that the investigators had made some inquiries at the Puget Sound Pilots' Association, the organization Rolf had belonged to for years, where, as its oldest member, he was a popular "grand old man." The pilots and their wives had had a number of parties since the prior August.

The last one had been in January. Of course, Rolf didn't attend — but Ruth did. And she had quite a bit to drink at the party. One couple there recalled that she'd made an odd remark. She'd said, "Rolf won't be coming home again; Rolf's in heaven."

Tvrdy asked her about that now, and she shook her head dismissively. "No, no —

that's not what I said. I said, 'Rolf would be in seventh heaven if only he could be here!' "

"What do you think Rolf is using for money?" the undersheriff asked her.

"He told me when he left that he'd be taken care of by the Ekeneses."

Later, although Ruth seemed to have an answer for everything, she finally outright admitted to Tvrdy and Clever that she had lied to them about going to Norway in October. Yes, she had left the island two months after Rolf walked out on her, but she hadn't flown to Norway. Instead, she had gone to Louisiana to visit her son and other relatives who lived there.

Now her story became really convoluted: She said she had been so mortified, knowing Rolf was with Elinor, that she hadn't even told her good friends and relatives what the real story was. She told one Lopez Island friend that she was going to Norway, and another that she was going to Louisiana.

"You see, I read a letter that was addressed to Rolf, and sent to the Pilots' Association," she said sadly. "It was from Elinor. Rolf always told me that he didn't want a divorce from me. But Elinor sued us for seventy-five thousand dollars to support her two sons. She was going to cause trouble for Rolf by telling that he lied about his age back in

1917 so he could get his first-mate papers. He said he was born in 1897, but he was really born in 1900."

That was true enough, but the sheriff's investigators didn't realize at the time of this interview that this was a story very similar to what Ruth had told Rolf two decades before to keep him from leaving her. It had worked then, and now she used another version of it to bolster her story about his elopement at the age of eighty with Elinor.

"Just before Rolf left me, he told my brother Robert that Robert had to stay here with me," she added, explaining that her brother had been visiting them in August. "He told my brother, 'She's going to need you,' and I realized then that Rolf was going to be gone a long time."

One thing that Sheriff Sheffer and his detectives knew about Ruth cast a shadow of doubt over her version of the end of her marriage: Just as Ray Clever had once told her, it had been easy to check on her travels the previous fall. Clever had simply contacted all the airlines that flew from the Seattle-Tacoma Airport to Norway. Ruth Neslund's name didn't appear on any of their passenger manifests on October 10 or any other date in October 1980. Before she ever admitted her lies to them, they knew the truth.

Even more interesting, they knew exactly where Elinor Ekenes was, and Rolf wasn't with her. Elinor might have traveled to Norway, but she had gone with another man — her new husband. They learned that she and Rolf had remained friends through the years, but she was anything but a femme fatale who was trying to lure him away from his wife.

The investigators allowed Ruth to ramble on about her theories, knowing all the while that Rolf's disappearance had nothing whatsoever to do with Elinor.

SIX

Although he had emigrated to America, Rolf had kept in constant contact with his family in Norway. Working with Interpol in Oslo, Ray Clever learned that none of his siblings or other relatives had heard from him.

Even before they heard from his friend Gunnar Olsborg, Rolf Neslund's brothers and sister had become very concerned. Harald Naeslund, from the city of Drummond, and Eugenie Naeslund Lindboe, who lived in Oslo (both used the Norwegian spelling for their last name), had always been in close touch with Rolf, and the family not only had rituals they observed on special days, but they had planned to visit Ruth and Rolf in October 1980.

Naeslund was a well-known name in Norway, particularly in the shipping industry. Rolf's siblings were quite wealthy now and owned a shipping line in their native country. They could well afford to visit him and

Ruth in America, and he looked forward to having them in his home.

But Eugenie had received a strange phone call in October 1980, from Lopez Island, from Ruth — not Rolf. "I was missing Rolf," Eugenie said, "and we talked about him. She said he was gone, and she didn't know where. Ruth and I said we would call each other if we saw him. She said she wanted to come to Norway and talk to me. She said she would come in a fortnight. She never called me again."

Eugenie recalled that Ruth said later in that phone call that she thought that Rolf had gone to "the Greek islands."

Harald and his wife had been planning to visit Rolf and Ruth that October so they could celebrate a number of family birthdays together. Harald had been relieved that Rolf seemed truly serene in his retirement and not especially distressed about the bridge incident. In fact, he'd written to Harald in June 1980.

"I am very satisfied," Rolf wrote. "I don't need to go out anymore to sea. There is too much to do from early in the morning. The swimming pool will be ready when you arrive — hurry up and come."

And again, on August 4, just a week or so before Rolf disappeared, he had written his brother enthusiastically, "We are waiting for the day you come!"

And then there was nothing. No communication at all from Rolf to his beloved siblings. Such a thing had never happened before, and they wondered if they might have offended him in some way. They didn't want to go to America if they weren't welcome, but there were no more calls about their planned trip in October.

Finally, on September 10, Ruth called Harald. "She told me that there was no need for us to come to visit," he said. "She said, 'Rolf's not here.' She said he drew twenty-five thousand dollars from the bank and was going to Europe. We canceled our plans to come to Lopez."

On November 3, 1980, Rolf Neslund's true birthday, his sister Eugenie had phoned the Neslund house to wish him a happy eightieth birthday. But he wasn't there — and neither was Ruth. A stranger to Eugenie answered the phone to say Rolf wasn't there, and Ruth had gone to visit her relatives. Although Eugenie didn't know her, the house-sitter was Winnie Kay Stafford, one of Ruth's closest and most devoted friends. She and her daughter had agreed to watch over the Alec Bay Road home while Ruth was gone back East.

Winnie Kay and her daughter moved into Ruth's house when "they" — allegedly Ruth and Rolf — "went to Massachusetts" and she stayed for two weeks. Winnie Kay didn't actually see Rolf leave, although, when she spoke about the Neslunds' East Coast trip, she always said "they" and "them" in referring to Ruth's travels that fall. When the deputies questioned her later, Winnie Kay said she had received many phone calls while she was staying at Ruth's, and she had advised callers that Ruth and Rolf were en route to Massachusetts. Winnie Kay asked Ray Clever "not to bother" Ruth with questions because it would be "a waste of time."

Harald and Eugenie were troubled. If Rolf had left on a trip to Europe or just to Massachusetts, surely he would have contacted them, and he almost certainly would have told them about his trips before he even left home. Now even Ruth was completely out of touch with them, and some stranger was living in their home.

Almost four months later, when he checked with the Norwegian Consulate, Ray Clever learned that if Rolf was in Norway in the late summer and fall of 1980, he could only have stayed for ninety days. After that, as an American citizen, he would have been required to ask for an extension of his visitor's visa. But there was no record of that at the consulate.

Gunnar Olsborg placed ads in Washington State newspapers offering a twenty-five-thousand-dollar reward for any information on Rolf Neslund, to no avail. Apparently, no one had seen him, and there were no takers even for a hefty reward.

As the holiday season approached in 1980, Ruth had received sympathetic messages from her relatives and friends who were worried about her because her husband had, according to her, abandoned her.

"Dear Ruth," two old friends wrote, "all of us down here were stricken by the news of Rolf. Buddy told us.

"It must have been so hard on you. You're a strong lady, but there are limits. Hang in there, girl. We pray for you."

And so, as the spring of 1981 approached, Rolf Neslund remained among the missing. Ruth told the sheriff's men how she had found his beloved Lincoln Continental on the other side of the Anacortes ferry run, apparently abandoned there. Had he driven it onto the ferry and then down the ramp to the mainland himself, or had someone else left it there? If Rolf had left his favorite car behind, how did he get to Seattle or the airport or anywhere else, for that matter?

People on Lopez Island were used to Rolf Neslund's being gone for weeks at a time, but that was before he retired after the West Seattle Bridge incident. Now he was retired and no longer had a job that would take him out to sea or on Puget Sound, steering ships into port.

As suspicious as the deputies were — and they were — there was no solid evidence that Rolf had not left his home of his own accord. It would take a lot more than his "abandoned" wife's ever-changing stories to bring charges against her.

The San Juan County Sheriff's Office expanded their inquiries into Rolf Neslund's life and habits. They talked to his neighbors and his many friends, especially the ship pilots who knew him so well. Every interview indicated that he was a man of precise habit, a man who was gregarious and who kept in close touch with both his relatives and his friends. Ray Clever doubted that such a man would have voluntarily walked away from his life six months earlier. It didn't make sense.

Sheriff Ray Sheffer, Undersheriff Rod Tvrdy, Greg Doss, Ray Clever, Joe Caputo, and Perry Mortensen, along with other deputies brought into the search for Neslund, didn't know what had happened to him, but they were determined to find the old ship's pilot — alive . . . or dead.

It would not be easy.

The investigators began to examine Rolf Neslund's life as minutely as if they were looking through a microscope. Could they find some forewarning, signal, or hint about where he might be? If he was alive somewhere, surely he should have been in contact with someone. And if he was alive, was there some way to entice him to walk out of the shadows?

If he was dead, where were his remains? Perhaps hidden in the depths of the Strait of Juan de Fuca? There are so many stretches of open water around the San Juan Islands and Seattle, and there had been several instances where people had simply vanished from ferryboats wending their way between the mainland and the islands of Washington: suicides, accidents, deliberate disappearances . . . or, perhaps, murder. Under the darkness of night, all it would have taken was a leap over a ferry's rail or a swift push from someone stronger and younger than Rolf Neslund was.

Maybe he was buried somewhere on Lopez Island. He wouldn't be the first victim to be dispatched and then buried in a hidden — but shallow — grave. Most of western

Washington is made up of anything but rich loam. Without heavy-duty equipment, a makeshift grave is of necessity a shallow grave; any shovel hits rocks just beneath the surface. As one forensic anthropologist testified in a murder trial, "All makeshift graves in Washington State are 'shallow graves.' "

Joe Caputo spent a lot of time walking the fields around the Neslund property — both on- and off-duty. "I'd get permission from property owners to do my 'walk-abouts' scrutinizing the fields and brush. If Rolf was buried there, I didn't want the site turning up years later."

But Caputo didn't come across a lonely grave. And unless a body is discovered, it is very difficult to prove unequivocally in a court of law that a human being is no longer living.

Laymen tend to believe that the term "corpus delicti" refers to the actual corpse of a homicide victim. In truth, corpus delicti is the body of the case — not the body of the victim. But if detectives and prosecutors can come up with enough circumstantial evidence to convince a "reasonable man (or woman)" that a murder had occurred, it isn't technically necessary to show a jury or a judge photographs of a body, a crime scene, or an autopsy report.

If it looks like a rat, squeals like a rat, smells like a rat, acts like a rat, then it just might be a rat. That would be an example of circumstantial evidence and deductive reasoning. Still, in the early eighties there were very few cases in Washington State — if any — where murder convictions had resulted when no body was ever discovered.

The San Juan County investigators believed that Rolf Neslund had been dead for at least twenty months, but they had to find a way to prove that.

All of us who are still breathing can be tracked by paper trails — credit-card purchases, phone calls, tax filings, bank deposits or withdrawals, medical care sought, letters, sightings, or chance meetings. Rolf had a bank account in Norway where he kept the several thousand dollars left to him in his mother's will. He had not withdrawn any of the money there, nor had he tried to access any of the bank accounts he shared with Ruth for substantial amounts of cash — not after August 8, 1980.

All the checks written were signed by Ruth.

There were endless paper trails for Ruth. She had continued her life without a ripple. On August 14, only days after Rolf left her, Ruth put an ad in the *Friday Harbor Journal,* paying $9.10 to offer several items for sale: "Commercial meat grinder $550.00. Antique sewing machine $50. Potbelly Stove, $100. Office furniture, sofa, and chair — $125. Record-A-Call $350, Steel desk, $100. AND 1968 Plymouth 9-Passenger Station Wagon — $500, 1964 Ford Fairlane 500 — $450, 1955 Mustang Fastback, pony seats, $2,000."

How odd that she put Rolf's prize Mustang up for sale almost before the door slammed behind him. . . .

Ray Clever wondered what might have occurred during the first ten days of August 1980 that would have caused a major rift between Rolf and Ruth. They had battled with words, fingernails, household objects, and fists for years — but they continued to live together, however uneasy the détente.

Clever suspected that there had been some kind of a sea change that summer, something so cataclysmic that there was no going back. Several of Rolf's longtime friends had visited at his home or run into him in June and July 1980. They recalled that he was happy — "bouncy" almost, one said. He was in such good physical condition that he seemed barely to have aged in the last few decades. His mind was described as "very sharp," and he had the muscles of a much younger man.

And then Ray Clever met a woman who had information that helped him find a loose end in the tangled skein of conflicting stories. He pulled at it and began to unravel the case by talking to a colorful witness named Kay Scheffler, who lived in the north end of Seattle. Kay was an old and platonic friend of Rolf's, a large, rumpled-looking woman who resembled Marie Dressler or Marjorie Main as they looked when they played "Tugboat Annie" and "Ma Kettle" in famous movies of the past.

Kay told Clever that Rolf had come down to Seattle on July 29, 1980. He told her that he needed some cash, and he hadn't asked Ruth for any that day, so he had gone to one of their banks to cash a seventy-five-dollar check.

"They wouldn't cash it for him," Kay said. "They told him he had insufficient funds."

Puzzled and sure that it had to be a mistake, Rolf had stopped in to see Kay Scheffler. She loaned him thirty dollars. And then Rolf asked her about the mortgage he and Ruth held on the house she had bought from them.

"He asked me when I would be paying it off," Kay said. "And I told him, 'Rolf, I paid that loan off in 1975 — five years ago. I paid Ruth.'

"He was shocked."

Rolf had told Kay Scheffler that Ruth said the loan to her hadn't been paid off. He himself had no idea about how much money he had — Ruth was in charge of that. She was the one who collected his retirement pension, and any other money due them. She did all the banking.

"He said he gave Ruth power of attorney to do all that," Kay told Ray Clever.

Rolf was suddenly concerned; he didn't know where his money was, and it sure wasn't in the bank where he had tried to cash a check. He thought he had close to eighty thousand dollars in that account. Now, at his age, even though he was healthy, he was facing his own mortality. "He said he wanted to change his will so that he could leave something to his sons," Kay told Clever. "I told him I'd try to help him, and he said he would be back to see me on August 5."

Rolf Neslund came to Kay Scheffler's house again on the fifth, and he told her he had taken care of some of his problems. Without Ruth's knowledge, he had secretly taken the power of attorney document out of their safe.

"He thought that's all he had to do," Kay said. "That, if he had the papers, Ruth couldn't say what to do with his money. I told him that wasn't enough — that he had to hire a lawyer to revoke her power of attorney."

Rolf then asked Kay if she'd help him find an attorney and she said she would. He was also worried because he'd found out that Ruth had applied for a mortgage loan on their Lopez home — which had been free and clear for years. But she hadn't told him anything about that. Rolf wanted help getting the title so he could see what was going on. He told Kay he also intended to see that his pension payments from the Puget Sound Pilots' Association came directly to him — and not to Ruth.

"I told him I'd help him," Kay said, adding that Rolf had been agitated and that before he left, oddly, he actually said he was afraid of Ruth. They had made an appointment for him to come back on August 12, when Kay Scheffler would have the title report on his house for him.

"But he didn't show up," she added. "I haven't seen him since."

Once he'd been alerted to the problems with his bank accounts and the fact that Kay Scheffler had paid Ruth the last of the money on her mortgage five years earlier, Rolf visited or called several old friends. Among them were Margaret Ronning and her husband. The couple had also purchased real estate from Ruth and Rolf. He stopped at the Ronnings' house on July 29, after he left Kay's.

Rolf asked Margaret if they owed him or Ruth any money, and she shook her head. Like Kay, Margaret Ronning had paid off everything — to Ruth — a long time back. Rolf told Margaret, too, that he was trying to discover where all his money was, and that he'd just found out there was no money in his account in the bank he had always used.

Rolf went back to the Ronnings' house on August 5, but they had other company and he didn't stay. "He said he would come back another time," Margaret said, "but we never spoke with him again."

The old man had also gone to see Elinor Ekenes on those same two days — July 29 and August 5. His long-ago sweetheart saw that Rolf was very upset, and he told her he was determined to change his will. He wanted their sons to have a fair share of his assets, and he promised Elinor he would find a way to put that in his will.

"If I die," he said bleakly, "please see that there is an autopsy on my body."

Elinor had stared at him in surprise as he explained he was living in fear for his life. The slender woman told Ray Clever that it was his wife, Ruth, that Rolf was afraid of.

It was out of character for Rolf Neslund to be afraid of anybody or any thing, but Elinor said she felt he was truly fearful. She knew from her own experience that Ruth did strange and disturbing things.

"Sometime in the winter of 1979," Elinor recalled, "she called our phone and asked to speak to my son, Erik. I told her that he wasn't home, and she told me to give him a message."

"What was that about?" Clever asked.

"She said, 'Tell him his father is dead.' "

That, of course, turned out to be untrue, but it was the kind of statement that could stop a heart in midbeat.

Elinor told Clever that from the first month Rolf had married Ruth, he talked about leaving her. "The last time I saw him — on that Tuesday, August 5 — I suggested that he should just go to Norway and not return — just stay there, because his life was so miserable. And he told me, 'You have no idea how many times I've tried. They've always caught up with me.' "

"They?" Clever asked. "Who would that be?"

113

Elinor wasn't sure, but she thought Rolf meant Ruth and some members of her family because she seemed to be in close touch with them, and often had her relatives staying with the Neslunds.

"That day," she recalled saying to Rolf, "I told him I was going to Norway in a week. But we had no plan to go together."

It was Elinor's belief that Rolf feared Ruth was planning to poison him, and he was worried that, without an autopsy, she would probably get away with it.

There was no question that Rolf Neslund was nervous about what Ruth might do, but apparently he wasn't convinced he had only a short time to live, because after he left Elinor, he had ordered his new glasses. He obviously expected to live to wear them. His optometrist's receptionist told Clever that Rolf had never come to pick them up. She had sent several bills to his home on Lopez Island in the fall of 1980.

"Mrs. Neslund finally sent us a check in the first part of March — March 1981."

Clever realized that would have been about two weeks after he and Greg Doss had called on Ruth and begun to ask questions.

Although Rolf had access to all that money in a retirement account, he hadn't withdrawn any of it. However, his pension checks had been cashed, endorsed by Ruth. That was also true of his Social Security checks. That hadn't raised any red flags because she routinely did all their banking.

Rolf Neslund himself had left no paper trail at all. He was in the midst of life in the second week of August 1980, and then he seemed to have walked into the mist that sometimes clings to the shoreline and country roads of the San Juan Islands at dusk.

No one had heard from him since August. For more than fifty years, he had personally written and addressed Christmas cards. The address list that had once numbered 150 had dwindled to only about twenty-five lifelong friends as he aged and his friends died off. Contacted by the investigators, not one of his close friends had heard from him during the Christmas holidays in 1980.

As Ray Clever and his fellow investigators continued to follow an ever-changing path to Rolf Neslund, they became more baffled. There were just too many stories. Now they learned that Ruth had told one of her neighbors that Rolf was in New England with some distant relative, and that she planned to go there and bring him home.

Naturally, the question arose: "If Rolf Neslund was alive, what was he living on?" He hadn't accessed any of his usual sources for money. When she was asked about how much cash Rolf had taken with him, Ruth came up with varying amounts — from six hundred dollars to twenty-five thousand dollars.

It had been easy enough to find out where Rolf was during the first week of August 1980. But one day seemed to be the last day he was seen. He'd conveyed his concern and his outright fear of his wife to several friends, and then gone about his errands. On August 5, he ordered the new glasses, but he hadn't picked them up. His personal physician had prescribed the drug Orinase (generic name: tolbutamide) to treat Rolf's adult-onset Type 2 diabetes.

Ruth had apparently failed to understand his illness, or she was lying to the investigators. She was wrong when she told them that alcohol "poisoned" Rolf's blood. That was the opinion of someone with little medical knowledge; alcohol was not good for someone with diabetes, and it would certainly have aggravated Rolf's condition and raised his blood sugar, but it didn't "poison" him. Because he did drink, it was essential that he not run out of his Orinase prescription, and yet he had failed to pick up his medicine from the pharmacy, and he had never called his doctor for a renewal either.

Besides missing his appointment with Kay Scheffler, Rolf had also arranged to meet with one of Ruth's nieces, Donna Smith, on August 12. He hadn't shown up and that puzzled Donna.

The San Juan County sheriff's investigators had now narrowed the dates of Rolf's "leave-taking" to August 7 and 8. By the middle part of August, Rolf hadn't shown up for any appointments he'd made.

When he left, he had no money, no car, no glasses, no medicine, no extra clothes, no lucky cuff links, no watch, none of the items he would need for a long journey.

But where on earth did he go? And how could he possibly mingle with other walk-ons onto a ferry headed off-island without someone recognizing him?

SEVEN

The search for Rolf Neslund was ultimately frustrating. Several weeks after their initial visits to Ruth Neslund in her Alec Bay Road home, the San Juan County sheriff's investigators had little doubt that Rolf was dead, but they had not one iota of physical evidence that might prove that to a jury. Cases can go forward with a preponderance of circumstantial evidence, but they were pretty sure that no prosecuting attorney would want to take on the case as it was. It was all smoke and mirrors and theory, nothing to take to the San Juan County deputy prosecuting attorney on criminal cases, Charlie Silverman. If they did, he would surely send them out to get more physical evidence.

Furthermore, it really didn't seem likely that a woman of Ruth Neslund's age, who was overweight and claiming to be in poor health, could have the strength to carry out a grisly murder. Still, when this information was lumped with all the other bits and pieces of circumstantial evidence the sheriff's investigators had gathered, it was at least enough to allow the investigators to obtain a search warrant for the Neslund property.

They got their search warrant.

On April 13, 1981, Donald K. Phillips, a supervising criminalist from the Washington State Patrol Crime Lab, traveled to Lopez Island. It was barely light when he boarded at Anacortes, and Undersheriff Rod Tvrdy met him on the ferry landing at seven-forty-five that morning.

It was going to be a beautiful spring morning. Trees and bushes were just leafing out with bright green new growth, fruit trees had blossoms, and daffodils, forsythia bushes, and Scotch broom dotted fields and yards with bursts of buttery yellow.

And so, eight weeks after Greg Doss and Ray Clever had first interviewed Ruth Neslund about her missing husband, a phalanx of official cars turned down the dirt lane that led to her backyard. Sheep nibbling in the pastures ignored the convoy.

Phillips, accompanied by Doss, Clever, and Caputo, was about to search for evidence that might prove that the old sea captain who had lived here had been dead for months — that he had never left home at all.

All of it seemed surreal.

The men located several green plastic garbage bins behind the red house. They were filled with burned and partially burned debris. When it was spread out on a screen and examined, they found a single spent .22-caliber cartridge and bagged and labeled it. The burned and partially burned material in the green garbage cans wasn't unusual — only insulation, beer cans, blackened metal, glass jars, and some carpet.

Nearby, they saw that a blue metal burn barrel contained still-burning coals. Without garbage pickup on the island, everyone along the rural roads had burn barrels. This one was new, its paint barely singed, far too new to hold the remains of a man who had disappeared eight months before. Still it made the hairs on the back of their necks prickle to think that it was possible that Rolf Neslund had been disposed of in a similar barrel. But when they looked in, the glowing ashes looked to be only papers and normal garbage.

The searchers spread out over the yard and into the pastureland beyond, their eyes focused on the ground as they looked for some sign of what might have been a grave. They found no suspicious dips or humps.

Next, they moved into the residence and

searched it meticulously. The search warrant had listed the specific evidence they were allowed to look for: bullet holes in the wall and/or bloodstains. Phillips tested a number of stains he found to see if they were blood. They weren't.

At some point, Joe Caputo sat with Ruth in her living room. He noted a book on her coffee table, a Reader's Digest condensed edition. He read the title to himself — *To Catch a Killer: How to Get Away With Murder.* Ruth saw him glance at it, but said nothing.

A Chevrolet station wagon parked outside was also tested for bloodstains. There were none.

The search team spent two days going over the Neslund property, but in the end there was nothing at all in the homey house that could be construed as physical evidence in a murder: only a single bullet cartridge. That didn't mean much out in the country. Ruth herself was known to be skilled with guns, and those Lopez residents who lived in the country sometimes fired rounds at dogs to scare them away from stalking sheep.

Donald Phillips took sixteen photographs of the house which he had enlarged and later gave to Greg Doss.

One lawman who asked to be anonymous said, "We have a suspect, we have a motive, we don't have a body, but we think there was one here once."

Ruth Neslund was scornful and triumphant as she crowed to friends that the detectives hadn't found anything. Why should they? She assured them that she would never have hurt Rolf.

She told several people that he was most likely "sitting in the Greek islands, waiting for all of this to blow over — and then he'll come home."

But the months passed and seasons changed, and Rolf didn't come home.

EIGHT

The missing persons case, or, more likely, the possible homicide case, stalled.

Just as the deputies had suspected, Charlie Silverman was hesitant to bring charges against anyone without more proof or information. And for good reason. Should someone be charged with murder, tried, and acquitted, that would be the end of it. New evidence wouldn't matter because double jeopardy would attach. No one can be tried for a crime again after he has been found not guilty. It was better to wait, but it was galling for the sheriff's deputies who believed that Ruth Neslund knew exactly where her husband was.

Ruth's supporters were steadfast, and they formed a circle of protection around her. She certainly wasn't a pariah, and her life continued almost as usual. She was free to entertain her friends, to visit with them, to leave the island whenever she chose.

With the case becalmed, and the sheriff's investigators backing off — or so Ruth thought — she went about her business. She had already sold Rolf's Mustang a few months after he disappeared. In June, she placed an ad in a local paper, the *Friday Harbor Record*'s classifieds. She offered to sell her house and land, listing the property for half a million dollars. Even though she advertised it both locally and in the *Wall Street Journal,* at that price, she got no serious offers, only a few lookers. Eventually, she changed her mind, and took it off the market.

By December 1981, Rolf had been gone for sixteen months, and Ruth said she needed some kind of resolution about their finances. Wherever her husband was, she had to live, and to do that she needed some income she could count on. Back in the spring, the Puget Sound Pilots' Association had moved to block her from getting Rolf's eighteen-hundred-dollar-a-month pension payments. She had always resented the way Rolf handled that money because she knew he had given some of it to Elinor to help out his children.

"All he wanted," Kay Scheffler said, "was six hundred dollars for the house, six hundred dollars for her [meaning Ruth], and six hundred dollars for himself. Ruth told me that she said to him, 'I'm not going to give it to you; you're just going to give it away!'

"He was figuring he'd give his share to his sons," Kay continued. "She [Ruth] figured to hold on to it."

In her petition to be appointed trustee of Rolf's property, Ruth complained to San Juan County Superior Court Judge Howard Patrick that she was barely scraping by. She said her current income was only about five hundred dollars a month.

In a hearing held on December 16, Rolf and Elinor's younger son, Erik Ekenes, twenty-one, requested that he or "some other suitable person" be appointed as the trustee — anyone but Ruth. But even Erik's attorney acknowledged that civil law decreed that the preferred trustee of the estate of a missing or incompetent person is normally that person's spouse. And that, of course, was Ruth.

Judge Patrick appointed Ruth trustee — but with several conditions. The Court ordered her to file an inventory and an appraisal of the property. That would be used to fix the amount of bond she would be required to post before her trusteeship became official.

Erik and Rolf Ekenes agreed not to interfere with Ruth's activities in any way. They weren't after their father's estate, because they didn't believe there was anything left of it. Surely, Ruth had either already spent the money or hidden it away. What they did want was some resolution and some kind of justice for their father.

On January 8, 1982, Ruth dutifully appeared before Judge Patrick with her handwritten inventory. More realistically, she now valued her home at $266,533.73, a little more than half her asking price six months earlier. The judge ordered that 70 percent of that figure would be her bond, and he also stipulated that she could pay herself considerably more than five hundred dollars a month from income accruing to the property.

For the moment at least, Ruth Neslund's life took on a modicum of serenity. Rolf was still missing, but she had her home and enough to live on, and she continued to buy and sell antiques and other items ranging from furniture to small parcels of real estate.

But any exultation Ruth may have felt over her small win in Judge Patrick's courtroom would not last long. Sheriff Sheffer's department had no intention of dropping their investigation into what might have happened to Rolf Neslund.

They continued to receive hearsay and tall tales that were circulating around Lopez Island.

All of it led exactly nowhere.

And then, Ray Clever's reporter brother, Dick, wrote a story about the disappearance of Rolf Neslund, and it appeared under a prominent headline. It was enough to spur two women to come forward — even though they were afraid of vengeance if someone should be angry with them.

They were Ruth's nieces, who were concerned about the way their "Uncle Rolf" had disappeared. They weren't sure what the true story behind that might be, but they were worried. And they wrote to the Puget Sound Pilots' Association.

Ruth's older sister, Mamie, had two daughters in their thirties: Joy Stroup, who lived in Circleville, Ohio, and Donna Smith, who lived in Washington. The information the women sent puzzled those who opened mail at the Pilots' Association, but longtime pilots Captain Gunnar Olsborg and William Henshaw followed up on the information they had sent. Both of them, especially Gunnar Olsborg, remained among Rolf's closest friends. They read what sounded like a fearsome story: Joy Stroup had made a bizarre and shocking accusation against Ruth.

Joy wrote that she wanted to talk to someone in authority about her aunt Ruth. Ruth had evidently called her many times between November 1979 and July 1980. Most of the time, she had been drinking and said crazy things like, "I'm watching Rolf out the window," and, "I could shoot him from right here." Sometimes she spoke of "wasting Rolf " or "burning him."

Joy's sister, Donna Smith, lived in the Seattle area. She was the girl who had been like a daughter to Ruth when she was younger, but Donna remembered the time Ruth had locked herself in the bunkhouse to keep Rolf away. Ruth had called her, saying, "If he comes back here, I'm going to shoot him!"

That was in the fall of 1979, and Ruth had threatened violence toward her husband in numerous phone calls since. Indeed, there had been so many phone calls when Ruth was inebriated that her relatives tended to dismiss them as drunken ravings.

But Captain Gunnar Olsborg had a sinking feeling about Rolf. He suspected his longtime friend was dead, his body hidden from view.

San Juan County authorities made arrangements for Joy Stroup to fly to Seattle for a meeting. The Puget Sound Pilots' Association paid for Joy's trip. Joy Stroup, Donna Smith, Gunnar Olsborg, San Juan County's Chief Criminal Deputy Prosecutor Charlie Silverman, Ray Clever, and an attorney met in the Columbia Tower, a soaring building in downtown Seattle.

This was a clandestine meeting for many reasons. Joy and Donna were afraid of reprisal from their aunt and from other family members, and neither the San Juan County Prosecuting Attorney's Office or the Sheriff's Department were able to act on what they heard that day. If anything that the young women described had, indeed, occurred, it still had to be proven.

An investigation like this would be difficult for a big-city police department and prosecutor; it seemed almost impossible for a small county sheriff and a prosecutor who was far better versed in civil law than in criminal proceedings. Silverman, newly elected, admitted that he felt he was in over his head. Beyond that, San Juan County had few citizens per square mile and their tax base didn't spew out wealth to pay public servants and court costs for massive investigations.

Fortunately, the legislature in Washington State voted in a new law in 1981, a statute that would be central to the Rolf Neslund investigation. The State Attorney General's Office now had a Criminal Division: prosecutors and investigators who, along with the Washington State Patrol's criminalists, were available to assist some of the state's smaller and less-affluent counties when they were involved in major probes. Attorney General Ken Eikenberry was sending his top team in to work beside the San Juan County detectives.

Senior Assistant Attorney General Greg Canova and Criminal Investigator Bob Keppel (the same Keppel who was the first King County detective assigned to the Ted Bundy cases in 1974, and who would later advise the Green River serial murder task force) were young, but they were already two of the smartest and most admired men in Washington State criminal law. Together the AG's team would soon successfully prosecute murderers years after the killers thought they had, quite literally, gotten away with murder. The Neslund case would be their first.

Canova and Keppel weren't taking over — the San Juan County investigators were still principally involved — but the two AG's men would be there to help, both in the investigation of the Neslund case and to assist in any trial that might evolve.

Joining the two offices together — the attorney general of the State of Washington and the San Juan County Sheriff's Office — had to be done tactfully. Luckily, they were not adversaries nor did they encounter "turf wars" over which assignments belonged to one or the other. Indeed, Ray Clever and Bob Keppel would have nothing but praise for one another, and Charlie Silverman, recently out of law school and more versed in civil law than criminal proceedings, said he was relieved to have Greg Canova come on board. The job ahead promised to be difficult and there was every chance that they could not bring charges against anyone because they had no corpse and apparently no witnesses brave enough to come forward and testify in open court.

Investigating disappearances and murders wasn't something that deputies on a small and mostly friendly island were often called upon to do. They had to keep performing their regular duties, and most of the deputies kept their own files with them. Computers certainly weren't part of their filing system — nor were they standard equipment in either Seattle or Spokane law enforcement offices at the time.

Ray Clever was a man who made lists. When he found what he sought or finished performing some task he felt essential to his investigation in the Neslund case, he checked it off. And then he made new and longer lists. If what he discovered seemed positive, he wrote "Bingo!" in his notebooks. Initially, he didn't have many "Bingos!"

Bob Keppel was also a detail man. Known as a brilliant interrogator, Keppel's other forte is organization. Even when computers were in an embryonic stage when the "Ted" serial killer was still roving in Washington, Oregon, and Utah back in the midseventies, Keppel used a "stone-age" computer to winnow out a half dozen names from a roster of thousands of "Ted" suspects. One of those names was Theodore Bundy.

By 1982 Keppel had mastered the art of organizing information and evidence in criminal cases. He was able to take all the different working files of the San Juan deputies and coalesce the information into a tightly organized narrative of the disappearance of an eighty-year-old man.

The question remained: Could such an impressive lineup of lawmen prevail over one sweet-faced, elderly woman who might, indeed, have a problem with alcohol, but who continued to present herself to the world as a woman scorned, a long-suffering wife betrayed, a lone woman who wanted only to keep her home, grow her flowers, visit with her family, and find some happiness in her "golden years"?

And would Joy Stroup and Donna Smith be brave enough to come forward with what they knew in a court of law?

NINE

It had not been easy for either the lawmen or those who rushed to support Ruth Neslund. The *Journal of the San Juan Islands* and the *Friday Harbor Record* were sometimes thorns in the Sheriff's Department's side, continually nagging at them to do something, or even worse, suggesting that they were humorously incompetent.

But they also printed rumors that upset and angered Ruth. Wary now, Ruth "lawyered up," first with Mitch Cogdill of Everett and then switching to Fred Weedon, who had been in charge of the Public Defender's Office in Pierce County in Tacoma. Weedon was a savvy criminal lawyer who spent vacations on Lopez Island and Ruth considered him a "neighbor" she could trust.

Cogdill and Weedon were vocal in their criticism of law enforcement. The local papers printed their statements dutifully, and half the county seemed to feel Ruth was being unfairly besieged.

The sheriff's men were thwarted in their efforts to investigate further. They had followed through on their search warrant back in April 1981, and they'd found nothing. Ruth was now officially Rolf's trustee, and it looked as though she was going to win her jousting with the Pilots' Association and continue to receive his eighteen-hundred-dollar-a-month pension.

Rolf's disappearance was far from an ordinary case, and it had to be worked "backward." Because there was no body, it didn't really seem like a murder case. Washington courts had yet to convict a murderer when there was no corpse to establish that a crime had been committed. There was always the possibility that Rolf would come home and that there might even be a happy ending. Even if he was dead, there wasn't the sense of tragedy about the demise of a man who was somewhere between eighty or eighty-three that there would be if the victim had died young. Rolf had had a good life, a fulfilling life. His reputation as a man who had known many women was familiar to the pilots he worked with over the years. But they also agreed that his libido had probably cooled considerably as he grew older. Still, was it possible that Ruth was on target as she continued to claim he had left her for more sexual dalliance? If Rolf had managed to sneak away with a lover (definitely not Elinor Ekenes, but perhaps some other woman), then he might even serve as a shining example of senior citizen virility to other men of middle age and even beyond.

Both Rolf and Ruth had remained close to their extended families over the years; Ruth had been a second mother to Donna Smith, her niece, and often welcomed other family members for extended visits in the Neslund home. Ruth went back to visit her family in Illinois, Ohio, and Louisiana just as often as, if not more often than, Rolf kept in touch with his siblings in Norway. Despite some of her sisters' belief that Ruth had "hurried" the death of their mother to collect her insurance, she was still welcomed by other family members in the Midwest. Her older brother, Robert Myers, was visiting during the summer of 1980, and, as she had said in one of her many statements to deputies, Rolf had asked Robert to look after her as he left.

Robert had been very ill early in 1980 with failing kidneys and prostate trouble, but he had slowly regained his strength after having surgery. He had looked forward to spending many months with Ruth and Rolf, and both of them had welcomed him.

If Rolf had indeed asked Robert to take care of Ruth after he left, Robert apparently had done that. He had remained with Ruth into the autumn months.

Any argument Ruth and her sister Mamie had once had over how to raise Donna Smith had long since been resolved, and Mamie wrote to Ruth often from Mt. Sterling, Ohio. The family letters were normal, like any letters one gets from older relatives. It was hard to imagine that anything as dark as bloody murder could be a part of their lives.

Mamie wrote to Ruth on September 26, 1980: "I was terribly worried about you. I am afraid you are overdoing it. I guess you know why I was so glad you had Bob with you now. I hope you get along all right with him. I'm sure you will.

"Don't you worry about me. I know I will be allright [sic]. You can let me know how you are . . . I know you are worn out. You rest as much as you can.

"I hope you come out ahead with Rolf. It's a shame he is so greedy."

(Obviously, Ruth had told her sister that Rolf had left her without funds, and that he was a stingy man.)

Mamie Anderson wrote about her own

arthritis, visiting the cemetery to pull weeds from relatives' graves, and of various family members who were ailing, in the hospital, poor, or, in some cases, dead.

"Gladys is doing allright. She has no income now — except for [her] Veteran's Widow's Pension. She will have to work 3 years before she can get S. Security."

Ruth promptly sent checks to help out.

It did seem that having her brother Robert with her was a blessing for Ruth. Robert was her escort even to social events. Oddly, Ruth hadn't mentioned one of the Pilots' Association parties to Clever and Caputo. Captain Gunnar Olsborg had phoned Ruth and invited Rolf and Ruth to a retirement awards dinner to be held on August 17, 1980 — a party where Rolf was to be honored. Ruth had cheerily accepted for them. But when the evening came, Rolf wasn't there. Ruth brought her brother Robert along instead.

Robert had extended his visit at the Neslund home for some time after Rolf left, but he eventually returned to his home in Beardstown, Illinois. There was a long delay during that trip when none of his relatives heard from him. Ruth and Mamie were worried about where he was. Ruth and her son, Butch, were especially concerned about who he was talking to.

Another brother, Paul Myers, was supposed to be somewhere in the Northwest.

Finally, Robert wrote to say that he had arrived in good shape in Illinois. His letters from the Midwest were just as down-home as Mamie's, although his spelling and grammar were not up to hers. He wrote to Ruth from Mt. Sterling after he returned home. Ruth had bought him an old log patrol boat so he could fish off Lopez Island. Robert spent a lot of time cutting it in half and rebuilding it, only to find that he could not get it licensed in Washington State, so he had loaded it onto a trailer Ruth owned and headed for Illinois.

His first letter read:

Dear Sister,

I guess you wonder why it took me so long to drive across the country, the reason was because I couldn't drive over 30MPH. When I tried to go faster, the trailer would sway. The Boat weighs 4 1/2 tons. The trailer and Boat Weighs 11000 lbs. The next ride for The Boat will be 7 miles to a Ramp on the river at Meredosia, Il. Then I'll Run it to Peoria.

Robert and his son, Carl, were planning to make money in building a few boats for other fisherman so Robert could finish up his boat. He wrote that they would use ash, elm, oak, and sassafras wood. He seemed elated with his gift from Ruth, and he planned to do a lot of fishing. He wrote of having supper with their shared family, eating "high on the hog" enjoying wild duck and venison.

But Robert's long trip home from Lopez hadn't been without mishaps, even at thirty miles an hour. As he explained:

That Hit and Run deal was this way. There was close quarters getting out of that station. Two men took over signaling me out of the Driveway and the station attendant went back to pumping gas. After maneuvering the boat around as Directed to get clear these men signalled me to go out all clear, I left then I got about 16 or 18 miles out of Town, This County Police man stoped me and arrested me for hit&run and Damage to proprity. I felt nohing or herd nothing This Policeman built his case on the Station attendants lies, his pop machine was an old machine, and it didn't have no dents or scratches on it and realy I don't think it ever got knocked over.

I'm getting rested up some now IM

glad you are feeling better, tell all hello for me and I think of you all by with Love

Your Bro Robert

Yes, Ruth Neslund's health and well-being seemed very important to her family. They worried that she wasn't well-rested and that she didn't have enough money. Still, she seemed able to send them checks and to give them magnanimous presents like boats, cars, and checks for college tuition and living expenses.

Ray Clever had heard the rumors that Ruth had said some shocking things to her relatives around the time Rolf disappeared. That was nothing new. For a long time, neighbors had heard her yelling things at her husband like, "I'll see you dead before you get a cent to give to those bastards!" Whenever she caught Rolf giving money to Elinor or his sons, most of her friends and neighbors knew it. For Ruth, death threats aimed at Rolf weren't unusual. She was certainly a woman of violent mood swings and she didn't care who heard her when she was angry.

Although Ruth didn't want Rolf spending money on his own sons, she had been quite generous with her family, or, rather, it was possible that she was helping certain members of her family financially to assure herself that they would keep any dangerous secrets she had within the family circle. But as solicitous as she was to Robert, she didn't seem to care for her brother, Paul, at all.

Paul Myers was a man of the sea, too, but he never reached the pinnacles Rolf had. Paul was rumored to have been in the Merchant Marine, and he sometimes worked fishing boats headed for Alaskan waters. Once, he put together a thick bankroll, but he had entrusted Ruth with his savings when she promised to invest it for him. By 1982 he had been sending her his paychecks and his Social Security checks for some time.

As it turned out, he might as well have put all his money in a pull-tab machine in a tavern. To his dismay, Paul learned that Ruth had spent his money on some land in Whatcom County, but she put the deed in her name and in the name of Ruth's younger son, Butch. Paul wasn't listed at all.

Ruth could talk her way out of anything, though, and she managed to convince Paul that she would give him a car she owned to make up for the money she had weaseled away from him. She also promised to send him checks for keeping his mouth shut about her business.

In January 1982, Paul finally smelled the

coffee, and, desperate, wrote a last angry letter to Ruth:

Dear Sis,
I have called you several times and I have finally come to the conclusion you have made a mistake.
Love and affection that I have for you and the Blind addiction to your needs, I believe, have given you the impression that I can be treated like a dumb sucker.
I'm not going to call you anymore or write you anymore.
You get the money together that is mine and get it to me or send me the [unclear] and I'll come get the car. If you don't I'm going to Seattle and I'll show you who is a sucker.

Your Bro Paul
(P.S.) Send me any mail you have for me there.

Paul showed up on Lopez Island in February 1982, to claim the vehicle that Ruth promised him. However, when he got there, she had changed her mind. She told him the car was gone. He was convinced that Ruth and her neighbor, Winnie Kay Stafford, had colluded to hide it from him. Despite the fact that she was about fifteen years younger

143

than Ruth, the two women were very close friends. Ruth could talk Winnie Kay into almost anything.

A man who knew them both said, "Winnie Kay can be crazy as a hoot owl sometimes. She just got sucked in by Ruth and Ruth's money."

The state of Winnie Kay's mind may have only been one man's opinion, but Ruth had a much stronger personality than she did. As one of Ruth's "dearest friends," she went along with Ruth and neither of them would tell Paul where the promised car was.

Stranded without a car on an island where he didn't know anyone, Paul went to a local restaurant and lounge where he proceeded to get drunk. He met a man there, Marty Beekman,[*] who agreed to give Paul a ride out to Ruth's house, where he planned to plead once more for the car she had promised him. But when he got there, it was all locked up, and no one responded to Paul's frustrated pounding on the doors. Muttering, Paul turned to Beekman and said, "I've got a mind to talk to the FBI or someone about what Ruth got me into! She killed him and Bob cut him up . . ."

Beekman didn't pay much attention because it sounded like an angry drunk talking.

However, he later mentioned it to some of the regulars at the lounge and that information soon became yet another juicy bit of gossip to spread around Lopez. Greg Doss eventually heard about it, and he arranged for Marty Beekman to talk to the San Juan County criminal prosecutor, Charlie Silverman.

It was just one more instance of the alleged facts of a brutal murder being passed around, and the backward case was now becoming circular. As Ruth Neslund continued to reclaim her life and planned happily for her next business endeavor, the investigators were as disheartened as a Californian would be by the clammy fog that sometimes envelops Lopez Island, blotting out the vistas of the sea and pastures.

There seemed no way through to any clarity or truth in their search for Rolf Neslund.

Had Ruth Neslund killed her husband and masterminded a gruesome plan to scatter his body?

Or was she only the innocent victim of a whisper campaign to destroy her reputation?

TEN

Ray Clever would not give up on solving the case and indicting the killer. He kept making lists, checking out his theories, and trying to find physical evidence that would validate the scuttlebutt. Sheriff Sheffer backed him, saying, "Go for it, Ray. I don't think you're gonna solve it — but go as far as you can."

While Ruth seemed unfazed by the gossip, the San Juan County Sheriff's Office, and the inquiries of the county's criminal prosecutor, Ray Clever was determined to find her brother Paul. He figured that Ruth's angry and disappointed brother might just be the witness who would tell Clever the truth, and he set out to find him. This proved to be a complex endeavor. Even today, Clever won't go into detail about those who helped him locate Ruth's brother — a policeman's prerogative — but he did manage to locate Paul.

It sounded as though Paul Myers might be

the weakest link in the chain of family members who surrounded Ruth. Paul was something of a nomad. He and Ruth were definitely reported to be at odds, according to her friends and neighbors. Ruth kept shutting doors in Paul's face, counting on his continued loyalty to her, no matter how she outfoxed him in business deals.

By 1982, Ruth was trying to put the tiresome investigation into Rolf's disappearance behind her as she prepared to launch a very high-end bed-and-breakfast lodging for tourists visiting Lopez Island. As she pointed out, she was all alone now in her big house with extra bedrooms and wonderful views of the water. She was a good cook, specializing in baked goods and her homemade sausage, and she had always enjoyed entertaining. She would call her home The Alec Bay Inn, stressing the beautiful vistas. There would be virtually no start-up costs, and she looked forward to meeting new people and having some company. She calculated that she could clear $150 to $200 a night for each room.

Paul heard about her plans and figured Ruth owed him a share of her future business income. He didn't have a steady job or a house or any money in the bank. Since she had burned him on the car deal, he planned to convince Ruth that she needed a man around the place to help with chores and for protection. He would go into partnership with her on the bed-and-breakfast. Their brother Robert wasn't in very good health, and Paul argued that he himself was the obvious choice. Ruth shook her head. She didn't need a partner.

Turned down for that, Paul asked her for a loan. It was the least she could do, but she was even less enthusiastic. And she didn't want Paul to think he could stay at her house; she needed all her space for her guests.

Without Ruth's help, Paul Myers was reduced to driving a "junker" from spot to spot on Lopez, sleeping in the old truck. Sometimes, Ruth allowed him to come visit, but he knew he took a distant second place to Robert. Paul felt that Robert literally "worshipped" Ruth, did whatever she asked, and was a quiet man who caused her no trouble. He was also quite deaf. That was the kind of man Ruth preferred to have around.

She had no patience with anyone who rejected her plans or who failed to do what she told them to. Within a week or so, Paul Myers was no longer seen around Lopez.

Paul Myers was still among the living, however.

It took awhile, but Ray Clever finally located Paul living in Scappoose, Oregon, a small town near the Columbia River in the far northwestern chunk of the state. A Scappoose police patrolman knew Paul and said he was living on the property of one of their reserve officers.

Clever talked to Paul's friend, who said he had met Paul a year earlier on the beach at Garibaldi on Tillamook Bay some sixty-five miles from Scappoose. "We became friends," the police reserve officer said, "and I told him he could put his trailer up on my property."

After returning from Lopez Island in February 1982, Paul had appeared jumpy and nervous, his friend said. "He seemed to have some idea that he might be an accessory to murder. He kept saying his sister had 'sucked him in.'"

That certainly sounded promising for the investigation. At 6:30 A.M., Clever approached the front door of the house where Paul was reportedly staying. He quickly spotted Myers. He could hardly miss him. He was a male version of his sister, short and round all over, just like Ruth.

Clever showed Paul his identification, and said he wanted to ask him some questions.

Paul Myers looked at Clever a little apprehensively and then blurted, "Uh, oh — I know who you are and why you're here . . ."

"Let's talk," Clever answered.

Surprisingly, Paul Myers seemed relieved to talk about his sister. He related how Ruth had tricked him out of his money and a car. He was mad and disappointed when she refused to let him share her bed-and-breakfast venture.

But that was the least of it. "I'm scared to death of her," Paul admitted. "I really think she planned to kill me."

Paul said he owned some property down in Garibaldi and that Ruth kept insisting that he meet her and one of her women friends — Wanda Post — down there. He'd been very reluctant to do that.

Garibaldi was a popular spot for both Oregonians and tourists, as it was situated right on the Pacific Ocean near the famous Twin Rocks, a towering natural rock formation that was a familiar image on postcards. There were only a thousand people living in Garabaldi, and there were miles of rugged coastline where Pacific Ocean waves crashed endlessly onto the rocky beach. Their roar would easily drown out a voice calling for help — or a shot ringing out.

"She wanted me down there on a trip along the Oregon coast," he said, "and I

150

never thought I was going to come back alive, so I didn't go."

What Paul Myers told Ray Clever that early morning in Scappoose, Oregon, would become the basis of an affidavit filed to request another search warrant for the red house on Alec Bay Road. Paul's was, indeed, a harrowing story, but one that had to stay under wraps for some time. After Paul gave Clever a statement, Clever arranged to fly him back to Friday Harbor where he could give testimony to the court of inquiry looking into Rolf Neslund's disappearance. Superior Court Judge Richard Pitt listened to what he had to say and read the affidavit that Ray Clever and Charlie Silverman presented, asking for a second, more massive, search of the Neslunds' property.

Judge Pitt granted the investigators another search warrant. To the disappointment of the press and public, it was sealed and whatever juicy details might be included would be kept secret. Sheffer explained that it "has to be confidential because it involves so many people."

And indeed it did.

The first search warrant had listed a restricted number of items the detectives could look for; this one was far more sweeping.

On March 2, 1982, Senior Deputy Joe Caputo, Ray Clever, Greg Doss, Perry Mortensen, and Criminalist Don Phillips knocked on Ruth Neslund's door. They had been authorized to search her five-thousand-square-foot house and the almost eight acres of land around it, and they were going to look for anything they might find that would give even a hint about where Rolf was.

Winnie Kay Stafford and Ruth were present when the second search began at 11:02 A.M. The disgruntled women left two and a half hours later, but Ruth came back the next day to pick up her blood-pressure cuff and a hot water bottle, complaining to everyone within earshot that it was terrible that an ill woman should be treated so badly, forced out of her own home while cops pawed through her belongings.

She snarled at Ray Clever, "There are about fifty people who would like to come in here and squeeze your head!"

A few minutes later, she phoned the searchers and demanded that they turn off the outside lights, even though it was she who had absentmindedly left them on in the daytime.

Ruth's attorneys called the search "preposterous." Neither they nor their client had seen the affidavit listing what the searchers were looking for. "We think there's no basis for it. We have no problem with them taking a look at what's there, because maybe that will shut them up once and for all."

Still, her lawyers were scornful about how the investigators were carrying out their search. "They're just going along on their merry way."

Ruth, he said, was taking the search "very hard. It not only creates a physical hardship by her being displaced from her home — but serious emotional trauma as well."

Furthermore, even though she had no formal charges levied against her, Mitch Cogdill said Ruth was being tried by "innuendo" and hinted darkly that there might be a civil suit against the Sheriff's Office forthcoming because the deputies and criminalists had "appropriated her property, damaged her property, and made obvious charges against her."

The baffling case was gaining more publicity all the time, and now residents of Seattle and the rest of the state were watching the search on the evening news. KOMO-TV sent a helicopter to fly over the house on Alec Bay Road, and photographers filmed the bare earth that appeared here and there in the pastureland where a backhoe had scraped the ground looking for, perhaps, a grave.

KOMO news anchors also revealed the matter of the meat-grinder. Ruth had owned one, but she sold it in mid-1981 to a couple who owned a meat-packing plant on Lopez. Jean Plummer, a Lopez butcher who lived on Port Stanley Road, turned over the items she bought from Ruth: (1) meat-grinder, (1) grinding auger, and (4) grinding and cutting attachments.

Fortunately, the Plummers had never used the meat-grinder, possibly deterred by the rumors. Joe Caputo picked it up from them, but when the Washington State Patrol Crime Lab ran tests on it, no speck or stain of human blood was present in the mechanism.

Even so, the meat-grinder version was the most steadfast of all the rumors circulating about the fate of Rolf Neslund.

Those who had enjoyed Ruth's sausages in the past lost their appetites.

During the ten days of the 1982 search, life went on on Lopez Island, and Ruth was sometimes relegated to the back pages of the local paper. As the search continued at her house, the *Journal* ran another story with seemingly more interesting local news: The girls' basketball team from Lopez High School was welcomed home by a huge crowd after being the first team from Lopez

Island to have participated in the Washington State final play-offs. Even though they didn't win, the teenagers had a police and fire department escort with sirens wide open.

There was also a long feature on a crackdown on Lopez Island dogs — warning their owners to keep a closer eye on them. There wasn't a leash law yet, but there could be if the canines kept chasing livestock.

All the while — and for almost two weeks — investigators swarmed over the Neslund home while Ruth complained that she had to depend on the kindness of friends or stay at motels.

The April 1981 search of the Neslunds' home and acreage had netted only that single bullet. Fortunately for the investigators the current search a year later was much more successful in terms of physical evidence. Or perhaps it would be more accurate to say that the second processing of the property finally opened doors for further investigation.

The law enforcement officers moving in and out of Ruth's house kept scrupulous logs, noting the time each one entered and left, and every scintilla of possible evidence that they had bagged and marked. As the detectives and criminalists moved through the house, it was silent except for their own breathing and subdued voices. Was Rolf Neslund's ghost here? If something awful had happened in these rooms, any overt residue of violence had clearly been hidden — wiped up, cleaned up, covered over. To the casual eye, Ruth's house was now in immaculate condition, spick and span enough to attract guests to a bed-and-breakfast.

The searchers had to keep reminding themselves to look beyond the obvious, to stare at the slightest stain on a wall, or a baseboard, or even on the ceiling. Did any furniture or wall or floor covering look newer than the rest of the house, new enough to have been purchased since August 1980?

Ruth Neslund apparently kept all manner of receipts, records, and contracts. Now, despite her indignation, those fell within the scope of the search warrant. Her life and her habits and interests were all there. Few people were as meticulous as she was.

Ray Clever filled numerous notebooks in his remarkably small, careful printing, listing what he had found, and made out receipts that would be given to Ruth Neslund to indicate possible evidence the deputies had removed. (In the end, there would be more than seven hundred items!)

Ruth Neslund's banking and tax records were precise and organized. She had apparently saved every receipt, letter, card, and bill she ever received. The couple held mortgage contracts on a number of properties. Clever saw eight full-size, four-drawer filing cabinets in her office area, and every drawer was full to bursting.

"As it happened," Clever says, "I had taken a speed-reading course. It's both a blessing and a curse. If I'm reading a really good book, I'm sorry that I read at the rate of twelve hundred words a minute. But during that search warrant, it was a blessing. I read through everything Ruth Neslund had filed, and I took all documents that seemed to be relevant into evidence."

Tediously, Ray Clever jotted down a long list of documents. They might prove to be totally useless in the probe, or there could be information in the stacks of files and notebooks that could either link Ruth to Rolf's sudden vanishing or clear her of any culpability or motivation.

It was likely Rolf never sat on the couch that was currently in the living room; her records indicated that Ruth had purchased a new couch just two weeks after she said Rolf left her. Earlier photos of the Neslunds' living room showed the old couch, and bills from Hanson's furniture in Mt. Vernon, a town just east of the Anacortes ferry landing, were for the present couch and matching love seat, purchased on August 23, 1980.

Clever and Joe Caputo agreed that portions of the living room carpet looked newer than the rest of it, although the pattern was exactly the same. Ruth had gone to Willett's Carpet in Anacortes on August 16, 1980, and bought eight square yards of carpeting and seam tape. That was only eight days after her husband disappeared. And then on March 23, 1981, after Clever and Greg Doss first questioned her in late February, Ruth had gone back to the same store to purchase still more new carpeting and tape. This carpeting, which Ray Clever saw in Willett's style book, matched the present rug in the master bedroom.

It wasn't as if she had completely redecorated her home. Instead, certain sections had been patched or replaced so that the rooms would look to the casual observer exactly as they were when Rolf was there. Ruth had often said in a sentimental tone that she "wanted to keep our home just the way it was, so he will see that when he comes back to me . . ."

The two investigators cut only that carpet that seemed to be recently installed.

Beneath the new carpet, the padding was stained deep, dark red.

ELEVEN

"Ruth's bedroom was a small armory," Joe Caputo said. "Loaded handguns and rifles up against the walls, under the beds, in closets, or in the drawers."

The search warrant listed any weapons Ruth might possess. According to those who knew Ruth, she was quite familiar with guns. They had seen her take a bead on a deer from her front door, and she also shot at cats to scare them away from quail on her property. She could shoot rifles, shotguns, and handguns. Indeed, a search of the Neslunds' master bedroom netted a Smith & Wesson .38-caliber revolver in the bottom drawer of a dresser. They bagged it carefully so that it could be tested for back-spatter or other evidence that indicated it might have been used to shoot a living creature. Its barrel would also be compared to the lands and grooves on any bullet casings they might find.

"Ruth was a hell of a shot," one neighbor had said, and no wonder.

Clever and Caputo found a Colt Python in a pouch, along with six rounds, and a Winchester .22 Magnum rifle with a scope, which had eleven live rounds in the chamber. There was also a Marlin with a scope and eight live rounds, an Ithaca 20-gauge shotgun, a 30-06 shotgun, and at least two dozen boxes of bullets, ranging from .22s to 30-06 for a shotgun.

There were numerous knives of every size and a "chopper," as well as hatchets and hacksaws, machetes, axes — not what most people kept in their homes. But this was, of course, the home of people who lived in the country and who often did their own chores, who sometimes hunted. Still, what might seem expected in ordinary circumstances now took on a macabre feel. The large ornate steamer trunk had a gray hair caught in the hasp. What did that mean? Ruth's hair was tinted a dark auburn; Rolf's was straight and gray.

They found a homemade "voo-doo-type" doll with a nail driven through its chest. Odd . . .

Joe Caputo searched Rolf Neslund's bedroom, but there was little to find. "It reminded me of my own grandfather's bedroom," Caputo said. "Very spare — with few items in it beyond his bed and dresser. It was like a simple hotel room."

He took the wood-and-leather jewelry box with Rolf Neslund's jewelry, including his favorite Viking ship cuff links, his broken wristwatch, and his "Medic Alert" tag. Rolf's clothes still hung in the closet.

During one of the last days of the ten-day search, Ray Clever and Joe Caputo paused in their search to rest. It had become habit for them to keep their eyes focused on what might be in such plain sight that they had missed it. Now Joe lay on the carpet and gazed up at the ceiling. As he tipped his head back to stretch his aching neck, he caught his breath.

There was the faintest mist of something dark brown against the ceiling tiles.

The faint dots weren't all over the ceiling; in fact, it looked as if most of the ceiling had been resurfaced with a textured paint product. But one section had been missed. It was stained with what looked like high-velocity blood spatter — the fine spray resulting from a gunshot wound.

"It was right over where Rolf's Easy Boy chair was," Joe recalled. "He always sat there. I can remember Ruth sitting on her bed and telling me about how Rolf had hit her, even though she never had a mark on her, and Rolf sitting in that chair with scratches and cuts all over his face."

The two deputies grabbed a saw and carefully cut that section out to be tested in the State Patrol lab.

Now they looked down. There was a concrete floor slab in the shadowy area behind the couch. It was porous enough that it, too, had absorbed some darkish liquid. They discovered that another concrete slab leading to the master bedroom was also stained. Not only were both areas marked with some fluid deposited there, they tested positive for some strong chemical designed to clean concrete. The investigators located a product called "Crete-Nu" among Ruth's cleaning products.

It hadn't worked as well as the label promised it would.

They would have to take these large and unwieldy chunks of evidence away with them. "We tented off the area to keep concrete dust from floating around the living room," Clever says, "trying to keep the rooms as clean as we could."

"But it was like a dust storm in there," Caputo put in.

Clever and Caputo took turns with a jackhammer until they were finally able to lift and remove a number of the concrete slabs for testing. Despite the Crete-Nu, the lab would be able to tell if the dark stains were blood, and, if so, if they were human blood.

"That's the first time I ever had to use a jackhammer in a crime scene," Clever says. "And we couldn't use a wet saw to cut through the concrete because it might have diluted any blood there. There was so much concrete dust. We vacuumed several times, but Ruth Neslund was still furious afterward because of the dust."

All of the blotches, drips, and sprays were subtle, nearly invisible to the naked eye, but they glowed when the searchers sprayed the area with Leucomalachite Green or Luminol. What looked at first glance like rust or grime showed up as blood left on the frame of the sliding glass doors of the tub in the master bathroom, and they found similar stains on the walls of both the master bedroom and bathroom. There was even a faint path of droplets between the master bedroom and a bathroom on the other end of the hallway. A large stain resembling the imprint of a hand appeared on a carpet pad in the living room along this path.

The handles of a wheelbarrow reacted to the chemical agents, too.

With further testing, all of the stains

proved to be Type A human blood. In certain areas — like the concrete slabs — there was so much blood that the person who had bled there would have to have suffered a major wound, probably a fatal wound.

The two most common blood types are A Positive and O Positive. Ruth Neslund had A Positive blood, but no one knew what blood type Rolf had.

When the stains, spatters, and mist the detectives found proved to be human blood, the only further information criminalists could determine was the blood type. It was 1982. There wasn't enough to test for enzymes that might isolate the blood by racial pattern. But it was A Positive. That could have come from Ruth's veins sometime over the many years she had lived in the house.

They couldn't be more specific; DNA would not come into play for another dozen years.

The deputies and criminalists were collecting so much possible evidence in their second search that they had to go back to the judge and ask for an extension of their search warrant, but, in the end, it was worth it. They had bagged and labeled hundreds of pieces of physical evidence from the tiniest of possible blood specks to those heavy chunks of concrete floor.

One of the last items they bagged into evidence was the Reader's Digest edition of *To Catch a Killer.* It had never been moved from Ruth's coffee table in the year between searches.

"This time we took it," Joe Caputo said. "It seemed pertinent."

It was March 12, 1982, before Ruth was allowed to return home. She confided to anyone who would listen that the damnable lawmen had almost destroyed her home, complaining that they had left her house in shambles, pawed through her papers, left their muddy footprints, dust, and dirt, without regard to her nostalgic feelings about the home she had shared with Rolf for so many years. She claimed that her front door was damaged, her septic field and lawn dug up, and her peace of mind erased.

Caputo was one of the searchers assigned to the septic tank — not the most palatable job. "It was pumped out and it was pretty clean, but we had to do a close inspection of the drain filter."

The other job that nobody wanted was wading through the swimming pool that Rolf had been so proud of, that he'd been anxious to show off to his brother and sister when they came from Norway. "It had about six inches of duck crap and mud in it," Caputo recalled. "And that all had to be sifted. Ruth said that Perry Mortensen shot holes in the pool to let it drain, but that was not a true story. Perry was a hilarious guy, but he did not shoot holes in that pool."

Ruth, however, said she had been almost ready to open a lovely bed-and-breakfast so that she would have some way to support herself. Things were in wonderful shape, and now that was delayed for heaven knew how long. Ruth even told the *Journal* that she had found several uncapped liquor bottles and believed that the sheriff's men had been drinking her liquor while they searched!

It was a ridiculous charge, but it appeared in print. Sheriff Sheffer defended his men. They had worked many hours of overtime, and were exhausted when they finally cleared the Neslund house. And, of course, they hadn't touched Ruth Neslund's liquor supply.

"The only thing we drank in there," Clever remembered, "was some terrible grape pop that we brought in with us."

Ruth no longer liked Joe Caputo. She told her attorneys to be sure and mention in her documents demanding compensation for the losses she had suffered from the search that she had been shocked to find that he had "snuck his wife in there — in my house and she stayed over! I was stunned."

So was Caputo when he heard that rumor. "I didn't have a wife," he said. "I didn't even have a girlfriend at the time. I don't know why she said that."

Sheffer told reporters that the biggest handicap they worked under was the time that had passed — at least a year and a half — since Rolf was last seen. Ruth certainly hadn't reported him as a missing person; it had taken his fellow ship pilots to sound the first tentative alarm and that came six months after Rolf had gone missing. The first search had been so restrictive in scope that they had found only the .22 bullet casings in the burn barrel.

Following behind the backhoe, the four deputies had sifted through dirt on the chance that they would find bones. This had taken many hours, but they found only occasional animal bones.

Now Ray Clever set out to determine Rolf Neslund's blood type. The old man hadn't donated blood, one source that often worked in detectives' inquiries. His siblings and sons were currently in another country, and while their blood types might help in determining Neslund's type, it wasn't a sure thing. It was a "catch 22" situation. They were trying to prove that Rolf was dead, but if he was alive, medical personnel had to protect patient personal information. They refused to release the information that Clever needed to show that Rolf was deceased. And he didn't have enough probable cause to get a search warrant to allow that. Clever checked with almost every hospital in the Seattle area to see if any lab had a record of Rolf's blood type.

"It got increasingly difficult to get any information," he remembered. "But finally someone let me know that there was that information in their records, although they were not able to tell me the blood type. Still, just my knowing the answer was there proved to be enough to get a search warrant to find out the blood type."

Rolf had had surgery in Northgate Hospital for prostate problems, a common ailment in men over sixty. And some of his prostate gland had been retained after his prostatectomy. But there could be a problem with that. The tissue had been preserved in formaldehyde which might have altered the blood chemistry, making it impossible to determine his blood type.

Bob Keppel started a search for a lab that might be able to isolate the blood type despite the presence of formaldehyde. He located a Dr. Reubenstone in Chicago who had had some luck doing that.

Clever held his breath. Luckily, they were able to determine Rolf Neslund's blood type.

It was A Positive.

Other crime lab findings on the items and swabs removed from the Neslund home also revealed that the person who had shed so much blood there had Type A Positive blood.

The .38-caliber revolver in the dresser drawer of the master bedroom bore silent evidence. With the expansion of hot gases as a bullet is fired from the barrel of a gun held at close range, "back spatter" — blood from the target — is drawn back toward the gun, sometimes into the barrel, sometimes on the cylinder. That was the case with this gun, even though it had been wiped cleaned since it was last fired.

Michael Grubb, a Washington State Patrol criminalist, wrote in his reports that some of the blood spatter found "was from a gunshot wound to the uncovered and hairless area of a human body or an animal, shot from a distance of less than three feet."

It would seem that charges would be forthcoming.

TWELVE

If this had been fiction, deductive reasoning would have dictated that someone who was living in the Alec Bay Road house in early to mid-August, 1980, would surely be arrested at any moment.

But it didn't happen. The Neslund investigation was an uphill battle for the San Juan County Sheriff's Office, Criminal Prosecutor Charles Silverman, and the attorney general's team, Greg Canova and Bob Keppel.

Ruth Neslund was proving to be an uncommonly popular woman on Lopez, and she had a crowd cheering for her. Curiously, she became more popular all the time. She didn't need to hire a publicist; her own comments and those of her attorney, Fred Weedon — who was taking a leave of absence from the Public Defender's Office down in Tacoma so that she would have solid legal representation — made her image as a "poor old woman" quite believable.

The *Seattle Times* printed quotes from island citizens who praised Ruth. "I don't think she had anything to do with his disappearance," one man said. "She's too kindhearted."

"It was common knowledge that he was going to Norway," another commented. "Something probably happened to him a long way from here. It didn't happen on the island. I'm mad as hell at the deputy sheriffs! Why did they wait a year and a half to start tearing up the property?"

"They were just an old couple, and they seemed to get along all right," a woman eating dinner at a very popular eating spot, the Islander-Lopez Restaurant, told a reporter. She had heard on good authority that Rolf had been seen in Hong Kong.

Someone said that the investigators better have a good reason for "doing what they're doing. Otherwise [Ruth] will have a lawsuit that won't quit."

Disappointed and besieged, the sheriff's men kept building their case. Ray Clever worked to establish the state of Ruth and Rolf's relationship, only to end up with twenty-three statement forms from couples and individuals who had known the Neslunds over the years — some through business dealings, and others socially. He was surprised to find that every one of them described Ruth and Rolf as a relatively happy couple, not unlike scores of others on Lopez. What he had would be of more help to the defense than the state.

"Would you testify to that in any trial?" he asked at the end of each interview.

"Yes, of course," they answered, to Clever's dismay.

There were those who had once laughed at the Neslunds' unfortunate dinner parties, but as time passed, even they modified their recollections. It was the deputies who had responded to the "domestic violence" calls who knew how fierce the fights were. They had arrived after the "company" departed and seen how the Neslunds' arguments had ended with broken crockery all over the floor, and bruises, scratches, lumps, bumps, and even bite marks left on the participants.

But the rumor mills kept churning. Much more than even a small town, everyone on a sparsely populated island seems somehow connected. The evolution of the disappearance of Rolf Neslund as a folk tale was becoming entrenched. The case belonged to Lopez Island, a somewhat suspect bit of popular culture or of island history. Rolf's vanishing under such eerie circumstances was becoming, as some said, a "tourist attraction."

The goriest gossip said that Ruth had killed Rolf and reduced him to bits in her meat-grinder; it was a story right out of *Grimm's Fairy Tales* or *Sweeney Todd.* Irreverently, some jokesters referred to Rolf's alleged death as "The Meat-Grinder Murder," and whispered that local restaurants would be serving "Rolf Burgers" soon.

Ironically, Lopez Island had long been touted as a most friendly spot where newcomers were welcome, and a tradition had grown where people in cars passing one another always gave a cheerful wave. One entrepreneur ordered dozens of T-shirts and had them silk-screened to show a drawing of a burn barrel with a hand sticking out. Beneath that, words were emblazoned to say, "Wave! You're on Lopez Island!"

The sheriff's men didn't see the humor, and few would blame them. Wherever Rolf was, it was their job to find him, and they weren't making much progress.

"That's what got to us the most," Ray Clever remembers. "Some people didn't think Ruth was capable of harming Rolf, and others believed she had killed him, but they didn't care."

It was disheartening to see how public opinion was gradually swinging over to Ruth Neslund. The public, of course, did not know about the lab results that suggested the Neslund residence had probably been a virtual abattoir at one time. And they didn't know about what Paul Myers had told Clever. Or about what had happened in the Columbia Tower meeting with Ruth's nieces, Joy Stroup and Donna Smith. That information, and all the forthcoming information, was sealed tight, waiting for the right moment.

Within the year Fred Weedon would represent Ruth in bringing suit against everyone and anyone connected with the execution of the second search warrant. Ruth was on the offensive, threatening to sue for $750,000 in damages to her home. She claimed poverty and illness, but she exuded confidence as everyone involved in the 1982 search of her property — the San Juan County deputies, the sheriff, the State Attorney General's Office, and the Washington State Crime Lab — was warned that they might be sued.

If she prevailed, Ruth would have no need to proceed with her bed-and-breakfast business. She could have lived quite comfortably for the rest of her life. Still, she said she looked forward to running her home business.

She just naturally liked people, she said.

THIRTEEN

The lay public of Lopez Island could not see a motive for a sweet, "kind-hearted" old woman to kill her husband. And the San Juan County sheriff's investigators and the AG's Office had to bite their tongues and continue with their probe. They weren't in a popularity contest; they were looking for the truth and if it turned out to be what they believed it was, they knew the day would come when they could charge Ruth Neslund with murder.

Ruth's banking records validated what they already suspected. Rolf Neslund had left money matters up to his wife and she had quite probably robbed him blind. He'd always said, "I trust her and she's better at it than I am."

In those last few days before he disappeared, Rolf had finally begun to see the first indication of the enormity of his wife's betrayal. He knew that his bank account was almost empty — with too little in it to cash his seventy-five-dollar check. When he talked to Kay Scheffler, he learned that she had paid off her mortgage five years earlier. It was the same with the Ronnings. Ruth had lied to him for at least that long. She had kept the Ronning and Scheffler payoff money without telling him.

Had he remained in the picture, Rolf would have discovered much more. Ruth's bank statements showed that, silently and secretly, she had been taking money out of their joint accounts for a long time and putting it into individual accounts in her own name — accounts that Rolf could not access.

She had done this quite subtly, taking out relatively small amounts at first, or simply depositing money paid to both of them to her own account. When he didn't notice these transactions, Ruth grew bolder. For example, on May 1, 1979, she transferred Rolf's entire pilot's retirement fund of $78,049.50 into two joint accounts — $50,000 in a certificate of deposit that earned high interest, and $28,049.50 into a savings account.

She waited about seven weeks for Rolf to say something, but of course he didn't. On June 25, Ruth removed nearly $80,000 from the two accounts and put it into an account in her name only.

By December 1979, she had transferred virtually all their money that had been deposited in their joint account at People's Bank in Seattle to an account in her name only in the San Juan County Bank.

Rolf knew he was getting his eighteen-hundred-dollar pension every month because Ruth kept putting his spending money in the dresser drawer, and he wasn't concerned about the rest. He counted on their savings to see them through their last years.

In August 1980, when Rolf tried to cash the check at People's Bank, he had access to only one joint account there. Its balance: $9.12.

With all their money available to her alone, Ruth had been cashing checks as she liked. She loaned money to some people on mortgages, but when they made payments, again at high interest, those went into Ruth's private accounts. She shared her largesse with her family, probably assuring herself that they would always take her side.

Moreover, between December 1979 and February 1981, Ruth collected Rolf's pilot's pension checks for eighteen hundred dollars every month, and endorsed them in his name, and then put them in her account. He never noticed. She did the same with his Social Security checks. She would continue to cash both until the Puget Sound Pilots' Association froze them. And then she sued them, too, furious that anyone would interrupt her money sources.

By the time Rolf vanished, the only account in the San Juan Islands where he could cash a check was at the San Juan Bank, where the balance was just forty dollars.

For years, smugly believing she could fool Rolf forever, Ruth easily kept him from discovering that she controlled all their money. It was only when Rolf became so miserable in his marriage that he considered going to Norway forever that he learned he had no money.

The motives for Ruth to want to get rid of her aging husband were quite clear, and as old as time. Money for one, and seething, mindless jealousy for another. With Ruth, the two combined into an even more powerful, conjoined motive. She had hated Elinor Ekenes for twenty years. Although she was misinformed, Ruth probably had convinced herself that Rolf loved Elinor — and not her — and that he was giving Elinor money. Indeed, he was giving her money, but it was for his sons. He wanted to leave something behind for the boys who were his flesh and blood.

Rolf was prepared to leave Ruth if he could, but first he had to get his money back. A confrontation was as inevitable as the collision of the *Chavez* and the West Seattle Bridge. Once the elements of disaster were in motion, there was no going back.

Rolf was afraid his wife was poisoning him, putting something in his coffee, and he was careful not to drink it or, for that matter, eat what Ruth cooked.

He didn't know that something infinitely more dangerous was sneaking up behind him.

FOURTEEN

Almost from the first time Rolf Neslund's disappearance made headlines in the Seattle papers, the investigators had heard about peculiar stories, stories purportedly originating with Ruth Neslund's relatives. But even followed back to the source, the information was diluted by Ruth's tendency to embroider the truth — if not outright lie. That, combined with the things she said when she was intoxicated, meant rumors had to be substantiated with solid physical evidence and believable eyewitnesses.

Ray Clever and Bob Keppel, the criminal investigator from the Washington State Attorney General's Office, realized that a trip to the Midwest to talk to other members of Ruth Neslund's family was essential.

Keppel and Clever met with Sheriff Carl Wubker at the Cass County seat in Virginia, Illinois. Wubker said that many of Ruth's nine siblings and their offspring still lived in the area. A lot of the Illinois branch of the Myers clan resided in nearby Beardstown. In their younger days, Ruth's brother Robert was rumored to have had dealings with Al Capone in Chicago. But that was a long time back and whether it had to do with Prohibition and rum-running or something darker, Wubker wasn't sure.

Keeping in mind the stories that there were bodies of old-time "Revenooers" (now called Alcohol, Tobacco, and Firearms agents) buried down in the swampland near the river, Wubker warned the two lawmen from Washington State. He said they should be careful with the Myers boys because it was rumored that they had "planted" more than one Revenuer in the mud flats. He insisted on sending a captain from his staff to accompany them when they headed out to talk to Ruth's male kinfolk.

Keppel and Clever wanted to talk to Robert Myers, Ruth's brother who had been living with the Neslunds when Rolf disappeared. Like his sister and brother, Robert was also short and round as a turnip, an old man so bowlegged that he walked as if he was on the pitching deck of a ship. He had huge arms, but he didn't seem like much of a threat any longer.

As they attempted to ask Robert about his

missing brother-in-law, they immediately observed that Robert's mind was cloudy. He appeared to be either senile or mentally ill. He might even be suffering from Alzheimer's Disease. Robert was nearing eighty now, and his recall of his last visit to Lopez Island was worse than hazy. Moreover, he didn't want to talk about his sister Ruth or his visits to Washington. Any questioning was a fruitless effort. It was clear that Robert Myers wouldn't make a competent witness for either the state or the defense.

Robert's son, Carl, was eminently competent, but he wouldn't talk to Clever and Keppel at all, and he grew more belligerent with each question. Whatever either man knew about Ruth and Rolf Neslund's relationship and what might have happened more than two years earlier, Robert couldn't remember and Carl refused to say.

Frustrated, Keppel and Clever headed back to Washington. They had certainly added to their belief that there were dark secrets in the Myers family. They also suspected that Ruth had been sending checks to be sure that none of them talked to the police about her.

Mamie, Ruth's oldest sister, was fiercely loyal to her. Long after Rolf left, Mamie continued sending her concerned letters.

"I want you to know, my dear sister," she wrote, "I love you very much. My heart goes out to you and I think of you most of the time . . . I am appalled at the things you have had to go through. I love you and pray for you and can only think of the good things you have done. You take care of yourself and remember 'I love you.' "

It wasn't surprising that Ray Clever's phone calls to Mamie's Ohio home elicited the same stony silence that he and Bob Keppel had encountered in Illinois. Mamie said she didn't know anything at all about Rolf's disappearance. She refused to answer any questions.

Ray Clever knew that Ruth was sending checks to Mamie.

There were still, thankfully, two very credible witnesses: Joy Stroup and Donna Smith, Mamie's daughters. Joy was as concerned as Donna was about the phone calls they had both received from "Aunt Nettie Ruth" on August 8, 1980.

Joy told Ray Clever that she was at work that day, estimating that it was noon in Ohio (3:00 P.M. in Washington State) when her aunt called her. They had a very brief conversation, not more than three minutes.

This was the most shocking recollection of all. This was the dread secret that had been hinted at when Joy's letter came to the San Juan County detectives through the Pilots' Association. This was the information that Joy and Donna had given in the secret meeting in Seattle, long sealed now until the Attorney General's Office team and the San Juan County Sheriff's Department and Prosecutor Silverman were ready to move.

According to Joy, her aunt Ruth had contacted her in the summer of 1980 and told her that she had shot Rolf and burned his body.

If this shocking news was from anyone else, it surely would have been reported immediately, but Ruth was known for making outrageous phone calls when she was in her cups. Nobody paid much attention to them. Over the previous years, many of her calls had to do with her anger at Rolf, or some fight they had had. She was somewhat like the boy who cried "Wolf!" and it was hard to take her drunken phone calls seriously.

Besides, Ruth's letters to her family were so typically those of a beloved — if slightly dotty — old aunt. She sent checks to her nieces, her sisters and brothers, and was always there for them.

They had all wanted to believe that basically Aunt Ruth had a good heart.

But her calls in August 1980 had been too

explicit to dismiss. Joy Stroup told the investigators what Ruth had said to her. There was little question that Ruth had spoken of killing her husband. "I was very busy at work and I just told her I would call her later," Joy said. "I didn't want to believe what she was saying. I thought she had been drinking again."

Two days went by before Ruth called Joy again, and over those forty-eight hours, Joy felt her first impression was right. Her aunt had been drunk and spouting nonsense as she often did. But then, on August 10, Ruth called again.

"She told me the same thing she did before."

"Did she ever tell you that was all a big story — say it wasn't true?" Clever asked.

"No."

After the San Juan County Sheriff's Department's first search of the Neslund property in April 1981, Joy said Ruth had called her. "She wanted to know if I'd given a statement to the police," Joy said, "and she said 'Keep the confidences I have given you.'"

Joy and Donna had been concerned enough that their aunt might not be making her grisly story up that they set out to find Rolf Neslund and make sure he was safe. But they could not locate him. Ruth easily

187

explained why. "She convinced us that he had gone to Norway and that she and Rolf were getting a divorce."

The young women had wanted to believe Ruth, and she was very convincing when she told them there was absolutely nothing to worry about. Rolf was safe and well — but her marriage was over. Ruth had appeared to be very well off financially, and she was very kind and generous. She wasn't grieving over the upcoming divorce, and seemed happy enough.

Still, as time passed, it struck Joy as strange that Rolf hadn't taken his clothes with him when he left. "She offered to send his clothes to me for my husband," Joy said. "They were about the same size."

Later, when Joy mentioned to her aunt that her daughter was having trouble with a boyfriend who was "too persistent," and Joy talked of her own plan to discourage him from bothering the teenager, Ruth said inscrutably, "I know a better way to get rid of him."

After that phone call, Ruth's words came back to worry Joy. What had she been trying to say? Joy hated to speculate on the meaning intended. Donna Smith knew that her uncle was alive on August 7 because he called her house. She wasn't home but he had a brief conversation with her babysitter, who was sixteen.

Joy told Donna about the two phone calls she had received from their aunt on August 8 and August 10, so Donna called Ruth on the eleventh. They exchanged pleasantries, and then Donna asked to talk to Rolf, explaining she was returning his call.

"He's out," Ruth said first, "but he should be back in a minute."

When Donna didn't hear his voice on the phone, she asked Ruth again where he was.

"He's out on the property somewhere," Ruth said vaguely, "but I can't find him."

Finally, Donna asked her why Rolf hadn't responded to Ruth's shouts to tell him he was wanted on the phone, and Ruth changed Rolf's alleged location once again and said, "Oh, he's over in Anacortes. I don't know when he'll be back."

By the time Donna hung up, she was highly suspicious. Why would her aunt give three different explanations about Rolf in one conversation?

Since Donna lived closest to her aunt and uncle, she was the one chosen to keep calling Ruth. Ruth told her the story about her upcoming divorce, and explained that Rolf had gone to Norway with Elinor Ekenes.

None of it had reassured Donna and Joy.

When they talked to their mother, Mamie, she said that Ruth had told her an entirely different story. Annoyed that Donna was questioning her so closely about Rolf's location, Ruth told Mamie that Rolf was in Maine and that she was going to drive back there to get him. "I'll show him to Donna," Ruth sniffed, "if that's what it will take to shut her up."

In still another call to her oldest sister, Ruth used one of her other explanations about her husband's whereabouts. "He's in Greece — waiting for this to all blow over," she said with just as much certainty as her other accountings for Rolf's mysterious absence.

With further phone calls from Mamie, there were more excuses. "Rolf's on a world cruise," Ruth said, without explaining why he would have gone on such a trip alone. "He's going to dock soon in Seattle. I'm going to bring him over to Donna's and bring her a dozen roses, too, to apologize to her."

By 1982, Ruth, in reality, was very angry with Donna Smith; she believed that Donna was the one who had told family secrets to the investigators. She phoned Donna on her birthday and said that she would be sending her "thirty dimes — thirty pieces of silver for payment for betraying me."

Donna told the detectives that she was deathly afraid of Ruth, and what she might do in revenge. Hers was not an isolated instance of fear. Almost every friend and family member Clever and Keppel talked to eventually expressed an intense fear of Ruth.

In a way, it seemed ridiculous that anyone would be afraid of this plump, short woman with dimpled hands and a tightly curled old-fashioned perm.

But then, Rolf was still gone, and gone within a day or so of his first expression of trepidation about his wife's dangerousness. Joy Stroup, Donna Smith, and Paul Myers were coming to the forefront of witnesses who would surely make an impact on some future jury. Ruth's phone bills showed scores of calls back to Ohio and Illinois, and also to Donna, who lived in the Seattle area.

When Ruth finally ferreted out information that suggested Joy had given statements to the investigators, she stopped sending her money.

In October 1982, Ruth Neslund was briefly hospitalized. The Sheriff's Office was told that she had suffered a stroke — which Ray Clever found was not true. Most people on Lopez Island believed she was at death's door.

FIFTEEN

By 1983, no one but the investigators from the San Juan County Sheriff's Office, the prosecutor's office, and the Attorney General's Office believed that Ruth Neslund would ever go on trial for the murder of her missing husband — or for anything else. Rolf had been gone from Lopez Island for three years, and she was still living at her Alec Bay home. She had apparently bounced back from her stroke, and was enthusiastic about her newest enterprise. One of the local papers wrote a glowing review as Ruth's long-awaited business venture debuted. It was remarkable in that there was not one mention of Ruth's infamy in the Northwest.

"Lopez's First Bed and Breakfast," the headline read. The large photograph of Ruth accompanying the article showed a sweet-faced older woman placing silverware next to a gold-rimmed plate, with a baroque mirror, a polished sideboard, and shining silver candelabra behind her, and a glittering crystal chandelier above.

The Alec Bay Inn had just opened, and Ruth Neslund was offering guests four "attractive and comfortable bedrooms, with queen-sized beds, and wood-burning stove in each. Two rooms feature private baths."

There was a music room, a library, sundecks, and a "magnificent view of Alec Bay." The pool that Rolf had once hoped to have completed in time for his siblings' visit was now finished, still another attraction at Ruth's new enterprise. Those guests who enjoyed the outdoors could look for driftwood on the Neslund home's private beach, or explore "the lovely pastoral surroundings."

Ruth knew what tourists sought; she had visited a number of similar establishments in picturesque settings around Washington. Every successful bed-and-breakfast had some kind of signature, or a "gimmick" to make it stand out. Ruth announced that she was featuring rare antique furniture in every room. She was considering adding an antiques store later on so that her guests could purchase items that would remind them of their visit to Lopez Island.

"I've always loved to cook," she told the reporter, Betty Horne. "This project seems a natural for me, giving me an income and utilizing the things I like to do best."

Rather than the token coffee, rolls, and fruit that many bed-and-breakfast homes served, Ruth offered a complete meal: "Eggs, hash browns, sausage, cereal, fruit or juice, homemade biscuits and bread, coffee or tea."

In the first month after she opened her home to guests, Ruth Neslund seldom had vacancies. People came from all over the Northwest, California, and even England to enjoy the serenity and hospitality of the Alec Bay Inn.

Whether the notoriety of what was rumored to have happened in the huge home drew visitors, who could say? The house that was once home to Lizzie Borden has been a successful bed-and-breakfast. Some said that Ruth's "gimmick" was not her antiques at all, but the possibility that a grotesque murder had occurred on the premises. Ruth Neslund was beginning to need a larger income. Her legal expenses were substantial.

SIXTEEN

By March 7, 1983, the witnesses, physical evidence, and circumstantial evidence that made up the case against Nettie Ruth Neslund were all in place. At long last, she was charged with first-degree murder, with a trial date yet to come. At her arraignment, Ruth looked like someone's grandmother in her navy blue patterned blouse, slacks, and a dark jacket, her heavily lined face solemn as Fred Weedon helped her up the courthouse steps at the county seat in Friday Harbor.

At her arraignment, Ruth quickly entered a plea of not guilty. Fred Weedon asked to have her bail lowered from $50,000 to $10,000 — to no avail. Ruth posted a property bond to cover the $50,000.

Finally, the macabre secrets that the prosecution team and the investigators had been forced to hold close to their vests for so long were public knowledge. Not only the San

Juan County papers, but both the *Seattle Post-Intelligencer* and the *Seattle Times* featured front-page coverage, quoting the affidavit of probable cause.

What gossips had been whispering about for almost three years was apparently not that far from the truth as the prosecution saw it. Both Joy Stroup and Paul Myers had given statements alleging that they had conversations with Ruth and Robert Myers about the events of August 8, 1980.

The Neslunds had had yet another violent argument that day. The impetus for their last quarrel would have been Rolf's discovery that Ruth had taken control of all his financial assets and was preparing to mortgage the home he loved. Ruth had claimed to Paul and Joy that Rolf had hit her. Robert Myers, their summer visitor, had pulled Rolf off his sister.

At that point, the state maintained, Ruth had grabbed one of her many guns and shot Rolf twice in the head as Myers held him.

The brother and sister were then alleged to have set about to get rid of his body and to hide all evidence of the crime. How they reportedly did that was allegedly far more gruesome than even the darkest speculations that had circled San Juan County for three years.

Despite island gossip, however, no meat-grinder had been involved.

Even so, to many, Rolf Neslund's disappearance and the way the case was playing out was too bizarre to be true. And there were more T-shirts and more dark humor. John Saul, the bestselling Lopez Island thriller author, penned an epic limerick about the Neslund mystery. Read aloud at one of Saul's frequent gatherings for Northwest writers, it was hilarious because the case had become almost mythic.

Saul has a keen wit, and he is especially good at satire. His humor is the antithesis of his suspense-filled books, which are undisputedly chilling and not to be read at night when the reader is alone. New stanzas to the Neslund mystery continue to emerge from Saul's facile pen every few months:

One night at the Alec Bay Innie
A drunk shot Rolf Neslund, the ninnie
    While dear Brother Bub
    Chopped him up in the tub
Ruth served a drink to friend, Winnie!

There once was a lady named Ruth
Whose problem was telling the truth.
    She shot up her hubby,

Cut him up in the tubby
And now needs a pardon from Booth!*

There was a Lopezian named Ruth
Who tippled a little vermouth
    She shot her man dead
    And cut off his head
The judge said that Ruth was uncouth!

Some said the old lady was kinder,
Than one who would use a meat grinder.
    Some said she stole money
    But Ruth said, "That's funny,"
Yet guilty was still how they'd find her!

Looking at the benign face of the elderly defendant, it was hard to visualize her participating in such a grisly crime. And the defense would certainly play on that.

After those who filled the courtroom for Ruth's arraignment got over the shock of the specific allegations — much less amusing now that they were said to be fact and not mere speculation — they realized they had something else to worry about. The second-floor courtroom had been so jammed with people that the floor beneath creaked and groaned ominously. It was a lovely building,

*Booth Gardner, then Washington's governor.

very old — antique, really. But the memory of the scores of people who died in the sky-bridge collapse of Kansas City's Hyatt Regency Hotel was fresh in America's minds.

Suddenly, everyone wondered if the San Juan County Courthouse would survive Ruth Neslund's trial, or, more urgently, if the gallery watching might not be in danger. It seemed that half the population in the surrounding islands hoped to attend at least some sessions of this long-awaited trial. Were they all going to plunge to their deaths when the floor gave way?

They would either have to have a change of venue to another county's courthouse, reinforce the San Juan Courthouse, or build a new structure. Surely, there wasn't enough time before Ruth's trial to do the last.

Somehow, the county found the money to begin construction on a new courthouse, and the march to judgment moved ahead ponderously as different motions slowed the proceedings to a snail-like pace.

Judge Richard Pitt would not be eligible to preside at Ruth's trial because he had been the inquiry judge who oversaw the second search warrant on the Alec Bay house a year earlier. San Juan County had very few judges to pick from; it had never been a problem before because they didn't have that much crime. On April 15, the county's only other judge, Judge Howard Patrick, was disqualified when Fred Weedon filed an affidavit of prejudice. The Washington State Supreme Court appointed Snohomish County Superior Court Judge John Wilson to hear the case.

Ruth's trial date was finally set: May 31, 1983. But then Deputy Attorney General Greg Canova — who would be representing the state — filed an affidavit of prejudice against Wilson.

Ultimately, the Washington State Supreme Court appointed Judge Robert C. Bibb, also of Snohomish County. Bibb had presided over trials of notorious defendants before — including the trial of Fred (now Kevin) Coe, convicted of being Spokane's "South Hill Rapist," as detailed in the late Jack Olsen's book: *Son.*

Anyone following the trail of Superior Court judges could be easily confused. "Bibb" who was now the trial judge replaced "Pitt," the inquiry judge.

Finally, neither side had any affidavits of prejudice left.

On May 18, 1983, Ruth appeared at a pretrial omnibus hearing where Judge Bibb would rule on which pieces of evidence he would allow into her trial. Not surprisingly, Greg Canova wanted to present virtually everything seized during the 1982 search of the Neslund home, much of it devastatingly incriminating for Ruth. Fred Weedon continued to be a strong advocate for the defendant, treating her with such deference that Ruth seemed as delicate and fragile as the crystal pendants on her prized chandelier. He asked Judge Bibb to suppress the search evidence, insisting that the team of detectives from the Sheriff's Office "grossly violated" Ruth's Fourth Amendment rights against unreasonable search and seizure.

Weedon was not convincing enough in his rhetoric. At the end of the hearing, Bibb allowed all five hundred pieces of evidence in, everything Canova asked for — except for some photographs.

Not to be outdone, Weedon filed a civil case shortly after the omnibus hearing. Ruth's threat to sue became reality as she filed a $750,000 civil suit against the investigators. Virtually everyone on the search warrant team was served with a subpoena.

The newest date of Ruth's criminal trial was set for August 1, 1983, three years to the day, less one week, after Rolf Neslund had vanished forever.

But the pace slowed again. Fred Weedon

and his co-counsel, Ellsworth Connelly, appealed to the State Supreme Court asking for a ruling on a discretionary review. He still insisted that Judge Richard Pitt had not been a "neutral" judge when he granted the second search warrant. How could he have been, Weedon asked, since he had also been the inquiry judge earlier in the investigation?

There would be no trial on August 1.

What Ruth Neslund's defense team was working toward, of course, was a complete dismissal of charges against her. If they succeeded in having the evidence thrown out of the trial, their next move would be to question whether Rolf Neslund was really dead. Not even a fragment of his body had ever been found.

Even though the A Positive blood that remained in the Alec Bay house was the same type as Rolf's, Ruth was also A positive. Furthermore, Connelly commented that he could see no way to prove that Rolf had not cut himself shaving, had a nosebleed, or suffered a household accident.

Through all the legal maneuvering, Ruth's trial date seemed farther and farther away. Aware that the courtroom floor had trembled as if the islands had sustained a major earthquake in Ruth's 1983 arraignment, officials had condemned the building. As it turned out, there was plenty of time to construct the new courthouse in Friday Harbor before Ruth ever went to trial.

What appeared to be the final date was announced: May 1985. The courtroom had been reserved for six weeks, and trial was only a little more than a week away. The curious looked forward to sitting in the gallery, but there were those who thought it was time to just forget about Ruth Neslund and what she might or might not have done five years earlier.

A man named Marcus E. Bonn wrote a letter to the "Speak Out!" section of the *Journal:*

Dear Editor:

I find that our esteemed county prosecutor is now proceeding with the prosecution of Mrs. Neslund. I wonder just how much of a chance he has of convicting her of more than poor housekeeping? He is coming to court with no corpus delicti; it has taken a couple of years to prepare enough "evidence" to start the whole program.

He is going to try a woman for murder — can he get enough of a jury panel of people that hate her to convict? (People that are merely neutral will laugh at the case.)

As one of the county taxpayers, having seen what can be wasted with that guy that was shot in the leg [an earlier county case that cost $50,000], I wonder just how much more will be wasted here?

If Mrs. Neslund goes to trial, it will be another big-time waste job on our money. She can't be convicted unless the jury is bribed or stupid . . . If convicted, what will happen? When you read the results of other trials, will it be "30 days with all but 10 minutes suspended?"

I say, let it drop. If Mrs. Neslund assisted her husband out of this life, she alone must live with it for her few remaining years. This trial will be a farce.

The letter demonstrated once again that the majority of laymen don't understand the meaning of corpus delicti, believing that a murder case without a human corpse is no case at all. It was no wonder that the San Juan County sheriff's investigators had to work hard to keep up their morale and belief in justice. It had been five years — no one seemed to care anymore about a trial, except to worry that it would raise taxes.

And, somehow, the fact that Ruth was a female seemed to make her a pitiful target, one incapable of doing any real harm.

Nevertheless, both sides were ready to go to court in August 1985. But then Ruth suffered what the defense said was a terrible fall; she broke her hip.

A courthouse regular walked beside Fred Weedon as he left the courtroom, having been granted one more delay. Sotto voce, the man commented, "All you have to do now, Fred, is see that she breaks her other leg."

SEVENTEEN

The latest trial deadline was Monday, October 28, 1985, but no one seemed to believe it would happen — not even Ruth Neslund herself. It had been so long, and her new life revolved around her successful Alec Bay Inn. Ruth admitted to a *Post-Intelligencer* reporter that she, too, felt as though she was only a spectator at a theater production. She was sixty-five now, but looked older, walking unsteadily with a four-footed cane, mentioning that her "stroke" had left her "legally blind."

"I still don't believe I'm involved in it," she said with apparent amazement. "It's like watching a bad movie. I don't really know how a thing like this can get snowballing — except it did, with some relatives who have never been very close to me."

With tears brimming in her eyes, Ruth said she felt that Rolf had probably committed suicide, explaining how depressed he had been after being responsible for his ship hitting the bridge. "Although," she whispered, "there are some days when I think he's going to walk up the driveway."

She spoke of hard times they had lived through, always together. Their first house on Lopez Island had burned. It had been a providential coincidence that Ruth was storing all of her valuable antiques in a trailer behind the house when it went up in flames, in a fire whose cause was never determined. And, luckily, she had thought to get insurance. She recalled that after they lost the house, she had given Rolf a special Christmas present — plans for a new house she had drawn herself.

"I had no thought we would actually build it; I thought we were too old, but Rolf looked at the plans for the better part of an hour, and he said, 'Ruth, why don't you build it?' "

With two part-time carpenters, she said, she had done just that. Rolf had painted it. "He was the captain, and I was the crew in the household. I was strong as an ox when I built the house. We moved in in 1978," she recalled nostalgically. But things had gone wrong after the bridge fell. "His mind was going," Ruth told reporters. "The captain was hallucinating some and drinking a lot. Ever since the ship hit the bridge, he brooded a lot. He would sit for three or four hours at a time, only getting up to fix himself a highball."

Rolf, of course, was not there to give his side of their story, and it was easy for young reporters to feel sorry for the aging might-be-widow. There were many on Lopez Island who raved about what a wonderful person Ruth was. "I was enthralled with her the day I met her," a male acquaintance offered. "She is extremely generous with her time and personal things. She'd hear about a child who didn't have a bicycle, and would say, 'Oh, I have one in my garage. Why don't they take that?'"

Ruth said she was hurt by those "who have found me guilty already. I do have some supportive friends, and I try to be strong and survive. I don't sleep very well. I wonder about it a lot. I wonder about my own mortality in this very stressful time."

Ruth said she kept busy running her bed-and-breakfast, playing the organ and piano by ear, and was diverting herself by learning to play the banjo.

Despite Ruth Neslund's fans and friends, and her newly docile and mild demeanor for the press, Ray Clever had his own opinions, based on the facts he and Bob Keppel and other deputies had uncovered. He snorted in disgust as he read her pretrial coverage. "She just radiated evil. I believe that she was fully capable of everything she was accused of."

EIGHTEEN

It was almost Halloween 1985, perhaps an apt date for a trial which promised ghastly details to start. At last, it was beginning. The Washington State Court of Appeals had upheld the prosecution's right to present the hundreds of items of physical evidence. Judge Bibb said he would allow Greg Canova and Charles Silverman to present their case in any order they chose.

Of all ploys that defense attorneys in high-profile cases usually invoke, a request for a change of venue — seeking to relocate a trial to a more neutral territory — is the most often used. But Fred Weedon and Ellsworth Connelly had never asked for that. Sheriff Ray Sheffer had a theory on that. Off-islanders seem to view the rugged folk who lived in San Juan County as a bit more "primitive" than those who live on the mainland. "There's absolutely a feeling about islanders," he suggested, "that there's a backwoods mentality, that there are a lot of moonshiners, and so on."

Perhaps if this trial were held in Bellingham, Everett, or Seattle, it might be more likely to end in a conviction, just because large-city dwellers might expect shooting and dismembering a spouse and then burning the pieces would be something islanders would do to solve marital problems.

It was all quite ridiculous, of course. People in Washington State who live on windswept islands may be individualists and close to nature, but they tend to be highly intelligent professionals, who visualize life there as more serene than city life, and are anything but low-browed renegades living in "hollers."

Today, the price of San Juan and other island property is sky-high, and there are virtually no waterfront lots available to anyone who cannot afford hundreds of thousands — even millions — of dollars.

Judge Bibb was on the bench, assisted by Mary Jean Cahail, who had decades of experience as clerk of the Superior Court of the Joint Judicial District combining San Juan and Island counties. Connie Burns (Sundstrom) was her coclerk, and Karen King, the bailiff. Except for Judge Bibb, they were a "hometown" group of court officers who had served in the antique courthouse, now replaced by the new structure built with amazing speed with this trial in mind.

Ruth Neslund sat quietly at the defense table, the perfect picture of a sweet grandmother type. She had said that she still half-expected to see her missing sea captain come walking up their driveway. So did some of those anticipating her trial.

Rolf Neslund was listed as a potential witness in his own murder trial!

What did that mean? For one thing, it meant that every time the courtroom door opened, heads jerked and everyone in the gallery looked to see who was coming in.

There was scarcely space to breathe in the courtroom; every seat was filled and some spectators stood. It remained that way throughout the proceedings.

Picking a jury for a case that had had sensational headlines and media coverage in minute detail for so many years is always difficult. Judge Bibb wrote to the pool of hundreds of potential jurors and asked them not to read or watch television news or newspaper accounts that proliferated as Ruth's trial drew near. He hoped not to have to sequester the jury during the trial, which was expected to last four to six weeks. San Juan

County could scarcely afford the trial, much less hotel and food bills for jurors for that long. The county had budgeted eighteen thousand dollars for the trial, and keeping the jury sequestered would cost at least twenty-four thousand dollars, an unheard-of drain on the county budget.

But from the beginning, everyone concerned, which, indeed, was most of San Juan County's residents, had worried about the possibility of a mistrial. They would hold their breaths and hope that no one got sick, that there was no misconduct, and that everyone from witnesses to jurors would show up on time for every session. If the jurors were not sequestered, there was always the chance that one or more of them might be approached or overhear something they were not supposed to.

It took six days before all but thirty of the original four hundred in the jury pool had been winnowed out by the state and the defense for cause, and for medical and financial reasons of individuals who felt serving on the jury would be a hardship.

And still, Judge Bibb felt that it had become necessary for more potential jurors to be called. On Veterans' Day, Lisa Boyd, an Orcas Island banker, was shocked to receive just three hours' notice that she must report to the courtroom in Friday Harbor. The county needed five more jurors. Although her supervisor at the bank wasn't happy to have her leave on such short notice, Lisa and five other citizens caught the ferry to San Juan Island just in time. Only one of that half dozen was dismissed, and finally, twelve women and three men took their places in the jury box. Lisa had become Juror Number One.

No one on the Neslund jury was from Lopez Island; they had all been removed "for cause" by the state — much to Fred Weedon's disappointment. Ruth had a lot of loyalty from Lopezians, despite all the "meatgrinder" folktales. Many of the potential jurors had mentioned the meat-grinder when they were asked what they might remember of the Neslund case, but said they didn't think that would influence their ability to judge the testimony fairly.

It was to be a trial full of fits and starts; Ruth's health and habits would interrupt her trial continually. Only a few days into jury selection, her blood pressure had risen dangerously high and she suffered a severe nosebleed. Every effort was made to keep this emergency from the potential jurors' eyes, but one person did see her as she was spirited from the courtroom, a handkerchief pressed against her face in vain, and her blouse already stained with blood.

She was flown to a hospital in Bellingham. Subsequently, she spent a week in a local convalescent center until she was deemed well enough to come back to court. Although the jurors didn't know it, Ruth had suffered from "the DTs" — delirium tremens — in the medical center. They were brought on by alcohol withdrawal.

Almost anyone on trial for first-degree murder might be expected to experience a rise in blood pressure, but Ruth Neslund looked ill when she returned to her trial.

But there was no mistrial. They had all dodged another mistrial bullet.

Finally, Greg Canova asked that the defendant, who was free on bail, be confined to the Islands Convalescent Center where she could have her vital signs and her consumption of alcohol monitored. Unless she was, Canova argued that she was "in a position to control this trial."

Judge Bibb agreed and ordered that during the week, Ruth should be in the center from 8:00 P.M. to 8:00 A.M. She would be allowed to go home on weekends.

She was, in many ways, a pathetic figure, a limping old lady. But Ruth was also a consummate chameleon. Throughout her life she had morphed from capable business-woman to persuasive mistress to Lady Bountiful to furious and combative wife to alleged murderess to kindly neighbor to gracious hostess, and finally, to an elderly invalid whose own community seemed to surround her with concern.

But who was she . . . really?

With all the delays, it was November 13 before opening statements began. The jurors looked at Charles Silverman expectantly. As youthful and inexperienced as he was, the man known to islanders as "Charlie" did a good job as he laid out the whole case for them in a comprehensive fashion. He characterized the relationship between the Neslunds as "rather vicious," growing from the "seeds of violence" that had been germinating in their home for some time, culminating in a terrible argument that was sparked by Rolf Neslund's discovery of his wife's financial manipulation of his money. Silverman promised jurors that Ruth's niece, Joy, and her brother, Paul, would describe what had happened in the last bloody day of Rolf's life.

He promised the jurors a plethora of physical evidence that would back up the circumstantial evidence that pointed to Ruth as her husband's killer.

Fred Weedon opted to delay his remarks until the defense began its case. Attorneys sometimes choose to hear the opposition's case before they lay out their own.

This was a small-town trial, but it drew tremendous interest. "It felt like being part of a real-life book," Lisa Boyd remembered. "There were lots of 'actors.' Greg Canova was very handsome — like the actor Pernell Roberts — and he dressed beautifully. Charlie Silverman was quite young then, and earnest. He didn't pretend to be an expert in criminal law, and we liked him for that.

"Fred Weedon was known for being a real estate attorney in the islands. He wasn't a big-time criminal defense attorney. Ellsworth Connelly — who I think was appointed by the state — wasn't familiar to us. He had a habit of jingling coins in his pocket. I don't think he was aware of it. And he always referred to Deputy Ray Clever as 'Cleaver' — like Beaver Cleaver.

"Ruth constantly wore what appeared to be that navy blue pantsuit. She didn't care how she looked. Her hair was straight and short, and stuck out every which way. It was gray and it often looked greasy or dirty.

"We could see that she had a cane or a walker, but we didn't know if she really needed it or not."

Joe Caputo, Ray Clever, and other detectives were local men, deputies from the small Sheriff's Office, and not like investigators from Seattle, Spokane, or Tacoma. Jurors felt comfortable with them, as they described what they had found during the sweeping search of the Neslunds' home three years earlier, telling things no one had heard before.

Joe had created an exhibit that would document exactly where the blood spots on the floor were found. "I had actually got a large roll of white butcher-type wrapping paper and spread the paper about the floor, and then connected them into a huge diagram which could be folded. I thought it was a good technique that was done in addition to the photographs."

The trunk, which Rolf had reportedly tumbled over when he was shot, still bearing hardened blood and gray hair caught in the metal corner, was brought into the courtroom.

For the first time, the community heard what had really gone on during the long search of 1982. Now, at last, they could understand why the case against Ruth Neslund had moved forward so slowly, and yet no one in the courtroom could possibly realize how many hundreds of hours of detective work had gone into linking Rolf's disappearance with that final horrific day in 1980.

When the sheriff's investigators finished their testimony, the mass of physical evidence became part of the court record. Some of it was minute; some were the large chunks of concrete, carpet, and the padding beneath it — still bloodstained.

As the investigation's results spun out, Ruth sat at the defense table, her demeanor seemingly calm. She scribbled notes on a yellow legal pad and whispered often to the man beside her. Fred Weedon had devoted many years to absolving her of any guilt. Ruth had used those years to create a "new Ruth Neslund," with her lovely inn, and her life without Rolf. Jurors who glanced at her were struck by her air of confidence; a few found her demeanor almost arrogant.

Still, they wondered what she was thinking as she watched members of her own family take the witness stand to testify against her.

On November 19, the trial was in its third week when Donna Smith, the niece who had been "like a daughter" to Ruth, took the witness chair. It was obvious that she was torn by memories of better days. Since she had come to Seattle from Ohio in 1968 — seventeen years earlier — she had been welcomed into the Neslunds' home by both Ruth and

Rolf. Rolf had encouraged Ruth to invite her extended family to reunions on Lopez Island, and Donna recalled happy times. But she spoke then of the disintegration of her aunt and uncle's marriage. In answer to Greg Canova's questions, she described the fights that began in earnest about 1979.

"My aunt called me to tell me she was in 'the bunk-house,' because they were fighting. She said, 'If he comes back here, I'll shoot him.' I was scared for both of them."

Donna Smith said a family reunion in July 1980 had been ruined because her aunt and uncle were arguing. At that time, her aunt had said to her, "I'm not going to have to put up with him much longer."

The witness said that she had become very concerned in the first week of August when her babysitter left a scribbled message on her chalkboard. Rolf had been watching a preseason football game and, according to her sitter, he was excited when he called Donna. "Great touchdown! Did you see it?" he had dictated. "Tell Donna Rolf called and to call him back!"

That was on Thursday, August 7. And Rolf had apparently been in a good mood. "I tried to call him all weekend," Donna testified, "but there was no answer."

And when her sister, Joy Stroup, had

phoned her on August 23 from Ohio with her concerns about what might have happened to Rolf on August 8, Donna testified that she had called the Neslunds again, hoping that Rolf would answer and she could put both of their worries to rest. But that was the call during which her aunt Ruth answered and gave her three or four different versions of where he might be.

Donna Smith said she had seen Ruth and her uncle Bob at a family party on September 5, but Rolf wasn't with them. "My aunt said they had decided to divorce and that he [Rolf] was gone to Norway."

But by April 1981, Donna had still neither heard from nor seen Rolf. And his sister and brothers in Norway contacted her to say that Rolf wasn't there, and they didn't know where he was.

At that point, Donna — with her sister Joy's approval — had gone to the authorities.

"My aunt phoned me ranting and raving because I had betrayed her."

Later, of course, Ruth had sent Donna the thirty dimes, calling her a Judas.

Joy Stroup took the stand. She recalled that she had been working at her restaurant job during the noon hour of August 8, 1980, when her "Aunt Nettie" called. Joy said she was used to Nettie Ruth's muttering about her frustration with her step-uncle — that she had often talked of "wasting" him, and said she could "burn" him. When she had been drinking, she was known for her wild phone calls to relatives. This phone call had begun like all the others, but quickly took on an ominous tone.

Joy was nervous now, and close to tears as she looked toward the defense table where her aunt sat calmly, her hands folded on the table in front of her.

Seeing the witness's discomfiture, Canova moved just enough so that he stood directly in front of her, blocking her view of her aunt. Now Joy would not have to look at Ruth.

Lisa Boyd, who sat in the first swivel chair in the jury box, felt for Joy. "It had to be the worst thing in her life," she would recall. "Having to testify against her aunt."

"And what did she say?" Canova asked of Joy. "Tell us just what you remember."

"That there had been a confrontation with her and Rolf," Joy said, "and he had hurt her. Ruth told me that Rolf had struck her left breast, and hit her in the nose, doing more damage than he had previously."

As Canova asked the witness to describe more of the phone conversation, tears began to course down Joy Stroup's cheeks, and her voice choked. "I can't say it . . . I can't say it."

There was a pause while Joy Stroup took deep breaths and a sip of water.

Finally, she sobbed as she testified, "She said, 'Uncle Bob held him and I shot him and he's now outside burning in a barrel!' Those were her exact words. 'Uncle Bob held him and I shot him and he's now outside burning in a barrel . . .'"

The courtroom erupted into gasps and murmurs and then hushed as Judge Bibb warned those in the galley. Ruth never changed expression.

Joy said that her aunt's words were so shocking that she could scarcely believe them. She had tried not to believe them. "I told her I was busy at work and would have to call her back. It didn't affect me then like it does now. I just don't know what I thought then. At the end of my shift, when I called back, she said it was true, but she didn't repeat those words . . ."

Joy thought that her aunt had mentioned something about calling a "sheriff," or that "the sheriff was coming," but could not recall exactly what Ruth Neslund had said.

During the ensuing weekend, the witness said, she had tried to call Ruth again, but there was no answer. "I was hoping it would be like other instances, that it would be [the next] morning, and everything would be all right."

It always had been in the past, no matter how angry her aunt was with her uncle. But there was only the shrilling of a ringing phone in an empty house, and that wasn't reassuring.

On Monday, Joy Stroup had heard again from her aunt. "She told me Rolf was in Norway, and she had gone to Bellingham just to get away from there for the weekend."

"Did you ask her again about what she had told you?"

"No. She never brought it up again, either — or denied it or took it back."

On cross-examination, Joy Stroup acknowledged that there had been a period of estrangement in her relationship with both her "Aunt Nettie" and her sister Donna after a "little spat" after her father's funeral in 1969. Actually they had not spoken for eight years.

Still, it did not diminish the impact of Joy's testimony — or of Donna's.

Robert Myers had not been charged with murder, nor was he called on to testify. He was lost in his own mind, unable to tell reality from nightmares.

But Paul Myers, seventy-two, was ready to

take the stand. He was not any prosecutor's ideal witness. Like his sister, Paul was a drinker, but he openly admitted it. He wanted very much to testify. Paul had been haunted by the story he heard from his sister and brother. He had confided to Ray Clever that he feared he might even be an accomplice to murder. He testified that he had been persuaded to haul a section of carpeting to the dump for Ruth. Later, she told him that there were bits of Rolf's body rolled up in it.

Now he told the jury what he believed to be the scenario of Rolf Neslund's last hour in his beloved home. He spoke of what Ruth and Bob had told him when he visited on Lopez Island.

"She [Ruth] told me she shot Rolf twice in the head and killed him."

"Did you believe her?" Greg Canova asked.

"No, I'd heard so many stories I didn't believe any of them."

Ruth had given Paul most of her standard explanations for Rolf's being gone. "She said he was in Norway. She told me he'd jumped off the ferry, [because he was] despondent over hitting the bridge with a ship. I knew that was false 'cause I knew Rolf."

"Do you know why Rolf was shot?"

225

"My brother Robert told me it was about money," Paul testified. Robert had explained that Rolf was angry when he found out that Ruth had transferred his pension and all his money into her bank accounts. "Rolf told Ruth to put the money back — 'or else!' Robert said he got 'or else.' "

Paul said he had overheard Ruth and Bob talking about what they had done. Apparently, Ruth had instructed Bob to hold Rolf while she went to her bedroom to retrieve her handgun. After she shot him, he had fallen backward over the couch.

Although he wasn't at the Alec Bay house when Rolf was killed, Paul Myers said that he had been sitting at Ruth's bar in the Neslunds' sunroom on two occasions when Robert and Ruth were telling two of her women friends, Wanda Post and Winnie Kay Stafford, about what had happened to Rolf. He heard them clearly as they'd made no effort to talk quietly.

Ruth was not as composed during her brother's testimony as she had been when her nieces spoke. From time to time, she shook her head firmly, and scribbled notes that she passed to Fred Weedon and Ellsworth Connelly.

Paul spoke like an automaton, showing virtually no emotion as he described a scene right out of hell.

"Bob and Ruth put Rolf on a sheet and dragged his body to Ruth's bathroom. Bob put Rolf in the bathtub and cut him up with a butcher knife and a broad-axe — and possibly a saw. And when she brought those, he shut the door and pushed her out of there.

"He butchered Rolf's body, cut it up in pieces and [Ruth and Bob] carried the pieces out to the back [behind the barn] in a wheelbarrow to a burning barrel. They burned the body parts with wood until there was nothing but ashes, and dumped the ashes in the cow manure."

Ruth had been concerned that the burn barrel itself might contain some residue, so it was cut into quarters and, with the body of a still-born calf, taken to the dump.

At this point, Ruth had told Paul that he had become an accessory to murder.

And so, five years, three months, and sixteen days after Rolf Neslund completely vanished, the story that everyone in San Juan County had whispered and wondered about had come to a gruesome and ugly climax.

That is, if Paul Myers was to be believed.

Some of the jurors said later that they had not found Paul Myers credible. "I don't know if he was drunk on the stand," one woman said, "but he talked so much about the alcohol he had put away."

On cross-examination, Fred Weedon had no trouble getting Paul to admit that he was drinking a half gallon of whiskey a day during his visits to Alec Bay.

"It sounds like you were drunk up here all the time?"

"Practically," Paul agreed. "Seven to eleven in the morning was about the only time I wasn't drunk."

"Does alcohol affect your memory?"

"I believe it does — but I was so shocked at what I overheard that it's indelibly marked in my memory."

And Paul's recital of Rolf Neslund's death was almost identical to Joy Stroup's.

It now became indelibly marked in the memory of all who heard it.

THE SEA CAPTAIN

Rolf Neslund, at age forty-five. He was one of the first seamen in the Puget Sound Pilots' Association, and this photo remains on display in their headquarters in Seattle. It would be fifteen years before he married Ruth Myers.

Rolf and Ruth Neslund sit by the fireplace in their Lopez Island home. Some who knew them said theirs was a love match. Others weren't so sure.

*Rolf and Ruth Neslund's dream house. They called it
"Shangri-La," but Ruth later called the sprawling rambler
overlooking the sea the "Alec Bay Inn," and ran a successful
bed-and-breakfast there.* (SEATTLE TIMES)

*Rolf Neslund in 1979, shortly after he retired as a ship's pilot.
He is sitting on a couch that his wife later replaced. He was a
robust man, even as he approached his eightieth birthday.*

(Left) *Rolf Neslund a year before he vanished. He was in great shape for a man of seventy-nine. But his marriage wasn't doing as well.*

(Above) *Rolf Neslund on his last Christmas. A year later, only a handful of people knew where he was.*

(Left) *Robert Myers, who played a horrifying role in the disappearance of his brother-in-law, Rolf. His sister gave him a boat, and rewarded him in many ways.*

Physical evidence gathered by the search team from the San Juan County Sheriff's Office and the Washington State Attorney General's Office. It was a large part of the state's case against Ruth Neslund. Plaintiff's evidence: shell casings, voodoo doll, jewelry box with Rolf's favorite cuff links, knives and sheaths, Crete-Nu container, scrapings of dried blood. The Neslund case has become the "Lizzie Borden" mystery of the mystic Northwest. (SAN JUAN HISTORICAL MUSEUM)

Evidence, bagged and tagged by San Juan County deputies after many days' search of Ruth Neslund's Lopez Island home. Much of it was shocking to island residents who crowded the courtroom at Ruth's murder trial. (SAN JUAN HISTORICAL MUSEUM)

Ruth Neslund's favorite voodoo doll. (SAN JUAN HISTORICAL MUSEUM)

Ruth Neslund seemed remarkably cheerful at one of her court appearances as she is supported on the arm of a deputy. She rather enjoyed her notoriety as the "talk of the San Juan Islands." (SEATTLE TIMES)

Robert Keppel, a chief investigator for the Washington State Attorney General's Criminal Division, worked with Ray Clever to find Rolf Neslund's blood type in the days before DNA. They were finally able to isolate it from a tissue sample retained after surgery Rolf had. Keppel also helped the sheriff's department investigators in other aspects of the strange disappearance of a man so well-known in his island community. He now teaches an extremely popular course on homicide at Seattle University.

(Above) *Ray Clever, right, and other investigators who participated in the days-long search of the Neslunds' home share a rare moment of laughter. They are sitting on "replacement" furniture purchased shortly after Rolf vanished. Although Ruth claimed they poured liquor from her ample bar, they are drinking only grape pop they had purchased earlier. This room held grisly evidence. (Below) Ruth Neslund detested the San Juan County sheriff's deputies who searched her house for evidence of foul play in her husband Rolf's disappearance.*

It was Joe Caputo who looked up at her living room ceiling and spotted the almost invisible flecks of blood there. And with that, the trail to Rolf's killer became clear.

Greg Canova, an assistant attorney general for the State of Washington, assisted Charlie Silverman in the prosecution of Ruth Neslund. Ruth hated him. Canova is now a Washington State Supreme Court judge.

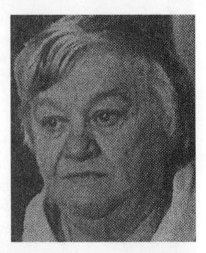

Ruth Neslund was stoic when she listened to the verdict at the trial for her husband Rolf's murder.

Ruth Neslund sits with her attorney, Fred Weedon, at her trial. He was very supportive of her, and did his best to see her acquitted, but would eventually speak of his own doubts.
(SEATTLE TIMES)

NINETEEN

People in the San Juans could hardly be blamed for talking about what was happening in the courtroom as the testimony became more and more shocking. Early on, court administrators had realized that the ferry ride to Friday Harbor and back to the home islands of jurors could very well be fraught with problems. The jurors were relegated to a particular section of the ferry decks, marked by tape, where they could not overhear comments by other passengers. At times, they felt almost ostracized.

Since they were not segregated, jurors could go to lunch on their own, and they did, in pairs or small groups. Two female jurors were in a restaurant when they heard a county politician from across the room as he commented loudly about trial testimony.

"We walked over and introduced ourselves as jurors," one of the women said, "and asked him to speak more softly. He was annoyed, but at least he lowered his voice so we couldn't hear his opinions."

Four weeks after Ruth's trial began, the prosecution was winding down. Earlier, the jury had heard Ray Clever, Greg Doss, and Joe Caputo describe the long search of 1982. What they found meshed with Paul Myers's statement about what he had overheard as he sipped whiskey in the Neslunds' sunroom. There was no question that Clever, Caputo, Doss, and Mortensen had, indeed, located the physical evidence that supported Paul's description of Rolf's sudden death.

Thanksgiving — to be celebrated on November 28 in 1985 — was drawing near as Donald Phillips testified to the dozens of stains in the Neslund house that had proved positive for blood. The concrete slab behind the couch had not only been scrubbed with Crete-Nu, an acid wash, but the defendant and her brother had apparently "ground" it down with a power tool in an effort to scrape off any remaining bloodstains. Much of the carpet had been replaced, and Ray Clever had the receipts and the salesmen's statements about Ruth's purchases of new carpeting.

Ruth had had a ready explanation for spiffing up her house so soon after Rolf's unexplained departure. She told her brother Paul that she was laying new carpets in her home because Robert Goulet, the well-known singer, was interested in buying it, and would be coming by to tour it. That caused a ripple of interest in the gallery.

One of the most effective witnesses on the bloody mist that had barely dotted the living room ceiling on Alec Bay Road was Sergeant Rod Englert, then a homicide investigator for the Multnomah County Sheriff's Office in Portland. In the next two decades, Englert would go on to become one of the most renowned experts in the world on blood spatter. The patterns that blood etches as it sprays, splashes, or drains from all manner of wounds — stab, bludgeon, or gunshot — are predictable. Englert was adamant that the high-velocity blood mist had come from a gunshot wound. The amount was too minute for him to say whether it was animal blood or human blood, but the Portland detective said positively that it had risen from the flesh of some creature who had been shot.

Criminalist Michael Grubb testified about the Smith & Wesson .38 found in Ruth's dresser drawer. Although someone had given it a cursory cleaning, he had examined it under a high-powered microscope. And he had found eight small blood droplets on the face of the gun's cylinder, one blood flake which was loose but still adhering to the extractor shroud, and two small blood spots under the thumbpiece (the mechanism that slides forward to release the cylinder). Each spot proved positive for the presence of blood. Whoever cleaned the gun would not have noticed those last spots when the thumbpiece was in its normal position.

The person shot would not have been more than three feet from the shooter, probably less.

Nellie Horan, the office manager of the *Journal,* testified that Ruth had placed classified ads on August 20, 1980, to sell Rolf's Mustang, camper, boat, and the home itself.

Ruth didn't advertise Rolf's clothing; she had offered that to Joy Stroup, whose husband was about the same size. Joy had declined.

Everyone had been afraid of a mistrial, but so far this trial had evaded any number of pitfalls. One thing nobody worried much about was the weather. Winter storms in the Northwest almost always meant heavy rain and high winds, but everyone was used to that. Snow didn't fall that often, and when it did, it rarely stayed on the ground. It usually melted within a day.

But during Thanksgiving week 1985, a

blizzard warning for the San Juan Islands caused a great deal of consternation. Two upcoming witnesses for the prosecution who drew a good deal of interest were flying all the way from Norway. Harald Naeslund and Eugenie Marie Naeslund Lindboe, Rolf's siblings, had waited five years to see justice done for their brother, and they were determined to tell the jury about him and the odd way he had suddenly dropped out of their lives.

But now there was a question of whether Harald and Eugenie's plane could land safely and if they could get from SeaTac Airport south of Seattle all the way up to Friday Harbor.

A foot of snow fell, completely transforming the landscape in the San Juan Islands, choking the roads and streets, and disrupting ferry schedules. The temperature stayed frigid, and the snow did not melt. It was lovely to look at, but almost every business was forced to shut down.

The trial did not. The jury was adamant that they would not allow a snowstorm to cause a mistrial, not at this point.

"We made up our minds we would get to court any way we could," Lisa Boyd says. "It was easier, of course, for the jurors who lived in Friday Harbor. For the whole trial, many of us had to catch the 7:00 A.M. boat from Orcas to San Juan and we didn't get home until 7:00 P.M. With the added problem of the snowdrifts, that was a challenge."

But not impossible. It was arranged that Deputy Steve Vierthaler would drive as close as he could to jurors' homes on what roads were still passable on Orcas, and they would hike out to meet him.

"I had to walk through snow up to my knees for half a mile," Lisa Boyd said. "We all had to, and then we had to share his vehicle with his German Shepherd K-9 dog, but Steve got us to the ferry."

It would be four days before the snow melted off the narrow back roads, but the Neslund trial continued without interruption.

One juror described the scene in Friday Harbor the day after Thanksgiving. "Several of us went out to dinner after that day of trial," she remembers. "We had to look for some place that was even open. Walking through Friday Harbor was like being in a Fairyland with all that snow. We felt like the only people on the planet . . ."

The roof of the new courthouse sprang a leak during the snowstorm. "We came to work one morning," Court Clerk Mary Jean Cahail remembered, "and, of all things, the ceiling had leaked onto the lid of the Neslunds' trunk where it sat right there in the courtroom! We wondered what else could happen, but, fortunately, it didn't hit the part of the trunk that held the stains and hair."

Rolf's brother and sister made it to Friday Harbor. And the next day, Harald Naeslund recalled the adventurous life Rolf had lived and his devotion to his family. Harald testified that five years earlier he and his wife had been looking forward to an October visit to Rolf and Ruth's lovely home. Harald's wife would be seventy, and Rolf would be eighty that fall, an occasion to celebrate for both of them. Their plane tickets were for October 29, just six days before Rolf's birthday.

Harald said that Rolf had been content to be home from the sea, and full of plans to fix up his house and property. On the stand, he read from a letter Rolf had sent him on June 17, 1980, saying how much he appreciated being on solid land at last. "There's too much to do from early in the morning," he wrote. "About 10:00 A.M. I get life in my body and begin to think about what to do."

His last message to his brother in Norway was dated August 4, 1980 — an enthusiastic postcard urging them to hurry and visit so they could swim in the Neslunds' new pool.

And then, nothing.

It was Ruth who called on September 10 to say that Rolf had left her, and there was no need for them to come because their brother wasn't there any longer.

Eugenie Lindboe was not a young woman, but she walked with grace, her head held high. Her hair was still dark brown and skillfully cut, and she wore a black sweater, a mink vest, and a plaid black and white skirt. Around her neck, Eugenie wore several gold chains with charms and coins, and her shiny black boots reached to her knees. She had clearly come from money. The Naeslund family background was aristocratic, and Eugenie and Harald obviously wanted to explain that their lost brother was not a throwaway person or a confused and senile old man who had been ready to die.

Eugenie walked down the courtroom aisle rapidly, and, with her back to the gallery and the defense and prosecution tables, she held her right hand high to take the oath.

Then she climbed the few steps to the witness chair, but she did not sit down immediately. Still standing, she turned deliberately, and rested her hands on the rail. For what seemed like minutes, Eugenie stared at Ruth

Neslund, willing her to look up and meet her eyes. Ruth would not do it. And then Eugenie shook her head negatively. Without saying a word, she had said whole chapters.

Finally, she sat down in the witness chair. Eugenie spoke English perfectly but, of course, with a distinct Scandinavian accent. She talked of happier times, her voice modulated but close to breaking. Rather than dissolve into tears, Eugenie occasionally fell silent until she regained her composure. She stressed that Rolf had not come to see them in Norway during the summer of 1980 or any time after. And Ruth had stopped calling her, despite her promise to stay in touch so they could find Rolf.

"He was not only my brother, he was one of my best friends," Eugenie said bleakly.

TWENTY

The state had hoped to finish its case before Thanksgiving, and the defense expected to begin after the long holiday weekend. They didn't make that time limit, but they weren't far off the mark. Now the big question was: Will Ruth take the witness stand? She had indicated even before her trial that she was anxious to tell her story, and she was confident that the jurors and everyone else would see that she had been falsely accused.

But it's a rule of thumb among defense lawyers in cases involving criminal violence that the appearance of the defendant on the witness stand is almost always bad news. Some may come across as too confident or cocky, others may irritate jurors, and some may give away too much information. Once a murder defendant testifies, he (or she) opens himself up to cross-examination by the prosecution and to questions that defense attorneys' wiser judgment never want to be asked.

No matter what Fred Weedon or Ellsworth Connelly advised, those who knew Ruth Neslund felt she would do as she pleased. She trusted Weedon and she had leaned on him for years, but she was a stubborn woman who, in the end, made her own decisions.

Fred Weedon answered all the questions that had been posed earlier on Monday, December 2, as he made his opening statements. He laid out his case for the jurors, and he exuded confidence as he did so. If he had tried to dissuade Ruth from testifying, he gave no indication. Instead, he said she would testify, and she "would welcome the opportunity to speak after years and years of island gossip."

Not only would the defendant give the jury the true story of her last night with her husband, Weedon promised to present witnesses who had seen Rolf Neslund after he was alleged to have vanished.

There would be testimony from people who had observed that Rolf was so depressed after the bridge accident two years earlier that he had spoken of suicide. "He was an eighty-year-old man who was getting forgetful, an eighty-year-old man who was increasingly concerned about his own mortality," Weedon reminded the jurors.

Hadn't Elinor Ekenes testified that she had dinner with Rolf on August 5, 1980, and that she had advised him to "run away to Norway"? Weedon portrayed Rolf as "a man torn between two loves," a situation that must have only contributed to his depression.

"I do not stand here to try to put a halo over Ruth's head," Weedon said easily. "It's not going to fit." Ruth was an admitted heavy drinker and her marriage to Rolf had become storm-tossed and angry. Yes, they had an argument on August 8. And, yes, Ruth had called her niece in Ohio. But Weedon insisted that Ruth and Rolf had made up after that call, and then they had sat down to dinner together.

And, yes, Ruth had transferred close to one hundred thousand dollars from their joint accounts into accounts in her name only. But that was only wise business sense. "She wanted to avoid possible losses that might come from the bridge accident."

A successful lawsuit could have wiped the Neslunds out financially.

The blood found in the house was just as easy to explain, Fred Weedon pointed out. During their fights, the Neslunds had drawn blood. Moreover, there had been accidents during the time that Ruth and those she hired built the house in 1976–78.

As for the .38-caliber revolver that the state dubbed the murder weapon, Weedon promised to present witnesses who would stipulate that that gun wasn't even purchased until December 1980 — four months after the alleged murder date.

Weedon's opening remarks were compelling. He was describing the case from the other side of the looking glass, and it was riveting to hear his "What if?" arguments that demanded jurors and court-watchers consider that Ruth Neslund might be a totally innocent woman who had been widowed through no fault of her own.

From where Fred Weedon sat, Ruth wasn't perfect, but she had done what she could — allegedly at Rolf's instigation to protect their retirement money. And Rolf — far from being the content retired man — was, instead, a suicidal, depressed, fading image of the robust man of his youth.

And then, Weedon suggested, Rolf would have suffered a crushing blow to learn that Elinor would not be waiting for him in Norway, but on her honeymoon with another man. Would that not have been enough to make an old man take his own life?

Perhaps. But the defense position on the blood evidence was hard to believe. It was difficult to envision that much blood flung, spattered, dripped, sprayed, and even vaporized from "building accidents" and domestic fights. Rod Englert had specified that the amount of blood that had soaked into the concrete slabs was so profuse that it remained there despite being treated with chemicals and scraped with a grinder. The Portland detective said there was "a large quantity of blood, consistent with very major artery bleeding." As the Neslunds fought, they had drawn blood by scratching each other, and left bruises, but "arterial bleeding"? No.

Nevertheless, Weedon and Connelly began the defense by questioning witnesses who said Rolf Neslund had been a different man after the bridge accident, a man likely to commit suicide. After the Coast Guard had found him negligent in his duty as a pilot, he had changed.

Acquaintances, men from Lopez Island, and those who had known him elsewhere or worked with him followed one another to the witness stand. They spoke of his supposed despair because he had been forced to retire from the career he loved.

"He'd been in it all his life," one man said. "[After the accident], the best way I can describe it is a whipped dog, a deflated ego."

Another said, "I think he was a lot different person after the accident. You could tell he was depressed and upset about it."

A fellow pilot, Captain Roy Quinn, testified that he had visited Rolf in February 1980, and Rolf told him that he was being named in a lawsuit seeking damages for the West Seattle Bridge. When Quinn warned him to be careful, and find somewhere to put his pension fund where it couldn't be touched, Quinn said Rolf had answered, "Mama and I have taken care of that. In my own name, I don't have a dime anymore."

Quinn felt that Rolf had been "disturbed" after the *Chavez* hit the West Seattle Bridge. "When we were talking one on one, he was depressed. When there were other people around, he put up a front." He added that Rolf had been forgetful and would sometimes "blank out."

"My father-in-law had similar spells, when he was in his eighties. And then he committed suicide. I told Rolf about that. He said to me, 'I think I'd do the same thing.'"

One defense witness bolstered Ruth's claim that Rolf had left her of his own accord. "He told me he was going to Norway in early August," the man testified. "He said, 'I'll be back before the holidays, and if I decide to stay longer, I will.'"

On cross-examination, this witness argued continually with Greg Canova. Ignoring courtroom protocol and Judge Bibb's repeated warnings, the witness offered his opinion without being asked a question. "I don't want to get intimidated by lies," he shouted at Canova. "You're getting the cart before the horse!"

When he complained to Fred Weedon about Canova, saying, "This sucker's trying to nail me and he ain't going to nail me," Judge Bibb told Weedon if he could not control his witness, he would find him in contempt of court.

After a sudden recess, the witness stopped offering comments, but he refused to budge on his stance that, as far as he was concerned, Rolf Neslund had gone to Norway.

A man named John Norman who had done odd jobs for the Neslunds swore on his oath that he had seen Rolf two days after the day he was supposed to have been shot to death. Norman was convinced he had seen Rolf riding the ferry to Anacortes on August 10. He was sure of the date because he and a friend were going to McDonald's to celebrate the friend's birthday.

At this point in his testimony, the witness began to cry, explaining that his friend had died since then. But he knew that date, and he saw Rolf Neslund sitting in the backseat of a car between a Lopez Island couple.

"He said, 'Hi Boss.' That's his nickname for me. He was kinda pale and he looked tired."

"You're certain that it was Mr. Neslund?" Weedon asked.

"Absolutely."

But Norman wasn't so sure on cross-examination by Greg Canova, who asked him if he and his friend often went to Anacortes to eat at McDonald's. He allowed that that was true.

"Isn't it true that you testified at a special inquiry hearing that the last time you saw Rolf Neslund was in 1979?"

"I hadn't heard that," Norman said somewhat vaguely. He was not an ideal witness.

Weedon called a workman who had helped Ruth build her house a few years before Rolf vanished. He recalled that he had smashed his thumb and cut his hand and dripped blood both times. Interestingly, he recalled the location of his bloodletting was in Ruth's bathroom, and along the hallway where the search warrant team had isolated blood the state said was Rolf's.

In a surprise move, the defense called Elinor Ekenes! She seemed an unlikely witness for

Ruth's side, but she had to respond to a subpoena to appear. At first, she recalled, Rolf had made jokes about the ship accident and he hadn't considered it a tragedy at all. It was his relationship with Ruth that made him "very unhappy."

Elinor acknowledged that Rolf had spoken about his will when she talked to him on July 27, 1980. He wanted to change it. "He said, 'I want you and the boys to get whatever I have left.'"

She also said that Rolf had been afraid of how he might die, and that he asked her to see that he had an autopsy to determine the cause if he passed away.

It was doubtful that Elinor helped the defense.

TWENTY-ONE

If possible, the courtroom was even more jammed with spectators than it had been earlier. On December 6, 1985, Ruth Neslund herself emerged from the elevator to encounter a gaggle of television cameras and reporters. Her son, Butch Daniels, was there from Louisiana to help her, and her attorneys flanked her protectively. She turned away from the microphones held out in the hope that she would give some memorable quote, and made her way slowly to the courtroom, leaning heavily on her four-footed steel cane. Her hair, a mixture of stark white and iron gray was straight and cut in a short, mannish style now, parted on the side. Her clothing was quite suitable for a heavy-set woman of sixty-five. She still wore the dark blue polyester slack suit that had become familiar to the gallery. She had changed only her blouses — from ruffled white to prints. Sometimes, she added a scarf, and she did on this day.

Facing the possibility of life in prison if she failed to convince her jurors of her innocence, Ruth seemed confident. At times, she was very serious and, when it seemed appropriate, she used a little humor.

She had told reporters a few days earlier that she "could hardly wait" to take the stand, and laughingly teased them by saying they should have followed her to the bathroom with their cameras. She seemed almost to enjoy being the center of attention.

Now, as she faced the gallery and its rows of acquaintances and strangers who seemed to lean forward in anticipation about what she had to say, Ruth Neslund stared back, her face arranged in an unfathomable mask.

She would seldom waver in her answers to Fred Weedon's questions, although, when she did, it was usually about specific dates. Not facts.

Once more, Ruth described the night when her husband had left her to go to Norway. She believed that he had arranged to join Elinor, the mother of his two sons. "He told me that she was going, and he was going, and I assumed they would go together or get together once they got there," she testified. It was something that she had to accept, something she had feared for many years. She spoke now of the way their marriage had disintegrated after Rolf retired.

"He was allowed to retire gracefully and could keep his papers without surrendering his license. After he retired, our relations changed considerably. Communications fell off substantially," Ruth said. "He would not stay in the same room [with me], and he would go off by himself."

She recalled that she was frequently left alone in the few months prior to Rolf's deserting her. "He would take trips to the mainland and be gone for days sometimes."

Asked about his state of mind, Ruth didn't use the word depressed. But she had seen a change in him after the bridge incident. "He did a lot of daydreaming. He lost a lot of his whistle and sing," she said. "His big concern was being sued over the bridge accident. He was afraid we would lose everything we had to the City of Seattle."

What they had enjoyed together during their twenty years of marriage was gone, and she had accepted that. And with Rolf's disintegration, their financial picture changed, too. She had always been in charge of their money, even before they were married. She estimated that about $120,000 had been "piddled away" during the first year of Rolf's retirement. "Sometimes he threatened to take the money and put it in kroner."

Ruth said she had tried to loan money for the interest and to make investments to keep them from bankruptcy. "He was very careless with money — he'd cram wads of it in his pockets — but he'd never take money directly from me. If I gave him a twenty, for instance, he wouldn't take it from my hand. I would have to cash checks and put money in his dresser drawer.

"He never wanted to be involved. He wouldn't even know how to balance a checkbook."

Fred Weedon asked Ruth how Rolf got the money for his flight to Norway, and she answered easily. "He said he had plenty of money already in Norway. When I asked him how he got it there, he said it was none of my business."

Ruth Neslund and her attorney were characterizing her as a loyal, commonsense woman who had been at her wits' end trying to save what she and her husband had worked many years to build. It was an effective stance. And now Weedon opened up the matter of excessive alcohol consumption in the Neslunds' house of cards. There was no avoiding it, and it was wise of him to encourage her to talk about it, in hopes of defusing the state's description of her probable alcoholism. Her own lawyer asked her to describe the exacerbation of her dependence upon drinking.

She nodded sadly. Drinking had been a constant thing in their home. "We called it the house that beer built," she said, "because we supplied a case of beer daily for those working on the house." (That in itself might explain why Ruth's workmen had so many accidents on the job . . .)

"We did do heavy drinking and drank too much every day. It sharpened the resentments Rolf had. He felt pretty much cooped up after his retirement and that would come out. He would make us drinks and then say, 'Drown yourself.' That would antagonize me and I'd say, 'You drown yourself.' This would lead into stinking little arguments which would grow into physical fights — up to three or four a month. We'd get up the next morning and sometimes not even remember the fights, except we saw our broken glasses, our bruises, a broken tooth, a broken lamp. We'd get along great in the morning. It was like the fights never happened . . ."

Ruth's testimony was not unlike the self-revealing admissions often heard at AA meetings. With Weedon's careful questioning, she was baring her soul. She said she hadn't thought of herself as an alcoholic in the summer of 1980, but in retrospect, she thought she must have been. She had been blind to so many things that happened. She, Rolf, and most of their friends drank continually.

Still, she recalled setting a limit for herself of three drinks a day. If she poured herself a fourth, she called it "a boomer," and said that she never drank that one.

Ruth wasn't surprised that a lot of blood-stains were located in her house. She had long suffered from high blood pressure, and often had nosebleeds (a common side effect). Sometimes, she had saturated up to four hand towels before she could manage to stop the bleeding.

Ruth had an even more elaborate explanation for how Type A Positive blood was found in the shower door frame of her bathroom. In yet another "household accident," Rolf had cut his fingers on a table saw. He was bleeding profusely, and Ruth said she had tried to take him to a medical clinic. He refused to go until he had taken a shower. "I told him to hold his hand in the air to keep it from bleeding [in the shower]."

There was the matter of Ruth's strange comments at the Puget Sound Pilots' party in January 1981. Why had Ruth said, "Rolf is in heaven"?

"Oh," she said with a faint smile, repeating a story she had told the sheriff. "I meant that to mean he was in Norway, because to my husband to be in Norway is to be in heaven! Never, by the wildest stretch of my imagination could I imagine Rolf being in God's heaven. Never . . ."

Whether she thought him too wicked to be in heaven or she was trying to say he wasn't dead after all wasn't clear.

It had been six weeks since the first day of trial when Greg Canova rose to cross-examine Ruth Neslund. Canova was a handsome man in his thirties with black hair and a luxuriant mustache, charismatic in the courtroom. But Ruth viewed him suspiciously.

She was dismissive and incredulous as the special prosecutor asked her about her alleged phone calls to her niece, Joy Stroup. Ruth said she had no recollection of those. When Canova asked her, "You don't recall telling your niece that you wanted to waste Rolf?" Ruth replied, "I've never used that word. I wouldn't know how to use it."

"You didn't tell her that you just shot Rolf and he was burning in the burn barrel?"

"I don't remember that specific call. Why would I say that? No, I didn't. There was no reason to . . . You can shout that from the housetops, but it is not true." And then she added, "I have relatives who would say anything you'd want to hear for forty dollars."

Ruth said she wasn't necessarily referring to Joy, but that some of her relatives could be bought. She said she might have made some phone calls on August 8. "I was upset and hurting because I knew Rolf was leaving. I got into my cups during those days, too. I think I drank quite a lot when I knew he was going."

As for Donna Smith, Joy's sister, Ruth was angry at her betrayal, but she didn't remember any phone conversations or particular incidents.

"Didn't you, in fact, call her and tell her you were going to be sending her thirty pieces of silver, a reference to the thirty pieces of silver paid to Judas for betraying Jesus?" Canova pressed.

"No. I wouldn't have said that because I don't consider her a real Christian," Ruth sniffed.

Ruth herself wasn't known for churchgoing; still, she took on a pious look.

Even though Greg Canova pointed out that Ruth had given different testimony in many areas in earlier hearings, she remained unruffled — and gave new explanations.

Now, after hearing Paul Myers testify

against her about what he had heard her say regarding Rolf's murder and the disposal of his body, Ruth deemed her brother "a pathological liar," and a thief, a heavy drinker, whom she had rescued from his filthy living quarters and tried to rehabilitate on Lopez Island.

But hadn't she praised Paul earlier in earlier hearings? Canova asked. "You said you were closer to Paul than to your other brothers and sisters?"

"I must say that I had mixed up pity for love," she answered quickly.

If she had given different testimony at the special inquiry hearing in 1981, in the areas Canova specified — and, indeed, she had — she explained that was because she had been "confused" at the time.

Ruth Neslund was implacable on the witness stand. She had an explanation for everything, even though her reasoning and answers didn't mesh with what she had said in the years just past, or with the physical evidence. She admitted only to being a too-trusting wife who was about to be abandoned, and to drinking too much in an effort to block out her emotional pain.

As for murder? No one had ever found even a smidgen of Rolf's body. He was alive when he left her, and for all she knew, he might still be alive someplace.

And when Fred Weedon asked her the inevitable and burning question on redirect: "Did you shoot Rolf Neslund?" Ruth spoke clearly and emphatically.

"I did not shoot Rolf."

Ruth's son, Warren "Butch" Daniels, testified that his mother hadn't even purchased the Smith & Wesson .38 that the prosecution said tested positive for blood until after the alleged murder. He insisted that it had been bought in December 1980 — four months after Rolf Neslund disappeared. She had bought it from a gun shop in Slidell, Louisiana.

On cross-examination, Canova suggested that it was not the Smith & Wesson she obtained that December and whose receipt was submitted as evidence by the defense, but the Colt Python that was also found in her dresser drawer.

"Mr. Daniels, isn't it correct that when your mother was there in 1980, the gun you gave her to take back to Seattle for her protection was, in fact, a Colt Python .357 Magnum, and this [Smith & Wesson] gun, this .38 caliber, was one you had given her on one of her earlier visits back in '79?"

"No."

Although Butch Daniels would not budge

in his testimony, Judge Bibb later ruled that the gun receipt would be excluded from consideration by the jury.

The final witness for the defense was called on Wednesday, December 11. Fred Weedon called the defense's own criminalist, a "freelance" forensic scientist, Raymond Davis. Davis said he disagreed with the Washington State Patrol's crime lab experts, and with Rod Englert. In his opinion, the splatters of blood drops on the ceilings of the Alec Bay home had not come from a gunshot. He told the jurors that the blood mist was "also consistent with medium-velocity cast-off blood," saying it could have come from an instrument or weapon that administered a blow. (Blood-spatter experts agree that it is very unlikely to mix up such diverse blood patterns.)

Davis said he had inspected the bathtub in Ruth's bedroom, but had not noted any chipping, gouges, dents, or defects at all. He testified that he would expect a broad-axe to have left such marks.

As a professed expert in the burning of bodies, Davis insisted it was not possible to reduce human body parts to ashes in an open burn barrel. "Large and long bones, perhaps flesh, would remain."

He was not correct with that information.

After two hours of intense heat, almost any human body will be reduced to only ashes.

It was the predictable "war of the experts." Who knew how the jurors would weigh what Davis had deduced against Englert's more professional presentation?

Ruth had her two close women friends on Lopez Island: fish-buyer Wanda Post and Ruth's neighbor, Winnie Kay Stafford. Wanda had testified that Ruth had never spoken to her about her husband's desertion or said anything about killing Rolf or disposing of his body.

"Isn't it correct," Greg Canova asked, "that she didn't have to tell you why Rolf left because she told you she'd killed him?"

"No, that is not correct."

"Remember," he warned, "you are under oath."

"I know that."

Wanda Post would not be shaken from her conviction, even though Paul Myers had testified that he had heard Ruth bragging to both Wanda and Winnie Kay over cocktails about how she had literally destroyed her husband.

The other witness who could be extremely helpful to the prosecution was missing. Winnie Kay Stafford was deathly afraid of testifying. Winnie Kay had once been utterly devoted to Ruth Neslund, and Paul said she, too, had been privy to many clouded secrets, but she didn't want to talk about them.

Winnie Kay had told other island residents that she was afraid of Ruth, so fearful that she had moved. Packing up her life and leaving the Alec Bay Road neighborhood wasn't very effective, however. Winnie Kay had first moved from the south end of Lopez Island to get away from Ruth, but her relocation was laughable; she only went as far as the middle of the tiny island, merely a hop, skip, and jump away from the Alec Bay Inn. Further, at any given time, Winnie Kay's location was easy to determine. She was a well-known island personage who showed up at almost all public functions on Lopez, and attended every party. She had once been a stunning woman, and now — in her midforties — she was still very attractive, slender, with long brown hair that she wore either up in a bouffant style or cascading down her back. Author John Saul's parents had known Winnie Kay for years, and the thriller writer often encountered her at parties. But now, suddenly no one saw her.

There was a rumor that someone in Ruth's camp had warned Winnie Kay that she would be better off far away from Friday

Harbor, and that testifying against Ruth would be "unfortunate" for her.

For whatever reason, Winnie Kay Stafford had driven south with a woman friend, headed for California. She had detoured into Arizona to drop her friend off, and now was reportedly "hiding out" in San Diego, California, with family members. Winnie had been full of anxiety about testifying. She was caught between her fear of Ruth and her concern that she might be prosecuted for being an accessory after the fact in Rolf's demise, or, at the very least, for perjury.

Winnie Kay had lied to a judge before to save Ruth, and she didn't want to be anywhere near Ruth's murder trial. She was afraid she might go to jail.

TWENTY-TWO

Despite the intense interest in Ruth Neslund's trial, life went on as it always had on the San Juan Islands. Residents crowded the ferries to do holiday shopping in Anacortes, Bellingham, and Seattle. Christmas lights appeared on the village streets and in the windows of homes, incongruous colored beacons, holiday counterpoints to the grisly testimony about blood, burning bodies, betrayal, and infidelity. As serious as the trial was, there was an almost "soap opera" feeling to it, as if it was still difficult to view as something that had actually happened to fellow island dwellers. Both Fred Weedon and Greg Canova were dynamic and attractive men — just like the lawyers on *All My Children* and *The Young and the Restless.* And while no one could describe Ruth Neslund as a glamorous woman, she did have a gift for the dramatic, an actress playing a powerful older woman who steadfastly denied any culpability in an alleged murder, seeming to be almost someone following a script.

But as each new spate of long-hidden information morphed from rumor to admission, whispers became shouts. What was happening was not only real — it was moving faster than any television soap. Celebrities like Robert Goulet had been mentioned and scores of people the locals knew — their own neighbors — were achieving a kind of overnight fame themselves as they testified. The nightly news on the ABC, NBC, and CBS affiliates in Washington State featured the Neslund trial at the top of the news. This was arguably the biggest media event ever to happen in San Juan County.

Christmas Eve was two weeks away. The trial was winding up when, right on cue, local papers headlined "Surprise Witness!" In real life, most trials hardly ever have such startling turns. It is the stuff of *Perry Mason* and *Matlock*.

Some expected that it would be Robert Myers, Ruth's alleged accomplice, who was coming to testify. But Robert was in a nursing home, long since lost to a mind full of clouds. He had been adjudged senile and unfit to be a credible witness.

No — it was the elusive Winnie Kay Stafford who had been located, Winnie Kay who was still petrified about testifying to the dynamite information she had kept secret. In the end, prosecutors had little choice but to offer her a plea bargain that would grant her immunity from perjury charges regarding her testimony at the special inquiry hearing shortly after Rolf Neslund vanished. She accepted the offer, and now she was coming home to take the stand as a rebuttal witness for the state.

Winnie Kay was, perhaps, the most nervous witness of all the frankly anxiety-ridden witnesses who had been heard from so far, and she had reason to be. She tried to avoid looking at her one-time best friend, averting her eyes from Ruth's stare. In answer to Greg Canova's questions, Winnie Kay admitted that she had gone to the Neslund home late on the night of August 8, 1980. Ruth had called and told her to come.

"Why did she ask you to come over?"

"I was her friend . . . Ruth told me she wanted me to come over. She said she needed me."

At the defense table, Ruth laughed derisively.

"Winnie Stafford seemed believable to us," juror Lisa Boyd said. "She was younger than Ruth was, kind of average-looking, and she didn't have that 'tough look' that Ruth had.

She looked like the woman next door."

As Canova questioned her, Winnie Kay's story spilled out. She recalled being summoned to the Alec Bay home around ten o'clock on that August night. It was warm outside, and twilight was just fading to darkness as she arrived. "Ruth let me in and she said she had killed him," Winnie Kay said, her burst of words shocking in the hushed courtroom. "She said she had shot him — shot Rolf."

But Winnie Stafford hadn't mentioned any of this when she appeared before the special inquiry judge, Robert Pitt. Now her recall was very different.

"Why did you lie?" Canova probed.

"I felt what had been done had been done, and I was protecting Ruth."

Winnie Kay described a grotesque tableau where she and Ruth sat on bar stools, sipping cocktails. Robert Myers was in the house, too, and Winnie Kay said she had seen him occasionally come to the sliding door of the room that adjoined "the music room" where the women sat.

"He smiled and looked in a few times," she said. "She [Ruth] indicated to me that she didn't want me to know any of the details," Winnie Kay said, breaking into tears. "She said Bob was in the bathroom. She said Bob was cutting him — Rolf — cutting Rolf up . . ."

Winnie Kay hadn't particularly wanted to know the details either, but they were almost unavoidable. It took strong drinks to soften the electric edges of panic she felt. She knew that just down the hall, Ruth's recently deceased husband was being disjointed prior to disposal. It was truly a psychedelic evening, a horror movie. She had told herself it could not be happening.

Some days later she had talked to Wanda Post, discussing what Ruth and Robert had done. Wanda offered that Ruth had also told her about what had become of Rolf.

"She [Wanda] had gotten Ruth intoxicated one night, and Ruth told her."

Winnie Kay testified that, sometime after August 8, Ruth had expanded upon her motivation for killing Rolf. Ruth told her she and Rolf had fought over money when he discovered that he had no access to any joint bank accounts. Ruth told Winnie Kay that she had to put their money into her accounts because she fully expected Rolf to take it all with him when he left for Norway with Elinor. She couldn't let him leave her penniless after all her years of managing their money so carefully — not when he deserted her for another woman.

When Winnie Kay Stafford's long-awaited testimony was reported in news bulletins, John Saul added a caustic stanza to his endless limerick.

When Winnie came down to the Inn
Friend Ruth had committed a sin.
　　Ruth then she did urge her
　　Her honor to perjure,
And offered Miz Stafford more gin!

Called to testify again on rebuttal, Ruth strongly denied that she had ever said any of the things Winnie Kay testified to. It was all lies. Winnie Kay was making it all up.

The trial was virtually over, and it was time for final arguments. Between them, Greg Canova and Fred Weedon would speak for four and a half hours.

Greg Canova went first. He knew that the concept of a murder without a body seemed strange to laymen, and he explained once again that it was not necessary to show photographs of Rolf Neslund's corpse to prove that he was, indeed, deceased. "All that was left of him [that was found] was blood on the concrete, and parts of his blood on the ceiling and on the gun that was used to kill him. Ruth Neslund must be held accountable for

266

killing Rolf Neslund."

The defense forensic expert had said that parts of Rolf might remain somewhere and suggested they hadn't all burned to ashes. Canova reminded the jury that the state had never claimed that Neslund's body parts had totally evaporated. What mattered was that they had never been found. The testimony from so many friends and relatives whom Ruth had confided in was far more compelling than finding the body parts. She had told numerous people how she got rid of Rolf's remains. Ruth had been unable to contain herself, and admitted to bloody murder many times, giving macabre details, particularly when she had enough to drink to lower her guard and loosen her tongue.

That the murder had occurred wasn't surprising. Canova commented that it had only been a matter of time before Ruth and Rolf — one or the other — would kill. They were deadly adversaries with "incredible animosity bubbling to the surface all the time." That had become the norm for them.

"What happened on August 8, 1980, was that it all exploded."

Canova deemed the defense's attempt to offer Ruth's nosebleeds and minor accidents as excuses for blood remaining in the house unconvincing. "Isn't it amazing how every aspect of this case that seems to have physical evidence happens to have been destroyed, or cleaned, or 'can't be traced'?"

There were numerous discrepancies, Canova pointed out, in Ruth's stories. For instance, Ruth had testified that she found Rolf's Lincoln Continental on the Anacortes ferry dock "a week or two after" Rolf left her "on August 14."

But the bills from the classified ads and her own phone records showed that she advertised his beloved car for sale on August 13 and 14. "The reason the ad was running was because she had the car at home," Canova said. "She knew exactly where it was. The car was never driven anywhere by Rolf after August 8."

Greg Canova found Ruth's statements, testimony, and the ensuing contradictions those of a woman "who knew exactly what she was saying when she was trying to cover her tracks. She just tried too hard and she got caught at it."

Over all, there was "compelling" evidence that Ruth had shot and killed her husband on August 8, five years earlier, and then helped her brother chop up and burn his remains. "Taken together, all the physical evidence is overwhelming beyond a reasonable doubt that Rolf was killed and Ruth killed him."

Fred Weedon's final arguments stressed that there was no reason to believe that Rolf Neslund was really dead. "Just because Rolf hasn't been seen since 1980, that's no reason to believe he's dead," Weedon said.

Perhaps, Weedon suggested, he had decided to start life over somewhere far away from Lopez Island, or he might have killed himself in a state of depression. Weedon told the jurors that Ruth was not obligated to prove what had happened to Rolf. He had been depressed, and Weedon reminded them of the witnesses he had called to establish that.

As for Paul Myers, Weedon denigrated his effectiveness as a witness. "He's a self-confessed drunk," Ruth's attorney said, a man with a blurred memory and a fogged-over grasp of reality. And Winnie Stafford — why hadn't she heard any sound in the house where Robert Myers was allegedly cutting up a body? "Imagine if you can, the sound of a broad-axe chopping up a body in a bathtub."

And why wasn't the fiberglass tub scratched or dented from the axe? Weedon declared Paul's testimony unbelievable.

Her attorney stood close to Ruth, his hand

protectively on her shoulder, as he once more acknowledged that she wasn't any angel. Yes, she, too, had a problem with alcohol, and she and her husband had been dealing with a marriage in trouble. But it hadn't always been like that. Once, they had been happy, and Ruth had been "a person who took care of his [Rolf's] every whim, his every need."

Fred Weedon had spent years representing Ruth Neslund, his neighbor when he spent time at his family's vacation home, a woman he seemed to sincerely believe to be innocent. He was emotional as he spoke of her travail, and the tears in his eyes appeared to be genuine.

Ruth Neslund was not a client any defense attorney might long for, but Weedon had worked very hard to show the jurors the other side of this case. What a travesty, he suggested, it would be if she was found guilty while Rolf might turn up somewhere . . . someday. He painted her as a humble and pitiable figure. Her bowed head and her clasped hands did make her look somehow innocent.

Ruth was only sixty-five, but she had aged a great deal in the prior five and a half years — either from stress or from alcohol. More likely a combination of both. She had dangerously high blood pressure, and she walked with a painful limp from her broken hip. But her life had been good recently. She loved her bed-and-breakfast, and her new life.

Would she spend her last years in prison? Or would the jurors find that there was not enough evidence to convict her?

On rebuttal, Greg Canova scoffed at the lack of marks on the Neslunds' bathtub. "Bob Myers was not a strong man," he said. "He wasn't swinging from his heels when he wielded that broad-axe. Can you imagine how long it took Bob Myers to do this terribly, terribly, gruesome thing?"

Up to this point, Washington State had never had a guilty verdict in a homicide trial where there was no body. There were many who believed it was impossible to convince any jury to rule for conviction in such a case.

But it was almost time for these jurors to wrestle with the two views of Ruth Neslund that had been presented to them. No one in the gallery envied them that task.

Now the fifteen jurors needed to be winnowed down to twelve. There had been no need to replace any juror during the long trial, no one got sick or had family emergencies, and all fifteen had listened to the testimony and remarks. Court clerk Mary Jean

Cahail drew three names at random, and those people were dismissed.

The dozen who remained left the court-room and Judge Bibb spoke to the attorneys. "I don't often compliment attorneys" he said, "because if you do it too often, I find it diminishes the effect. But I'm going to do it in this case."

He admitted that he had probably "snarled" at all four of them — Greg Canova, Charlie Silverman, Fred Weedon, and Ellsworth Connelly — at one time or another during the tense trial, but none of them "had lost their cool." Bibb said they deserved to be commended for that.

It was late. Just as the sun set far into the evening on the August night Rolf Neslund probably died, the reverse was true in winter. The sun disappears prematurely in the Northwest in mid-December, and it was pitch dark outside the courthouse on Wednesday night, December 11, when they finished final arguements.

The jurors would not begin deliberating until the next morning. They would be se-questered during those deliberations. In a day, it would be Friday, the thirteenth, hardly a propitious date for someone hoping to be found innocent.

Perhaps it would not take that long. Some said the jury would be back before noon on Thursday. A jury that returns rapidly usually means a guilty verdict. The longer they debate, the brighter things look for an acquittal. Ruth Neslund's jurors had four choices to consider: innocent; guilty of first-degree (premeditated) murder; guilty of second-degree (not premeditated) murder; and guilty of first-degree manslaughter.

If Ruth Neslund was found guilty of first-degree murder, a life sentence was mandatory. If she should be found innocent, she could go home to the Alec Bay Inn and resume her life, and never have to be wary of the San Juan County sheriff's investigators again.

The jury began their deliberations at 9:00 A.M. Thursday, December 12. Their first order of business was to elect a foreman. They were a diverse group — the youngest thirty-two and the oldest a woman in her late seventies. Someone said, "Who would like to be foreman?" A few people raised their hands.

One juror, an older man with snow-white hair, wanted that job, and was annoyed when he didn't win the show of hands. They elected Elizabeth Roberts as foreman instead. She had once owned a Friday Harbor restaurant. She proved to be an excellent choice.

One juror, a woman who worked in the medical field, had a scientific mind. They would rely on her for the forensic science and medical details. Several were involved in real estate, appraising, or banking. One man had played softball with Ruth's attorney, and some had worked on real estate transactions with him. Basically, it had been impossible to find jurors who had no history at all with the participants in the trial. But at the beginning, they had all been sure they could evaluate Ruth's guilt or innocence with an open mind.

They agreed to deliberate until 7:00 P.M. for as many days as it took. Many of them were emotionally exhausted from six weeks of trial already, but they were prepared to discuss the verdict ten hours a day until they agreed.

Two jurors said they should vote immediately. One man and one woman had been absolutely convinced by the prosecution. "It's a no-brainer," the man said. "Let's vote for conviction and go home."

The others shook their heads. Betsy Roberts led them through Charlie Silverman's overview of the entire case. She played "devil's advocate," taking the other side of dissidents' arguments.

They did not return a verdict on Thursday.

Nor did they reach a verdict on Friday, the thirteenth.

They elected to continue deliberating on the weekend. When the jury failed to reach a verdict by Saturday night, the defense team and the accused had reason to feel a bubbling up of hope. Surely, if the jurors were so torn after three full days, they must be leaning toward acquittal.

No one knew what was going on in the jury room. A long time later, some of the jurors talked about their deliberation.

"We just couldn't decide to convict," Lisa Boyd said. "We talked about how long someone has to plan a murder for it to be premeditated. Was it weeks? Days? Minutes? We finally realized it didn't have to be very long."

They talked about the fact that Ruth and Rolf had the same blood type. And time lines. And they wondered about the gun used. One man wanted "smoking gun" evidence — not necessarily a real gun — that would make the verdict easier. But there wasn't one.

A few of the women commented that Ruth had been ridiculously "cheap" when she had saved money by not replacing the blood-stained carpet padding, and for failing to texture her whole ceiling. Her stinginess had cost her a lot.

They all found Paul Myers a weak witness, but didn't rule out his testimony.

These twelve ordinary citizens were going through the time-worn process that had turned them into cohesive, thoughtful decision makers. But it was not without angst and tears and frustration.

Finally, near 5:00 P.M. on Sunday, December 15, the jurors signaled that they had a verdict. Word spread like wildfire around the islands. The principals hurried to the courthouse by ferry, car, and chartered plane. Judge Bibb had been attending a Christmas party, and he was flown in in a small plane. The dignified, white-haired judge still wore his large, bright red, holiday bow tie.

Superior Court Clerk Mary Jean Cahail got the call that the jury had a verdict from Fred Weedon. She said she and her husband would be glad to give Ruth Neslund a ride to the courthouse. Ruth had been staying at a Friday Harbor bed-and-breakfast while she and everyone else waited for the jury to return.

"We picked her up," Mary Jean recalls,

"and it was as if we were just going for a Sunday evening outing. She was very casual, and didn't seem worried at all."

The jurors themselves, who were fully aware of the waiting news helicopter and the covey of reporters on the courthouse roof, had developed strategies to avoid being ambushed by the media as they walked to the courtroom. On this night, as always, they sent their oldest member ahead. At seventy-seven, it took her longer to make the walk and she limped along with her cane. But she was wily and knew she was also sent out as a scout. She saw the reporters who were ready to pounce, ducked behind a sign, and gave a hand signal to tell the rest of the jury to take an alternate route.

The courtroom was full to bursting by 7:00 P.M.

Ruth Neslund sat stolidly as the jury filed in. They did not look at her, and several of them had puffy eyes. One female juror had tear-stained cheeks. That didn't bode well for Ruth.

If Ruth didn't feel a chill, she should have. In the last few moments before the verdict was read, the courtroom was hushed. There were no cameras, other than television cameras focused on Judge Bibb to catch the moment he read the verdict. The court had forbidden photos of Ruth Neslund or the attorneys, and he had warned against demonstrations or emotion.

Finally, the slip of paper holding the verdict was handed to Judge Bibb. He scanned it without expression and then he read it in a solemn voice: "We, the jury, find the defendant . . . guilty . . . of first-degree murder."

His words were a lightning bolt, unexpected and shocking.

Al Cummings, a very well-known Seattle-area personality who was both a disk jockey and a freelance writer, sat up and bolted from his seat — only to be chastised by Judge Bibb and told to sit down.

All the reporters present, including Keith Eldridge, from Channel Four in Seattle, were champing at the bit to get to phones, but they obeyed Bibb's instructions.

No one in the courtroom had expected this verdict. Ruth had also been found guilty of being "armed with a deadly weapon," an automatic five-year consecutive sentence that would be added to whatever her punishment for murder would be.

Fred Weedon turned to Ruth and hugged her several times, trying to comfort her. She rubbed her eyes several times, as if in disbelief.

As the jurors were individually asked if

they agreed with the first-degree murder verdict, each of them phrased their answer exactly as Juror Number One, Lisa Boyd, had. "Yes, Your Honor." One woman broke into loud sobs and the others had tears in their eyes.

The feeling in the courtroom was mostly one of shock. Virtually no one had expected that Rolf Neslund's murder would be deemed premeditated, planned in any kind of organized fashion. Even the judge admitted to being surprised. Almost everyone in the courtroom wore a stunned expression. Some had expected acquittal, and others thought that Ruth might only be convicted of manslaughter. But first-degree murder? It looked as though no one was prepared for that. There were no cheers and no smiles, not even among the prosecution team.

Ruth Neslund herself did not change expression.

She leaned heavily on her four-footed cane as she made her way slowly out of the courtroom toward the elevator, her skin the color of putty, her eyes beginning to redden. She was escorted now by Undersheriff Rod Tvrdy and Detective Ray Clever. Fred Weedon accompanied her, appearing far more distraught than she was.

Ruth was under arrest and headed for jail.

She waved off reporters who tried to either get a quote from her or help her up the steps to a waiting squad car. "I'll make it. I'll make it — it's all right."

It was not clear if she was talking about the steps or the prison sentence that lay ahead.

Fred Weedon came back to the courtroom and broke down. He had genuine tears in his eyes. In his eighteen years as an attorney, he had never had a client convicted of first-degree murder. Not until now.

As spectators, courthouse employees, and some jurors wept, Foreman Elizabeth Roberts spoke to reporters, representing the twelve. "It was a very difficult decision," she said. "We worked hard. It was not the decision we wanted to come up with. We wish we could have found a different decision. The evidence was too much. It was just one thing on top of another, on top of another. It was very difficult for all of us. I don't know what else to say. It was just a whole lot of details that added up . . ."

Juror Jeanne Barnes said that all of the jurors had started deliberations with a "gut feeling" that Ruth Neslund was guilty, but the evidence wasn't strong enough to convince all twelve that she was guilty beyond a reasonable doubt. However, on Sunday, they had discovered what they called their "smoking gun." It was an ad Ruth had placed in the paper on August 13, 1980 — one day before August 14, the date Ruth testified that Rolf left.

Ruth had advertised their house for sale. "If she was expecting him to come back, what was he coming back to?"

By Sunday afternoon, the jurors had gone from five to seven in favor of conviction, and then they had come down to one juror who was holding out for acquittal. They had dealt with the question of the unscarred tub and the element of premeditation. It was the fact that Ruth had apparently shot not once, but twice, that led them to decide Rolf's murder was premeditated, if only during a few seconds. Ruth had told so many people so many times how easily she could shoot Rolf. And the jury found that she had, indeed, planned ahead of time to kill her husband. If she had shot only once, they felt, premeditation had not been proven. But according to Paul, she had ordered their brother Robert to hold Rolf while she went to her bedroom to retrieve her .38, and then she had shot him twice.

But it had taken the newspaper ad to convince the final juror not to vote for acquittal.

Judge Bibb set January 13, 1986, as Ruth Neslund's sentencing date. He would later

281

say that if it had been up to him alone, he would have come back with a second-degree murder conviction. But Fred Weedon and Ruth Neslund had chosen a trial by jury.

Although they had been locked together while they deliberated, most of the jurors weren't ready to go home yet. Some of them had missed the last ferries home and had to stay overnight in the same two-story motel where they had been sequestered. But others stayed because they needed to talk. Even those who lived in Friday Harbor were reluctant to leave.

They gathered in one room to watch the television news flashes about their verdict, and then longer coverage. They had bonded during the long trial, and they still needed to talk about different aspects of the case that had troubled them.

They talked far into the wee hours of the morning. At length, this experience was over for them, although they would never forget it.

TWENTY-THREE

The day after the verdict came in, even though the long trial was over and Christmas was little more than a week away, there were still surprises. One of the male jurors contacted Fred Weedon and arranged to meet him at a Friday Harbor tavern on December 16, the day after the verdict's announcement. Bruce Cohen said now that he had misunderstood the evidence on one of the want ads Ruth had placed in mid-August 1980.

Cohen told Weedon that he had seen the newspaper ad that showed Ruth was selling a three-bedroom house within a week of her husband's disappearance. He believed it was her own home that she was selling, and now realized that it was not, but only a friend's. Ruth had only inserted her own phone number in the ad.

"If I'd known that," Cohen told Weedon, "it would have been a hung jury."

But the state had never said that Ruth was selling her own home, nor had Weedon offered evidence that she was not. Judicial precedent would not call for a new trial or a mistrial because of the manner in which a juror's mind reached an opinion. Not unless there was jury misconduct. Legal experts pointed out that there must be some finality in trials. If jurors' mental processes were to be examined endlessly, trials could go on forever. Whatever jurors think or view inside the jury room is permitted, but jurors cannot do investigations on their own — such as visiting crime scenes by themselves, talking to witnesses, or looking at exhibits that have not been admitted. That would be outside the pale.

Ruth had quickly put a number of items up for sale after Rolf left, but not her house. Not until she advertised it in the *Wall Street Journal* in May 1981, after Ray Clever and Greg Doss had begun to question her.

Juror Cohen's second thoughts did not lead to a new trial.

On January 13, 1986, after spending the holidays in jail, Ruth Neslund was sentenced to life in prison. While prosecutors argued for a thirty-year minimum, Judge Bibb said he would recommend a minimum of only twenty years. Even with time off for good behavior, Ruth would have to serve thirteen years and seven months. At sixty-five and in poor health, it was not likely she would leave prison alive.

But, for now, Ruth was still fighting. "I didn't kill my husband. I wouldn't. I couldn't," she said once more. She recalled that she and Rolf had their "ups and downs," and that the latter had become more frequent. She admitted that she had been feeling sorry for herself, and that her last few years had been "what the young people call a real drag."

Pleading with Judge Bibb to find some way for her to go home, Ruth said, "I wouldn't hurt Rolf, let alone kill him. Whether it's twenty or thirty years, it's not going to matter because I'm not going to last very long. You and I both know it."

Ruth went home on January 25. With the loyal support of eight San Juan County friends, who mortgaged their homes to raise the $150,000 security bond needed before she could be released, she returned to the home she and Rolf had once called "Shangri-La." While Fred Weedon appealed her sentence, she planned to return to running her bed-and-breakfast business.

Ruth Neslund had numerous islanders who believed in her innocence, many of whom were well-respected citizens. One was Charlotte Paul Reese, the author. Reese was a former member of the Washington State Board of Prisons and Paroles, and a presidential appointee to the U.S. Board of Paroles. She wrote to Judge Bibb to ask that Ruth be granted a retrial, or at the very least that she be released on her own personal recognizance.

Ruth could hold her head up high, reassured in the knowledge that influential people believed in her. She had always had a good grip on the English language, one that belied her lack of formal education, and she spoke to *Seattle Post-Intelligencer* reporter Larry Lange in an interview in which she castigated those who she felt had unfairly seen her convicted of murder.

She was very angry at Winnie Kay Stafford — who was despondent after she testified. She scoffed at the idea that Winnie Kay was competent enough to speak out against her in court. "If I have any feeling for her," Ruth said, "it's that she's loused up her life pretty bad."

As for her brother Paul, Ruth said that he had made up his testimony based solely on "gossip" he'd heard in local bars. She said he did that in an effort to claim reward money from the Puget Sound Pilots' Association for information about Rolf. She believed Paul had been paid by prosecutors and that he needed cash to support his craving for alcohol: "He has a thirty-dollar-a-day habit and a seven-dollar-a-day pension."

She gave Greg Canova short shrift, dubbing him "a cannibalistic prosecutor who bases every question on a [false] premise. He can kill me but he can't eat me."

Whatever that meant.

Ruth Neslund had little respect for the jurors who found her guilty of murder, claiming that several members "had never made a decision in their lives other than buying a used washing machine."

She was convinced that at least one juror had relied on something heard outside the trial, and felt that she had been victimized by the fact that some jurors lived on islands in San Juan County other than Lopez. "Those people look down on Lopez," she snorted, "as the 'hick island' in the group." She added that "competition between islands is terrific!"

How such competition might have made a difference in evidence in a murder trial was somewhat obscure. But Ruth Neslund hurried on, saying that she chose to treat her life as if everything was normal. She would continue to run the Alec Bay Inn, and wait for the hundreds of daffodil bulbs she had planted in her garden to bloom. She even invited the reporter to bring his wife and stay in her bed-and-breakfast.

She smiled benevolently as she said, "I really don't go around killing people!"

Despite the guilty verdict, life went on virtually unchanged for Ruth Neslund. Business was brisk at the inn, and she was a gracious hostess to all who stayed there. Her civil suit against the Sheriff's Department and the prosecutors — where she once sought $750,000 for alleged damage to her home during the 1983 search — was resolved quietly. She and her attorneys settled, in January 1986, for $6,000.

"We would have cleaned and repaired her house right after the search," Ray Clever said, "but she ordered us off the property."

On February 12, 1987, Ruth's other suit, the one against San Juan County, was dismissed.

TWENTY-FOUR

Ruth Neslund was still free in midsummer 1987, seven years after Rolf Neslund vanished, as her attorneys appealed her conviction on nine counts, involving the admission of the Smith & Wesson handgun, the handgun transfer receipt of December 1980, Ruth's alleged confessions and/or admissions, Paul Myers's testimony, premeditation beyond a reasonable doubt, testimony about Ruth's shooting of animals, Winnie Kay Stafford's alleged incompetence as a witness, and what the defense dubbed Greg Canova's alleged "improper comment" in closing arguments.

Ruth's life seemed serene. Her bed-and-breakfast business was more popular each year. Visitors came to stay there because they liked the view, the amenities, and Ruth's cooking — or, perhaps, because they enjoyed the mystery of the place, the fact that their hostess was a convicted murderess, and the possibility that Rolf's ghost might still wander the hall and walk the grounds through the mists of fog that descended on cool evenings.

Ruth gave an interview to the *National Enquirer* for their "Scales of Justice" series, and she smiled in the photo that accompanied it, posing as she filled hummingbird feeders on the veranda of her cozy inn.

She told the reporter with a sigh that she knew she had been convicted when she saw the jurors come back on that December night in 1985. But the verdict had been wrong. She was maintaining her innocence as she awaited the appeals court's decision. If they upheld the verdict, she said, "I'll go to the federal Supreme Court if I have to. But I may not live that long. I have high blood pressure and arthritis. I'm broke. I'll have to sell my house to fight this thing through."

Ruth recalled better days in her life, her eyes tearing up as she spoke of Rolf. "We had a lot of good times," she said softly. "On Mother's Day before he disappeared, The Captain gave me a big, beautiful greeting card. I wanted to show the jury how nice he had been to me — but I never got the chance."

It was an odd holiday for Rolf to celebrate. They had no children together, and Ruth detested the sons Rolf fathered with Elinor. Why would he have given her a sentimental Mother's Day card?

Now Ruth often referred to the lost Rolf as "The Captain," with a tone creeping into her voice as if she had idolized him.

Ray Clever sometimes caught a glimpse of Ruth as he patrolled in San Juan County. And it was a bitter thing for him and his fellow investigators to see her out and about, free as a proverbial bird. They had all worked so hard for years to see that she would finally have to answer for what they knew she had done to Rolf. Eighteen months after she was convicted, she seemed no closer to going to prison than she had the first time Clever saw her. Indeed, she seemed smugly invincible.

And then, something happened to change that.

On July 10, 1987, Ruth was about to make headlines once again. It was a lovely day and visibility along the roads of Lopez Island was perfectly clear as Ruth drove her 1975 Dodge van on Mud Bay Road near Islandale.

Ruth was considered "legally blind" as far as operating a motor vehicle; her driver's license stipulated that she could only drive during the day, and that she had to wear glasses whenever she drove. She herself said that she had lost her eyesight when she suffered a stroke, although her medical records failed to verify that.

The road was straight and traffic was nonexistent as Ruth drove close to the speed limit. She was not, however, driving very well as she came up behind two bicycling tourists who were also headed south.

They pedaled close to the edge of the two-lane road, aware of a vehicle coming up behind them — but not concerned.

Suddenly, Ruth Neslund's van veered off the pavement and sideswiped them. Her outside rearview mirror — possibly even her right-side fenders — struck one biker and sent him crashing into the other, a young woman. Both of them were knocked violently off their bikes, cartwheeling out of control from the impact.

Ironically, it was Deputy Greg Doss who responded to the report of a single car/bicycle accident. He found two moaning and weeping victims on the ground, bleeding copiously from their wounds. And there was Ruth Neslund, visibly upset over the collision and offering explanations. Doss's first concern was for the injured cyclists, and he radioed for an immediate response by the Lopez Emergency Medical Unit. The EMTs did what they could at the scene, and then transported the couple to a small plane that would rush them to St. Luke's Hospital in Bellingham.

Once more, Greg Doss found himself involved in an investigation of an all-too-familiar suspect. Ruth Neslund was very upset, but she was cooperating.

After all that had happened, Ruth Neslund was still there; it seemed as though she would always be there on Lopez Island. Sheriff Bill Cumming had also responded to the scene. "It was hot out there," Cumming recalled later, "and two people were on the ground screaming. She wasn't acting drunk . . . she had many medical problems and Deputy Doss was evidently concerned for her safety."

Ruth kept repeating, "I didn't see them . . . I just didn't see them."

Fearing that Ruth might actually have a stroke, Doss asked Richard Bangsund, a Lopez fire commissioner who had followed the aid unit, to drive her home. When he returned, he spoke quietly to Doss. Once she was inside his vehicle, Bangsund had noted a strong odor of alcohol coming from Ruth.

The terms of Ruth's probation specified that she would be supervised by the Washington State Corrections Department, travel only to adjacent counties, drive only on Lopez Island, have no firearms, maintain her residence on Lopez Island, and not use alcohol or have any new criminal charges.

Doss figured that Ruth had just blown through the last two clauses. Doss obtained a telephonic search warrant that would allow him to administer a Breathalyzer test from Judge Bibb and contacted Ruth's parole officer, Jack Zimmerman. At 3:43 P.M., some four hours after the accident, she blew a .06.

A .10 would have indicated she was intoxicated when she hit the cyclists, but human bodies metabolize alcohol at different rates, and she might well have tested at .10 four hours earlier. Given two more tests, her blood alcohol dropped remarkably to .01.

Ruth was mystified that any alcohol at all was present in her blood. After all, she said, she had only been driving because she was on her way to Coupeville on Whidbey Island to file a brief on one of her numerous lawsuits with Superior Court Judge Howard Patrick.

Why, she asked, would she have been so stupid as to drink when she was on her way to see a judge?

But then Ruth had made a number of "stupid mistakes" in her explanations about where her missing husband was.

Finally, Ruth came up with an explanation. She must have gotten hold of some orange juice that had begun to ferment. Yes, "bad orange juice" was clearly the culprit.

It was a ridiculous excuse, and she was cited for negligent driving.

The accident could have been worse — even fatal — but it was bad enough. Robin Lewis, twenty-three, of Chico, California, had been admitted to St. Luke's Hospital in critical condition, suffering from a broken pelvis, a fractured skull, and a deep four-inch cut on the back of her head. Scott Battaion, twenty-nine, also of Chico, had a broken left arm, abrasions, and contusions.

Robin Lewis was in the intensive care unit, and she stayed there as she gradually recovered to "serious" condition, and finally to "stable" on Monday, July 20.

On that same day, Ruth Neslund was arraigned on charges of negligent driving, a misdemeanor. When she was asked if she had been drinking at the time of the accident, she drew herself up and said "Absolutely not!"

"Do you think you should be set free?" the judge asked, and she said: "Absolutely."

Ruth's new attorney, James Lobsenz, argued in a somewhat peculiar take on the situation that Ruth should not lose her driving privileges, saying: "There is absolutely no connection between the act of murder and driving negligently."

Perhaps not — unless one should find that each demonstrated scant respect for the well-being of others.

And now it was obvious that Ruth herself knew that her days at Shangri-La were very close to being over. At first she said that nothing had changed, that her crash into the bicycling couple could have happened to anyone. But then she murmured, "This seems like the end of the world."

All of the men who had been on the prosecuting team to find some justice for Rolf Neslund and all of the sheriff's officers felt the time had come. "Based on a recommendation by Mr. Zimmerman," Greg Canova, commented, "because she violated her release agreement to have no alcohol, we think it appropriate for her to start her sentence now."

Judge Bibb seemed to concur, as he ruled that Ruth should be held in jail until a hearing on August 7 to determine if she had, indeed, violated her appeals bond.

For Ruth, it was, finally, the end of the world as she knew it. In that hearing held in Judge Bibb's courtroom in Everett, she was ordered to begin serving her twenty-year sentence.

She was furious to find Ray Clever as her escort-guard on the private plane that flew her to the Washington State Women's Prison in Gig Harbor, a small town on the Olympic Peninsula. Clever recalls that Ruth called him almost every unprintable name in her repertoire as they flew low over Washington State on their way to Gig Harbor.

Several infamous female felons would join Ruth at this prison, including Diane Downs and Mary Kay Letourneau. Although the women's prison is close to the water, Ruth would no longer have the breathtaking view that she had enjoyed at her bed-and-breakfast.

On February 8, 1988, the Washington State Court of Appeals handed down their decision: The appellate judges upheld all nine of the decisions made by Judge Bibb in Ruth Neslund's 1985 trial.

Ruth would remain in prison, a rapidly aging woman whose health was not good, whose options had finally run out.

During the Christmas season of 1988, the home Ruth had built, the one-time "Shangri-La" of the last good years of her marriage and the battlefield where she and her husband had fought until they bled, which had become the Alec Bay Bed and Breakfast, was sold for $190,000 to a couple in California.

In the end, Ruth received nothing for her one-time equity in the inn she had been so proud of. It had multiple encumbrances. Ruth, of course, had been made trustee of Rolf's estate way back in early 1982, while Rolf's sons were awarded 50 percent of the property. She had used her share of the property for the bond she had to put up. She was awarded the personal property at that time. And when she was convicted, it was her friends who had raised the bond that allowed her to remain free. She was essentially destitute.

Now there was a long line of people with liens on the Alec Bay Bed and Breakfast. After her conviction, Ruth was naturally removed as trustee, and Seafirst National Bank was appointed. Seafirst attorneys questioned her accounting of assets and won a $64,000 judgment against her. They agreed to accept only $14,500. There were many attorneys who had not been paid, and it looked as if they probably would realize only pennies on the dollar — if that. Ruth's share of the money was used up. But Rolf's sons would finally receive at least some of the legacy their father wanted them to have.

Ruth was a quiet prisoner in Gig Harbor. She occasionally tutored other prisoners, and corresponded with those members of her family with whom she was still on good terms. Alone in her cell, if she ever pondered what she had thrown away, allegedly to protect her fortune, she kept it to herself. In the end, she had nothing at all.

On February 17, 1993, Ruth Neslund was nine days past her seventy-third birthday when she suffered a fatal stroke in prison. Seven years before she had made her prophetic remarks to Judge Bibb as she asked to go home pending her appeal: "Whether it's twenty or thirty years, it's not going to matter because I'm not going to last very long," she told Bibb. "You and I both know it."

She was right.

Although there were no longer any major events to make people think about the ill-fated Neslunds, there were small bursts of interest and mysterious revelations.

Deputy Sheriff Joe Caputo was head of court security at the San Juan County Courthouse several years after Ruth Neslund passed away. Most courthouse regulars run into each other at the coffee machine on the third floor, and Caputo often talked with

Fred Weedon there. One day, half in jest, he asked Fred Weedon, "Did Ruth ever tell you what happened to Rolf?"

"Yeah, she did," Fred answered. "You know — in that first search, you were within ten or twelve feet of Rolf —"

"Are you going to elaborate on that?" Caputo asked, surprised.

But Weedon was already walking away. He called back, "No — read the book!"

But there never was a book — not written by Fred Weedon or anyone else. Al Cummings wrote some excellent articles for the *Seattle Weekly,* but didn't write an entire book.

One of those most obsessed with the Neslund case was a man named Gordon Keith, a local, who spoke often of having been a published author for three decades. Although he had never met Ruth before her trial, Keith took out advertisements in local papers after the guilty verdict to announce that he was writing a book that would tell the "real truth" about Ruth.

Keith had tape-recorded the entire trial, and he managed to get an interview with Ruth while she was out on bail. In it, she referred lovingly to "The Captain," and explained her rather unusual banking methods as the only way she had left to prevent "The

Captain" from frittering away all of their savings. She spoke about her brother, Robert, just as fondly — but blamed her brother, Paul, for lying about her just to get the reward the Puget Sound pilots were offering. As for Winnie Kay Stafford, Ruth said her testimony was just plain perjury.

Gordon Keith had what he considered a scoop, but his belief in Ruth's innocence really caught fire when he had a private reading with a psychic named Dr. Richard Ireland who had just given two lectures on Orcas Island. Gordon Keith was bedazzled by Ireland, the only person beyond Ruth herself who seemed to agree with his theories.

Ireland had been photographed with celebrities, including Mae West and Daryl Zanuck, and had once appeared on an early Steve Allen show. When the psychic told Gordon Keith that he could not visualize Rolf Neslund as dead, and, indeed, felt he was hiding near palm trees — not in Tucson or San Diego, but in Phoenix, Arizona — another bizarre chapter of the Neslund saga opened.

Although Richard Ireland claimed to know nothing of the case, he told Keith in 1988:

The only compelling or shocking evidence is to reverse the whole situation by

301

simply turning up with the man in his physical body. Then what can they say? I think this would cause a lot of red faces and, as a result, I imagine a lot of individuals will be unemployed.

Putting the judge and the prosecuting attorney in the spotlight is going to be quite embarrassing to a lot of people, including jurors and witnesses. And the way to accomplish this is to turn up with his body. I think he can be found. I think some brilliant young detective should go looking for him now.

That's what I'd do. I think she's going to get out of prison, because I feel as though Rolf Neslund is still in his body, and I think he can be found. That's your key. He's been seen by certain people who know he's alive, so follow the trail.

But, of course, the "trail" had been followed and followed and followed by a lot of brilliant young detectives.

Galvanized, Gordon Keith sent manuscript queries to several Northwest newspapers and television stations.

He was enraged and incredulous when he got either slight interest or no response at all. Keith then started his own newspaper, in which he could print his theories about

Ruth's innocence. He apparently had no copy editor and his articles were rife with misspelled words, and although he decried the way justice had been done — or not done — he gave no specifics to prove Ruth innocent. Keith was aghast that no one believed Ruth's answers to his questions in his "exclusive interview" with her, but they were just versions of what she had said so often. And only he believed in Dr. Richard Ireland's visions.

Gordon Keith died before he ever completed a manuscript about the Neslund case and Ruth's innocence. Dr. Richard Ireland is also dead, and cannot be reached to explain his condemnation of the state's case against Ruth and his visions of Rolf Neslund alive and well among palm trees.

Fred Weedon has never expanded on the remark he made to Joe Caputo at the coffee machine on the third floor of the courthouse. He might have been serious, or he might have been joking. Ray Clever had a somewhat similar exchange with Weedon in which Ruth's one-time attorney hinted that she had confessed to Rolf Neslund's murder.

Captain Richard McCurdy, the current president of the Puget Sound Pilots' Association, was living in Europe when the *Chavez* hit the West Seattle Bridge, but he heard that story and about Rolf's disappearance from the older pilots like Captains Bill Henshaw and Gunnar Olsborg. He never knew Rolf Neslund personally, but McCurdy was to have a kind of connection with him.

The *Chavez* had started out life as the *Pacific Carrier,* and then she became the *Chavez,* only to be rechristened the *Bahia Magdalena* after her bridge damages were repaired. On the afternoon of February 17, 1993, McCurdy was headed to serve as pilot for the *Bahia Magdalena.*

"It was Rolf's old ship," McCurdy recalled. "It had a comparatively small rudder and it was a little hard to control. I was taking it up the Duwamish that night to the gypsum mill, the same route that Rolf had piloted in 1978. I heard on my car radio that Ruth Neslund had died in prison. I had a strong feeling that Rolf's hand was on my shoulder that night."

Indeed, Rolf Neslund's spirit may still visit ships at sea or coming into dicey harbors; it would seem natural for a man who spent most of his life at sea, saving many lives and shepherding ships into port. And even today, there are some who live in the San Juan Islands who believe that Rolf Neslund did not die in "Shangri-La" at all, but managed to escape from his wife to live out his days in relative peace in the homeland he loved and returned to visit so many times.

Today, of course, if he should still be alive, he would be 106 years old. That he lived beyond the age of eighty in some Valhalla in Norway is possible, but hardly likely. Most people believe as I do that Rolf died in seconds, shot twice in the head by a woman who wanted him gone forever, so that she could have all his money and property, and that his body was, indeed, dissected into manageable pieces and burned to ashes. Ruth outlived him by thirteen years. Whether either of them occasionally returns to haunt the eight acres on Alec Bay that they once treasured is a question no one can answer.

Their story has been consigned to the lore of the islands, seeming, somehow, to be fiction.

But it is fact.

Were it not for the relentless detective work of men like Ray Clever, Joe Caputo, Greg Doss, Perry Mortensen, Sheriff Ray Sheffer, and Bob Keppel, and the superior prosecutorial work of Charlie Silverman and Greg Canova, Ruth Neslund probably would never have been arrested, much less convicted. Fortunately, they never gave up.

No one who lived in the San Juan Islands in the 1980s has forgotten the Neslund case. Evidence from the trial is on display at the Historical Society in Friday Harbor — even including the bath mat near the tub where Rolf was allegedly dissected.

On a Saturday night in October 2003, seventeen years after Ruth was convicted, many of those involved in the trial had a reunion. The *"State of Washington* v. *Nettie Ruth Neslund* — Revisited"* function was held in the San Juan Island Courthouse, with a reception following at the San Juan Historical Museum, where attendees could view the "Law and Disorder" exhibit there.

Since island dwellers who were interested were also invited, more than a hundred people showed up. The panel discussion in the courthouse included attorneys, deputy sheriffs, and jurors who were involved in the investigation and trial of Ruth Neslund. The original twelve-member jury had shrunk in the interim. Four of them had died and one had moved far away to Georgia.

Many of the half dozen jurors who attended had lingering questions about some of the facts of the case that had not come out in court. Charlie Silverman led them through the Neslund case once more, this time more able to answer their questions than he had been during the weeks of trial. They had never known much about Ruth's background before she came to Lopez. And that was as it should be in a murder trial.

Ray Clever repeated his opinion that "Ruth was without a doubt the most evil 'bad guy' I've ever dealt with in my thirty-five-year career. They were nasty people — we called Ruth's brother Bob 'Butcher Bob.' "

Clever spoke of the forensic techniques that revealed the many bloodstains in the Neslunds' home, and Juror Dick Saler told the rapt audience, "The forensic stuff was so critical."

Clever explained to the crowd how close Ruth and her brother had come to being caught twenty-three years earlier. The investigator had eventually learned that Bob Myers had passed sections of Rolf Neslund's body out the bathroom window, and used nearly a cord of wood to fuel the fire in the burn barrel as he cremated his brother-in-law. Then the burn barrel was loaded into Bob Myers's pickup truck to be disposed of. However, as Bob was pulling out of the Neslund driveway, a sheriff's car drove past.

"This scared him," Clever said, "so he took the burn barrel up into the woods and buried it. We never did find it."

Those who were brave enough studied the trial artifacts on display at the Historical Society, including the wheelbarrow used to carry Captain Rolf's remains to the burn barrel. There were still faint bloodstains on the rim, as there were on the bathroom carpet.

For those attending and for most jurors, it seemed as if Nettie Ruth Neslund's trial had ended only a year or two before. "It will stay with us forever," Lisa Boyd commented.

Lisa had been called again for jury duty in 2001. Charlie Silverman was, once more, the prosecutor — this time in a child molestation case. Lisa became the jury foreman, the others deferring to her experience gleaned from Ruth Neslund's trial.

And, as he has done so many times since then, Silverman elicited a guilty verdict from the 2001 jury.

IT (AIN'T) HARD OUT THERE FOR THE PIMPS

When I watched the Oscar awards in the spring of 2006, the "best song award" went to a group of rappers whose sentiments I found totally wrong. The winning song? "It's Hard Out There for the Pimps." The audience of stars and Hollywood A-List people clapped and cheered when the winners were announced, but I wondered what we had all come to. While I admired the group's enthusiasm and joy at receiving an Oscar, I wondered if they had any idea what they were really extolling.

A day or two before the Oscar ceremony, I watched an Oprah show in which she featured the star of a nominated movie — *Hustle and Flow* — in which the "pimp song" was featured. He told Oprah that he had done extensive research for his role by interviewing a number of pimps. "I found them rather sweet," he said. And Oprah, despite being a long-time supporter of underdogs and hapless women, nodded approvingly.

I could not believe my ears! The song's lyrics say that pimps have no other choice but to practice their trade, but I don't buy it. After writing about naive teenagers and desperate grown women whose safety, dignity, and hope have been sacrificed to men who treat them badly, I readily admit that I'm prejudiced against pimps. When I talk to working girls — a euphemism for prostitutes — they confide that they never set out to walk the streets. They listened to heady promises from seductive men about how great their lives would be, and most of them have been reduced to taking terrible chances night after night just to make enough money to pay for a cheap motel, a "Cup-of-Soup," or a McDonald's hamburger for supper. That is about the only thing they do for themselves. Almost everything they earn by having sex for money goes to support the men who once claimed to love them.

I won't equivocate: I don't like pimps. They sit in cocktail lounges, wearing expensive leather jackets, big-brimmed hats, flashy clothes, and "bling," while their stables of young women stand out in the rain trying to make enough money to please them, or at least to avoid making them angry.

Most pimps attract women by picking vulnerable victims and, initially, making them feel important and cherished. Sadly, by the time the women realize that the pimps don't love at all, it's often too late for them to escape. They have become mere chattel and they have no money of their own. They are trapped in a nightmare existence.

After writing *Green River, Running Red,* my opinion of the men who put their women out on the infinitely dangerous highways around Seattle dropped even lower. Many of them faked grief and remorse for the dozens of young women lost to a vicious serial killer, but I didn't believe them. Too often, they seemed to revel in the media spotlight, basking in the attention shown them by reporters as they mimicked concern. Soon, they all had fresh recruits working for them.

I happened to be writing the case that follows at the time I watched the 2006 Oscars. It seemed fitting that I should speak up for the girls of the street that I've met, and the hundreds I've never known beyond seeing their sad photographs in the newspaper or on television beneath captions that read "Prostitute Murder Goes Unsolved," or something bleakly similar.

So, I say, "No, it's not hard out there for the pimps. It's hard out there on the girls who work for them." In the following cases,

311

the tables were sometimes turned, with the weak striking back at those in power. I don't believe that murder is ever justified — except in cases of self-defense or in the defense of others who are unable to protect themselves. But this next case may well have been terrifying enough to make the desperate women in Seattle justified in striking back — before they, too, became targets of a brutal sexual criminal.

It was the first day of June. After a long, long winter, it should have been sunny, but the day dawned bleak and cloudy that year with the threat of a storm. The weather was the least concern of the terribly injured girl who crawled slowly from her concrete prison in the basement of a condemned building on Melrose Avenue in Seattle. Something was awfully wrong with her — something she couldn't quite focus on — and billows of what seemed like dark smoke kept blotting out her vision as she inched her way up worn steps. The sidewalk wasn't far, but it seemed a football field away to her. She didn't realize that she was completely naked; what reasoning power remained in her pain-befogged brain told her that she had to get someone to help her.

When she struggled to get to her feet, she fell — she didn't know how many times. Finally she gave up and scrambled crablike on her hands and knees, moving forward only by inches through the overgrown shrubbery that blocked the dirt path from the busy street beyond. She was headed for The Melrose, a once-grand apartment built in the 1920s. Surely, once she got to the street, someone would see her and call an ambulance.

Through sheer force of will, the girl made it to the sidewalk. Through her blurry eyes, she could make out the form of a well-dressed, middle-aged woman approaching.

"Please . . ." she begged. "I've been hurt. Please help me —"

The woman glanced at her with a combination of distaste and suspicion, and edged away. And then, incredibly, the woman quickened her pace and walked off without looking back.

The teenager crawled over to the grass-level basement window of the apartment building and rapped frantically on the window. But no one came. She began to black out once more and waves of nausea washed over her before she passed out again. When she came to, she was lying on the hard sidewalk. Then she saw a male passerby.

"Help me," she pleaded. "Please help me." The man, too, ignored her.

She began to wonder if she was invisible

and realized that she was probably going to die. Nobody could hurt this bad and live; perhaps she was already dead — that would explain why no one was listening to her. But then she saw another man move cautiously toward her. He stood there, watching her. Maybe she wasn't dead. Maybe he could see her, after all.

"Please," she whispered again. "I need an ambulance."

She struggled to her feet, only to collapse again.

"You don't have to come close," she gasped. "You don't even have to listen to me. I've been beaten up and raped. Just call me an ambulance."

The man walked close enough to note the address of the apartment house, and muttered, "Okay." But then he walked away. She prayed that he was going to a phone booth to call for someone to help her. After what seemed like a long time, she heard the wails of an ambulance approaching, and she allowed herself to sink back into the blackness again, barely aware of the paramedics from the Seattle Fire Department who were working over her.

If you could say that she was at all lucky, she was fortunate to have those highly trained paramedics trying to save her. Dr.

Michael Copass's innovative paramedic program was the gold standard in the nation. This team — Aid Unit 25 — was stationed nearby at the Harborview Medical Center, where personnel were fully capable of dealing with everything from heart attacks to gunshot wounds.

Medic One paramedics were used to seeing the results of violent accidents and assaults, but this young woman's broken body was as horrific as anything they'd ever encountered. It looked as if someone had used her for a punching- and kicking-bag. Her slender form was a mass of purplish bruises, her left breast completely discolored. She might have been pretty once, but they certainly couldn't tell that now. Her eyes were almost swollen shut, blackened by the force of blows. Her broken jaw wobbled and her cheeks were caved in. Blood leaked from her nose and mouth, and each breath was agonizing.

Although they doubted that she would survive, the paramedics started an intravenous drip with D5W (a dextrose-saline solution to keep her veins open) to stabilize her. They managed to get an airway tube down her throat so they could administer oxygen. Now, they gently lifted her to a gurney and raced to the ER Trauma Unit of Harborview, less than a mile away.

She had no purse, no identifying papers. Nothing. They didn't know who she was, and she couldn't tell them; she might never be able to tell them. For the moment, she was a "Jane Doe," admitted into the ER in extremely critical condition.

Seattle Police Patrol Officers H. J. Burke and R. S. Zuray had arrived at the Melrose apartment building within moments of the paramedics, and Burke had ridden along in the ambulance to the hospital with the victim to write down anything she said. It would be Res Gestae (spontaneous utterances), a virtual deathbed statement that would be admissible in court if she didn't make it. Burke also photographed her in the emergency room, feeling privately that they were already working on a homicide case, even though the victim was still, technically, alive.

Zuray, along with Officer Dave Malland, remained at the scene, trying to locate just where the attack might have taken place, while their sergeant, Beryl Thompson, radioed in that detectives were needed at the 1520 Melrose address. Before her transfer to Patrol as a sergeant, Thompson worked as a sexual assault detective for years, and she was particularly adept at preserving evidence of rape.

Detective Sergeant Don Cameron and Detectives Duane Homan, Gary Fowler, and Ted Fonis responded at once from the Homicide Unit on the fifth floor of the Public Safety Building. They sprinted to their cars and headed up the hill to the scene. Ironically, the victim had been found less than a mile from the Seattle Police Department's main precinct. By the time they arrived, the street in front of The Melrose was jammed with official vehicles.

The Melrose was a well-maintained relic of an earlier day, having long since ceased to be the fashionable address it once was when Seattle's high-society members hosted parties there, dancing the Charleston and drinking bootleg liquor. Their sprawling apartments had been sectioned off into smaller units for those who lived in genteel poverty, mostly elderly people living alone. They cooked on hot plates and watched a changing world through rain-spattered windows with faded curtains. Some of the occupants were younger, working for minimum wage, or getting money wherever they could. When they were drunk or drugged, or involved in "domestics" — fights between husbands, wives, and live-in partners — cops arrived, banging on doors. Every car in the Central

District knew The Melrose well. There was no longer anything grand or upscale about the old apartment house.

Next door to The Melrose, overgrown rhododendrons, camellias, lilacs, and laurel hedges were slowly being choked out by ubiquitous Himalayan Blackberry brambles. The thick growth almost obliterated a walkway leading to a deserted old mansion whose windows were boarded over. Just beyond that, there was a car rental agency. The area afforded tenants an easy walk to the downtown district to the west, or, going south, to the hospitals located on Seattle's "Pill Hill." It was the kind of neighborhood where residents try not to get involved in their neighbors' affairs, where fights and screams in the night often go unheeded because people are reluctant to face reprisal for calling the cops.

Zuray and Malland had looked around the area before the homicide men arrived and felt that the actual crime scene was probably at the abandoned house at 1516 Melrose. They pointed out what they had found to the homicide crew.

Jagged shrubbery was broken down along the walk leading back twenty-five paces from the street. Worn marble steps led down into the basement of the house. Nearby, a pair of tan knee-length nylons lay twisted on the walk. There were scuff marks on the sidewalk three feet from those steps as if a mighty struggle had taken place there.

The basement door appeared to have been forced open, and women's clothing had been thrown into the stairwell leading to the cellar.

"We found the coat over here," Malland said, pointing to a white leather coat with a fake-fur collar. "And blue slacks with blood on them. There's a bottle of Tylenol pills, too. None of it looks like it's been here long."

Two rusty nails that extended from the basement window casing had strands of long chestnut brown hair caught on them. It appeared that the victim had been dragged forcibly to the cellar entry, her clothing ripped off as she went.

The detectives moved into the concrete room at the bottom of the steps. Even though it was full morning light outside, the room was shadowy and dark; as a prison for a helpless girl, it would have been just what her attacker wanted to drown out her cries. Now it looked like something out of a horror movie, with fresh blood splashed on the walls and rubble-strewn floor.

A pair of black high-heeled sandals, a bra, and a T-shirt — all bloodied — were on the floor. Crimson-stained panties rested next to a bundle of kindling.

The detectives knelt to look at a length of yellow rope, which had been tied into a loop.

"She had rope burns around her neck," Malland commented. "It looked like someone dragged her by the neck."

Blood and hair marked all four walls of the tiny basement prison. The victim's attacker had literally bounced her off the walls in the savage attack. The picture in the probers' minds wasn't pretty: The girl had apparently been dragged from the street like an animal, with the rope around her neck, forced into this deserted room, stripped naked, and come very close to death. That she was alive at all seemed incredible, given the amount of blood that glistened on the floor and walls.

The only thing that the sadist had left of himself was the rope — and possibly an empty pack of Salem cigarettes that might have been his on the floor. Oddly, the detectives found two one-dollar bills wedged into a pipe that ran beneath the smudged window on the south wall.

Beryl Thompson approached the detectives with information she'd received from Officer Burke and the paramedics. "We've got a tentative ID on the victim and a very sketchy rundown on what happened to her.

Her name is Arden Lee, and she has a home address in West Seattle. She can't talk very well because her jaw is broken and her tongue is swollen, but Burke was able to find out that she came here with an Indian male — longish black hair, upper teeth missing — whom she knew as 'George.' She said that he beat and raped her."

There were probably five hundred Indian males in Seattle who would fit the description, but it was a start. Detective Pat Lamphere, of the Sexual Assault Unit, left the crime scene and went to Harborview to see if she could find out anything more about the suspect from the victim.

A police radio operator reported that they had had two calls from the area during the night. Nearby residents reported hearing a woman scream. "We sent a car at about 11:45 and again at 2:20 A.M.," the dispatcher said. "The officers checked the whole area, but they couldn't find anything, and there was no screaming by the time they got there."

Apparently, the victim had lapsed into unconsciousness in the dark corner of the basement both times the patrol officers were checking, and in the dead of night it would have been almost impossible for them to locate her.

Pat Lamphere and a social worker from the hospital attempted to question the victim, but it was very difficult. She was almost comatose and couldn't talk to them with much lucidity. She did, however, respond to the name "Arden," and she nodded when they asked if that was her name.

"Who did this to you?" Lamphere asked gently.

"George . . . Indian . . . teeth . . . gone . . ." the girl gasped.

"Did you know him?"

Arden Lee shook her head weakly. "Not really . . . met him . . . at the Korea Tavern . . . the bartender . . . introduced us."

The girl managed to tell them that she'd met "George" again the night before at about midnight and that he'd invited her to his house "for a drink." She'd gone with him, thinking he was okay because a friend had introduced them.

"Did you have a purse with you? We haven't been able to find it."

"No, no purse. Just a key — a ring with a key attached."

"Do you know what else you left at the house . . . where they found you?"

"Can't remember —" was the soft reply, and then Arden lapsed back into a coma.

The trauma team of physicians who had

323

worked on Arden Lee informed Lamphere that her condition was extremely critical and the most optimistic thing they could say was that she might survive — if infection didn't set in, or a blood clot didn't break free and travel to her lungs. "She's in shock; she's been beaten as badly as anyone we've ever seen," one doctor said. "The neurosurgeon's going to check her now for brain damage."

And Arden Lee had been violently raped and sodomized. She had clearly been trapped by a man whose sexual desires and need to hurt someone were almost beyond the comprehension of the normal mind. One trauma doctor commented that her body was far more damaged than those of most murder victims at autopsy.

Despite her broken teeth and jaw, Arden managed to tell Pat Lamphere that the man who had hurt her had had no weapon beyond the rope which he'd carried in his pocket. She had seen him pull the rope out, and before she could stop him, he slipped it over her head. And then he'd cinched it tightly around her neck to make her obey him.

The only link between Arden and her attacker appeared to be the Korea Tavern. Pat Lamphere and Detective John Nordlund started there. They had to wait until the daytime bartender came on shortly before noon. The woman behind the bar said that her brother was the night bartender, and he was proably the one who knew Arden. "I'll call him at home and have him come down," she said. "But I can't think of any 'Indian George' who comes in here. There's only one 'George' who comes in, and he's not Native American. Maybe my brother will know more."

Yung Kim agreed with his sister. There wasn't any "Indian George," only a man named George who was employed as a bouncer at the Exotica Studio at Seventh and Pike. Nordlund and Lamphere exchanged glances. The Exotica was a thorn in the side of the Vice Squad; it operated just on the edge of what was legal and often crossed the line. There were a number of "businesses" in the area that were not what they purported to be, using facades to disguise what really went on beyond their doors. Most were massage parlors. Others offered "mattress demonstrations," and the Exotica claimed to be a dance studio, with dance "lessons" performed by the women who worked there. Almost all of the storefront businesses were thinly disguised houses of prostitution. There were always women and runaway teenagers desperate to make money just to pay their rent and buy groceries. The owners of the sex-oriented businesses assured them that their tips would more than make up for the minimum hourly wage they got. But it didn't turn out that way. The men who managed the tawdry enterprises kept any big money that changed hands.

The Exotica practiced a kind of bait-and-switch policy. Many male customers left without ever getting what they thought they were paying for.

Even though patrol officers working along Pike Street kept a close eye on the Exotica, its windows stopped traffic day and night, because garishly made-up young women undulated behind the glass, beckoning to the men who walked and drove by to stare at them in their tight, short, transparent clothing. However, once the men were enticed inside, they were told that it would cost them forty dollars to view a "program" in one of the private rooms. They were promised "interpretive dancing."

"What's that?" one potential customer asked.

One of the dancers explained: "It's however you interpret it."

Borrowing from the old carny routine where the rubes were asked to pay more and more for each new revelation, the men who were gullible enough and had enough cash to get as far as the private rooms were given a new price. "The forty dollars goes to the house," the women were told to say. "We make our living from 'donations.' They begin at fifty dollars."

Some of the customers balked at that point, but many put up more money. They were then allowed to disrobe if they liked — and to lie on a couch to watch. The dancers stripped then to their bikini underwear and performed their interesting — if untrained — dancing.

But that was all there was. Ostensibly there was no touching. When the "program" was over, the customers were left as unsatisfied as they were when they came in. Some were only disappointed, but most of them were very angry. Many of the women were frightened at the rage that erupted. To keep them from quitting, the Exotica managers grudgingly installed a thick pellucid screen between the plate-glass windows and the half-naked dancers.

Several irate patrons of the dance studio returned to the Exotica after being ripped off, and they threw rocks to smash the windows. One man was so angry that he came back with a jackhammer and broke out two of the expensive windows, showering the dancers and the customers inside with shards of glass. Then, with a smile of satisfaction, he waited for the police to come and take him away.

The Exotica managed to stay in business, although detectives from the Vice Squad were frequent drop-ins to check out their business licenses and verify the ages of the girls who halfheartedly rotated their hips, shook their breasts, and cast what they hoped were suitably sultry looks at passersby. There always seemed to be new girls — none of whom lasted very long when they found how little they actually got paid. Promised one hundred dollars a night, they were lucky to get a fourth of that.

The managers and the bouncers got most of the money exchanged. Because Pike Street was the downtown "stroll" for Seattle hookers, and the Exotica's patrons almost always left angry, it took beefy bouncers to keep a semblance of peace.

Yung Kim told John Nordlund and Pat Lamphere that the George he knew worked in that capacity at the Exotica and frequently dropped into the Korea Tavern when he had time off.

"Do you know Arden Lee?" Nordlund asked.

"Oh, yeah, Arden — I've known her for about four years. She used to date a guy I went to school with."

"Did you introduce her to George from the Exotica?"

"Yeah — last week, sometime. See, Arden never comes in here because we all know she's only eighteen, so she knocks on the window if she wants to talk and we go outside. I guess that's when I introduced them."

Kim and his sister said that George had a pretty bad reputation, and they'd heard he'd beaten up a lot of Exotica customers. "None of the girls from there will date him because they think he's crazy. He wanted a job here as a bouncer, but we didn't hire him because we'd heard about him."

"You know," Kim's sister said, "it's funny. I didn't even know his name was George. He's the guy who always comes in to talk with me during the noon hour. Today's the first day he hasn't been in in weeks. I guess I never heard my brother say his name."

"Did Arden work at the Exotica?" Lamphere asked.

Kim shook his head. "She just comes by here sometimes to talk. She has a baby about eight months old, I think."

"When was the last time you saw her?"

"Last night. She came by twice — once

about nine or ten, and again about midnight. We were really busy, and I didn't go over to talk to her when she tapped on the window. I never did see her again."

"Did you see her with George last night?"

Kim shook his head. "She was alone when I saw her, never saw her with George at all."

The Kim siblings were certain that George was not an Indian. They thought he was possibly of Italian or Mexican extraction. "His skin is dark," Yung Kim said, "and he has teeth missing in front, but sometimes he wears his bridge."

"Anything else?" Nordlund asked.

"He's got black hair and he wears it long, but he's real careful about his haircuts and he's always combing his hair. Oh, yeah — he's got a big mustache."

"And a big belly, too," his sister added.

Nordlund and Lamphere headed to the Exotica Studio. They didn't expect a warm welcome, and they didn't get one. The only employees there at this time of day were two teenage dancers who were performing their desultory moves in the window. Business at two in the afternoon was hardly booming.

The girls sulkily insisted that there was no one in the place except the two of them; no managers, no bouncers. Lamphere and

Nordlund didn't believe them; it wasn't likely that the managers had left the girls alone in the Exotica after all the fights that had taken place there recently. The detectives felt hidden eyes watching them. But they didn't have a search warrant and they had to accept the dancers' word.

The girls did allow that they knew a George, who was the night bouncer. "But we don't know his last name or anything about him," one teenager said.

"We haven't seen him at all today," the other said, as if she had rehearsed it.

The detectives waited for half an hour in the Exotica for someone to appear who might give them more information on George — but no one showed up. They left and called vice detectives who told them to forget about getting any cooperation at the Exotica. "We've raided them so many times that they're not about to help us."

Back at headquarters, Lamphere and Nordlund spoke with five members of the Vice Squad, but none of them knew who George was. That meant he had to be a fairly recent employee of the flamboyant dance studio. They doubted that many questions were asked of would-be bouncers. If they were big, tough, and mean, they would meet the job qualifications of the Exotica.

"The only names we have for management there are Kit Mitchell,★ Al Rauch,★ and Roger Pomarleau," an undercover vice detective said. When Lamphere and Nordlund checked police files for these three "managers," they found that none of their physical descriptions meshed with that of the elusive and deadly "George."

Lamphere searched records to see if Arden Lee's name was there. She found only one prior for Arden — an arrest for "offering and agreeing to an act of prostitution." That was pretty small potatoes. There was no conviction indicated. Arden appeared to be more of a hanger-on than a working prostitute. It didn't really matter what Arden did for a living; in this case she was the victim of a devastating attack, and nobody should have had to undergo the torture she had endured.

After leaving a message for the Third Watch crew, Nordlund and Lamphere signed out for the day. They requested another attempt to contact George at the Exotica during the evening. But after their early afternoon visit, the doors of the dance studio were closed and locked. Stakeouts watching the studio reported that the doors remained locked all night. When the heat was on over any of the activities at the Exotica, the place was known to close down until things lightened up.

When Lamphere and Nordlund returned to work on June 2, they learned that Officers Burke and Zuray had arrested a suspect near the Exotica who fit the description given by Arden Lee exactly.

He was a Native American male, five feet, nine inches tall, and his front teeth were missing. His last name was George, and he even had a ring with a key attached on his hand! The detectives were elated; it sounded as though Arden Lee's attacker had been caught only twenty-four hours after he'd raped her.

"We arrested him in the 500 block of East Howell. He was so drunk he walked into a tree," Zuray said.

Pat Lamphere interviewed Delroy George,* who was considerably sobered up now, and advised him of his rights. The suspect had extensive bruising on his hands and knees which could have occurred during the attack on Arden Lee.

But Delroy George insisted that he'd just come back to Seattle from Canada. "I took the Greyhound, and I know I got in at two in the morning," he said weakly. "Ask my aunt. She'll be able to tell you. I came in on a bus from Vancouver."

Lamphere asked him about the ring he wore with a key attached, and he insisted that he owned the ring. "That's so I won't lose my house key."

"Do you go to the Korea Tavern?" she asked.

"Sure. I drink there sometimes, but I wasn't there this month because I was up in Canada."

Photos of the numerous abrasions and bruises on Delroy George's knees and hands were taken, and he was booked into the King County Jail. He looked good for the crime. Right name. Right neighborhood. Finger ring with a key. Everything seemed to fit.

Sergeant Noreen Skagen, head of the Sexual Assault Unit, agreed. She and Lamphere headed to Harborview Hospital to see if Arden Lee might be able to identify Delroy George. But if anything, she looked worse than the day before. Her condition was listed as extremely critical.

"We can't risk trying to reduce her jaw fractures until her condition stabilizes," the trauma attending doctor said. "But she wants to try to talk to you. Just don't stay too long."

Arden whispered that she remembered more about her assailant. "Most of what I said was right, but I think he was taller than

I said yesterday. He's probably more like six feet tall.

"And I remember now that it was that George from the dance studio."

"Are you sure he worked there?" Lamphere asked.

"Yes. Absolutely. Kim introduced him to me in a back room at the Korea Tavern a couple of weeks ago. He said he was a bouncer at the Exotica."

Lamphere showed Arden the ring they'd taken from Delroy George.

"That's not mine," Arden said faintly. "Mine was a ring made out of a spoon —"

Incredibly — but luckily for Delroy George — they had found information that let him off the hook. Detectives are all too aware of the fact that there are many instances where a suspect who seems to be perfect for a crime turns out to have no connection at all; only coincidence.

A very relieved Delroy George was released, swearing to give up drinking.

Skagen and Lamphere checked with Harborview to see if the patients' property room was holding anything belonging to Arden Lee. She had been naked and shoeless when the paramedics found her, but they learned that the hospital had Arden's ring. It was just as she had described it — a ring made by

335

bending a silver spoon into a circle; it had a key attached to it. The paramedics had removed it from her finger as she was being treated, and turned it in to the hospital's property room.

Skagen and Lamphere took pictures of Arden Lee, showing bruises that had become darker and uglier since the day before. Her body was black-purple from her chin to her waistline and her face was like raw hamburger. Her knees and hands were purple. She was on oxygen because her tongue was so swollen that she couldn't maintain oxygen levels beyond 85 percent through her own breathing. Most people's normal oxygen level is between 97 and 100 percent.

Her physicians explained that Arden was suffering from severe muscle spasms in her back. Her entire spine was pulled out of line, although they now felt the vertebrae themselves were not broken. She had sustained a concussion, but not a skull fracture. Her broken jaw and facial bones would be set when — and if — she got better. She would have to have a tracheotomy (a tube inserted through her throat into the airway) before the surgery could be accomplished. Her neck, burned by the rope that garroted her, was held rigid in a neck brace.

Both Skagen and Lamphere had interviewed many rape victims, but they had never seen anyone so badly hurt, not anyone who had survived.

An informant called to say that the Exotica had reopened. "I think several of the bouncers are there. They usually stay in the back rooms and out of sight."

Lamphere, Nordlund, and Larry Gordon of the Sexual Assault Unit, accompanied by three homicide detectives for backup, headed once more for the Exotica. There they talked with Roger Pomarleau, the dapper, bearded overseer who was currently on duty. An owner-manager, Pomarleau was twenty-four — although he looked older. He was a tall man, handsome in a dangerous kind of way, with thick, curly hair. He was not unfamiliar to the Vice Squad. He had several entries on his rap sheet — both as a victim and as a suspect. Pomarleau had been beaten up by a husband of one of the Exotica dancers who had claimed she was being held captive. Later, he was charged with assault on another girl. That case never got into court; Pomarleau took care of that by marrying the victim — who then refused to testify against him. The marriage didn't last long, only long enough to see that Pomarleau didn't go to court. The divorce came soon after, and Pomarleau, a marrying kind, married another of the dancers, a sixteen-year-old girl.

He had discovered that was the best way to have ultimate control over his women. He was a pimp as well as an instructor of dance, and control was extremely important to him.

Pomarleau told Lamphere and Nordlund that he didn't know the last name of his night bouncer. "I only knew him as George," he lied smoothly. "He's worked here for the last week. We let him live in a room just behind the window. But I'm afraid George is long gone. We checked his room, but he didn't leave anything but a bunch of torn-up papers. Nothing with his name on it."

How the Exotica's management team was going to follow IRS requirements for their employees without knowing their last names was questionable, but then the whole of their business operation was suspect.

Pomarleau was being remarkable cooperative, and he willingly called his fellow manager, Kit Mitchell, at home. Mitchell said that George had come into the Exotica between eleven-thirty and noon on the first of June. "He packed up all of his belongings. He told me he was quitting and was on his way to the bus stop. Seems like he had some kind of trouble and he was leaving town. He didn't say where he was going."

It figured. No one at the Exotica knew where George had come from, where he was going, his last name, or anything at all about him. Their business was not a place for close and continuing relationships.

The detectives went over George's "bedroom" and found nothing with his surname on it. Pomarleau promised to try to find out more about the man he'd hired as a bouncer. He was so oily and ingratiating that the investigators wondered what he was trying to hide.

One of the girls in the studio said she remembered that George's last name sounded "foreign. He was like a very dark Italian. Me, I'm mulatto and he wasn't as dark as me — but dark. His name might have been Rodriquez, but I'm not sure. Maybe it was Danny Rodriquez?"

Lamphere and Nordlund went through their computer bank and all the FIRs (Field Investigation Reports filed by patrol officers) for the prior six months to see if there were any hits on "Danny Rodriquez." They found no one matching the rapist's description. They hadn't really expected that they would; those who frequented the Exotica lived in a netherworld, moving in shadows and usually using several aliases. They wondered if they would ever find the man who had savagely attacked Arden Lee.

Pat Lamphere was surprised to receive a call from Roger Pomarleau. He said he had gone through some receipts and found the name "George Ayala" on them. "I might have a picture of him someplace," he added. "I'll look."

Since Roger Pomarleau had done his share of knocking young women around in the past, it seemed odd that he would try to help the police find his ex-bouncer. Perhaps he just wanted to make points against any future trouble he might have, but, whatever his motive, Pomarleau was the best informant they'd had thus far on the sadistic — and now vanished — George.

Joyce Johnson, another Sexual Assault detective, who was working the night shift, ran the name "Ayala" on the computer. She found some hits on Mexican Ayalas, but they were all older or they were in the computer banks under "victim."

There was a growing sense of urgency in this so-far-fruitless investigation. Ayala was still free, and he might assault other women. His rage against them was far beyond anything most detectives had ever encountered. Expanding her computer search into Oregon and California, Joyce Johnson contacted Salem and Sacramento to see if their state's computers had any listing for individuals named Ayala.

Sacramento detectives reported on June 5 that they had two "George Ayalas" in their computer banks. One was a burglar out of Los Angeles, and the other had gotten into trouble in San Francisco for sex and narcotics offenses. One was twenty-one and the other twenty-eight. "We're forwarding photos of both of them."

Arden Lee had finally recovered enough to speak with detectives in some detail about what had happened to her. John Nordlund tape-recorded his interview with her while Lamphere stood by. Arden remembered standing in front of the Korea Tavern around midnight on the night of May 31–June 1. "I ran into this man named George," she began. "I don't know his last name, but Kim introduced us, and I said, 'Oh, yeah,' and we started talking, just gossip, and then he asked me if I wanted to come and have a drink with him. He said he'd just bought a new house and we could go there. He said it was still boarded up, but he had the lower floor fixed up."

"Did you have any fear of him at that time?" Nordlund asked.

"Not when we were first walking up the street. A police car went by and he asked me

341

if there were any warrants out for me, and I said, 'No,' and he said there were for him, but that's about as much as he said then."

There was no point in telling Arden now that she had used very poor judgment in agreeing to walk off into the night with a man she barely knew. She had learned a terrible lesson, and even though it appeared that she was going to survive, what had happened to her would surely remain a devastating memory for all of her life.

Arden recalled that she became suspicious of George. "I was frightened when George started walking up a path through thick shrubs," she said. "They even shut out the streetlights, and it was very dark. It didn't look like a house at all — at least not one someone could be living in. It had a 'For Rent' sign on it, and he'd told me that it belonged to him.

"And then he started walking real fast ahead of me, and I said, 'I'm not going. I don't like it up here. I'm not going no further.'"

George had turned around then, and she'd seen the rope in his hands. She'd been afraid before when she saw the dark bushes and the "For Rent" sign on the house that was supposed to belong to George, but now, seeing the looped rope, she was terrified.

"I started screaming and running, but he tackled me and got the rope around my neck. He started choking me with it and I had to stop screaming."

"What happened then?"

"There was a little stairway with a metal railing. He made me take down his pants and do oral sex."

"How did you get down the path to that stairway?"

"He dragged me by the rope around my neck."

Arden said that when the act of fellatio was finished, George had dragged her down into the concrete room in the basement. There, he'd made her take all her clothes off, and he asked her for money. "I gave him the two one-dollar bills I had. I always carry a bottle of Tylenol with me because I get bad toothaches. And he took that, too."

"Now you're inside the room," Nordlund said. "Does he still have the rope around your neck?"

"Yes. He had the rope on my throat the whole time. After I got my clothes off — he ripped some of them off — he made me lie on my stomach.

"He unzipped his pants and tried to have intercourse in my behind — but he couldn't do it. He told me to put my hands behind my back, and he would tie me up and for me not to tell anyone what had happened. So I put my hands behind my back and he kind of sat on them, and then he pulled my head up with the rope."

At that point, Arden thought she had passed out — literally hung by the rope. Although tests had shown she'd been raped vaginally, too, she had no memory of it, nor could she remember the terrible beating she'd endured.

"The next thing I knew, I was awake and I didn't know where I was and I couldn't find my clothes. I was alone in that dark room and he was gone. First, I tried screaming and screaming and then I remembered where I was and I tried to find my clothes, but every time I stood up, I'd pass out and fall down."

"Was the rope still around your neck?" Nordlund asked.

"No. I kept trying to make my way to where the door was, but it was so dark and my eyes wouldn't focus very good. I kept thinking that I'd rest awhile and my head would clear."

It was obvious that Arden had lapsed in and out of consciousness — perhaps for hours at a time — all night.

"It finally got light out, but I still couldn't see very well. I got the door open — don't ask me how, because it was real heavy and you had to lift up on it. I called out, but no one came. I passed out two times on the path, and then I realized I had no clothes on. But I got to the apartment next door and tried to get help, but nobody answered the bell."

Arden described how three or four people had walked by her as she lay bleeding on the sidewalk, begging for help. She had only a vague recollection of the paramedics working over her.

Arden still thought she'd been attacked by a Native American, but she was also sure that George had told her he worked as a bouncer at the Exotica. He'd been clean and neatly dressed. She thought he weighed about two hundred pounds.

Pat Lamphere asked her, "Would you recognize George if you saw him again?"

"Yes . . . yes, I'm sure of it."

The interview was concluded and Arden was prepared for surgery to set her mangled jaw.

Pat Lamphere and John Nordlund headed back to their offices in the Public Safety Building, and they were surprised to find that Roger Pomarleau had called once again. "He said he found a photo of George Ayala," Joyce Johnson said. "He brought it in, and he told me that Ayala had been living in

345

some kind of 'youth hostel' before he moved into the Exotica. He may have meant the Green Turtle."

The Green Turtle was a no-frills building in downtown Seattle with clean beds and a kitchen where travelers on a budget could cook their own food. It was well-managed, and considered safe. Old buses and vans left regularly from the Green Turtle for California with a motley bunch of travelers who had signed up for a reasonably priced fare. If he'd behaved himself, no one there would have questioned Ayala. Arden Lee had described him as clean and neat.

Roger Pomarleau had told Joyce Johnson: "Ayala's probably a Caucasian-Spanish combination. He has such a big belly that he looks pregnant."

"Is he on drugs of any kind?" Johnson asked him.

And Pomarleau had shaken his head. "As far as I know, he doesn't use drugs or drink much," Pomarleau recalled, "except he sniffed some kind of a liquid out of a brown bottle. I don't know what that was all about."

Johnson reported that Pomarleau had found that Ayala had charged several long-distance calls at the Exotica and that he would bring those numbers called in to Pat Lamphere.

Kit Mitchell, another of the Exotica's managers, recalled hiring Ayala on April 16, paying him about one hundred dollars a week to bounce. Mitchell's and Pomarleau's recall of how long Ayala had worked for them didn't match. Pomarleau said he'd only been there for a week, while Kit said it was six weeks.

"He came in on the first of June and said he'd been with someone who did something wrong and he had to leave town on a bus," Mitchell said. "He said he was going to see his family. He sold most of his things: radio, TV — real cheap. He took his duffel bag and left in a cab for the bus depot."

Mitchell gave the detectives a list of the phone calls Ayala had made, the last two on June 1. The calls were to Walnut Creek, California, San Francisco, and Texas. The two numbers called in Texas were the last calls. These numbers seemed to indicate that the rapist had headed for the Lone Star State.

On June 12, a photo of the Los Angeles George Ayala arrived. This photo, along with the one of the George Ayala from the Exotica, was included in a mug "lay-down" with six other photos of similar individuals. The L.A. George and the Exotica George didn't look anything alike.

Lamphere and Nordlund went to Harborview Hospital and showed the photo montage to Arden Lee. She immediately picked number seven as her assailant. That was of George Allen Ayala, late of the Exotica. Yung Kim of the Korea Tavern also picked George Allen Ayala.

The investigators called the number Ayala had called in Texas on June 1. When they asked for George, they were told he was at work. Asked if George had recently returned from Seattle, the woman on the other end of the line said there were three George Ayalas in the family, and the "Seattle George" was the nephew. "I saw him just last Sunday," she said. But when she realized who was calling her, she suddenly turned frosty and refused to give any more information.

Apparently, there were many, many families in Texas cities with the surname Ayala, but Pat Lamphere felt they had reached the right family. On June 14, she sent a teletype to Austin requesting information on George Allen Ayala. Word came back that the suspect was born on February 11, 1950. As he hit his teens, he began to build a lengthy rap sheet in Texas. Since 1967, he'd been investigated for charges including assault to murder, vagrancy, felony theft, suspicion of burglary, parole violation, burglary with intent to commit theft, and assault with a deadly weapon. He'd been discharged from parole six years before the attack on Arden Lee.

The San Francisco charges involving commercial sex (pimping), sexual assault, and dangerous drugs had happened since. Arden Lee had made an almost-fatal mistake in judgment. George Allen Ayala was not the kind of man a girl would choose to follow down a dark path — or even a well-lighted one.

Nordlund and Lamphere placed another phone call to Texas City, Texas. This time they spoke to George Ayala — not the suspect but his uncle. He insisted he hadn't seen George Allen Ayala for some time, about seven years, although he called occasionally. "He called on the first of June and said he was in Seattle. I have no idea where he is now."

The man they were looking for appeared to have successfully escaped both from Seattle and from the detectives who tracked him. On June 27, Noreen Skagen received a call from Kit Mitchell. "I got a letter from George Ayala," he said. "It's postmarked San Francisco. I'll read it to you. He says: 'Sorry had to leave you. Had problems. Am home with family. Would appreciate your sending clothes. Sure is hot here in Texas. Will send address. George.'"

It was about to get even hotter in Texas for

George. On July 6 at 6:30 P.M., Nordlund and Lamphere received a phone call from Constable J. B. Cucco of Harris County, Texas.

"We've arrested George Ayala for burglary down here. Understand you'd like to talk to him?"

They would.

Ayala, in a talkative mood, had volunteered to Cucco that he knew he was wanted in Seattle for "beating up a whore."

"We've got a good burglary case on him," Cucco said, "but we probably won't proceed with it if you want him."

The Seattle detectives said they would be more than glad to extradite Ayala and would send specifics of the warrant down to Houston, the seat of Harris County.

"George seems to want to talk," Cucco remarked. "I think I'll go on back and see if he'd like to waive extradition."

Ayala told Cucco and his partner, Billy Mathis, that he thought he'd just as soon go back to Seattle. It was 6:00 A.M. on July 18 when John Nordlund and Detective Danny Melton arrived at the Harris County Jail. They took custody of Ayala, who said he would "ride this beef out in prison," but he also hinted that he might commit suicide. He knew he was going to prison, but preferred Washington penitentiaries to those in Texas.

During the flight back to Seattle, Ayala inquired about Arden Lee's health. Nordlund reminded him that he didn't have to talk about the incident.

"She was a whore who said she'd get me off twice for forty dollars, but she went back on her promise."

He seemed to feel he was justified in doing what he'd done to her. He said she'd tried to steal his wallet.

Nordlund and Melton stared at him, this cold man with no remorse at all for what he had done to another human being. Ayala seemed to feel justified in what he had done. "Well," he sneered. "She tried to steal my wallet."

Neither detective believed him.

When they landed in Seattle, Ayala seemed oddly anxious to return to the dark basement where the rape and beating had occurred. He was taken back there and he showed detectives the route from the Korea Tavern and how he'd gotten Arden into the basement. His statement agreed with Arden's except that he insisted that she'd agreed to go with him for money. Finally, he admitted that he had put the rope around her neck and forced her into the cellar.

"She promised she wouldn't tell the police," he said, "but I got paranoid and I picked up a stick and started to hit her.

"I went back to work. I thought I'd go back later and check on her, and maybe call an ambulance, but I didn't get around to it."

Ayala's written statement to Nordlund showed more violence on his part than he'd admitted during verbal statements. "I hadn't bought the house. I just wanted to get her there. I was ahead of her and I think she started getting paranoid. She started screaming 'Help me' or something like that.

"I found the rope next to a bush and put it around her neck. I dragged her down the stairwell. She was crying. I didn't want to hurt her or anything — I just wanted to talk to her."

Ayala said that the victim had offered to perform fellatio, but that he'd stopped her because he didn't want it then. "We were in the basement. It was dark in there. I took the rope off. I hit her. She was on the ground. I hit her with my hand open. I didn't know if I should let her go or not. I picked up a stick from the floor and I hit her about eight times. I could hear her kind of foaming from the mouth. I put my ear on her chest. I could hear her breathing. I closed the doors and took off."

Ayala admitted he'd been in the Exotica the next day when Lamphere and Nordlund came looking for him, but he said the girls covered for him, giving him a chance to escape. "After you left, I closed the place and split."

Ayala had hopped a bus for Galveston and gotten off in Houston. It was quite possible that he thought he'd killed Arden Lee when he left her in the basement of the deserted house. If she had not managed to crawl out to the street and finally summon help, she probably would have died alone with the rats and the spiders. As it was, she barely survived. Even as she seemed to be getting better, she developed pneumonia; somehow she fought that off, too.

She did recover, somewhat scarred, and with a niggling fear of the dark that she will probably always have.

George Allen Ayala pleaded guilty to an amended charge of assault and received a forty-year sentence.

One of the most helpful informants in the Arden Lee case did not fare as well. Roger Pomarleau, the owner-manager of the Exotica, was always on the lookout for fresh young talent to feature in the center window. He recruited a new employee in mid-September — only two months after George Ayala was arrested. Cheri Schak was a tiny blonde, only nineteen, and she was thrilled when she listened to the usual spiel that she would make one hundred dollars a night and tips for gyrating in the window of the Exotica and giving dance "programs" in the back rooms.

Since Pomarleau invariably ended up collecting a hefty percentage of "his" girls' earnings, he was pleased with Cheri, who was more attractive than most applicants. He was so pleased with her that he invited her to his spacious, new condominium. He drove her there in his new gold Cadillac. His hospitality was so warm that Cheri was invited to share Pomarleau's king-size bed.

It was an odd invitation since Pomarleau was still married to his sixteen-year-old wife. He assured Cheri that it wasn't for any sexual reason. But, even so, he refused to drive her to her own apartment and she had no way to get home. Pomarleau slept in the middle of the bed — with Cheri on one side and his wife on the other.

Roger always had an excuse why Cheri should stay in his condo, and in no time at all Cheri realized that she was trapped. He told her that if she wanted to keep her job, she would have to live with him and his wife.

Cheri's enthusiasm for the scam run at the Exotica began to fade after a week or so. She didn't want the job any longer, and she didn't want to live with the Pomarleaus. There was no big money for her — Roger took it all. She had a boyfriend whom she never got to see. Roger kept filling her head with promises, but she didn't feel it was necessary to be so devoted to her new career that she had to spend twenty-four hours a day either dancing or living in Roger's condominium.

Cheri Schak was a captive. Roger wouldn't let her leave. And she couldn't get away from him at work, or sneak out of his condo. Soon, he began to knock her around, and then he choked her.

"I have 'committed' you to other people," he told her obscurely. "If you leave, it might mean my life."

She wasn't sure what he meant, but then he spelled it out: She would have to sleep with strangers whenever Roger ordered her to.

Later, vice detectives differed somewhat in their opinion of Cheri's situation — when they had encountered her in the Exotica, she seemed cheerful enough as she danced in the window in a nearly transparent blouse. Roger hadn't been on the premises, or so it appeared. If that was true, she could have left whenever she wanted to. But then Roger Pomarleau often hid so that he could observe what was going on. Cheri never knew where he was, but she often felt as if she was being watched.

Cheri hated the ménage à trois that Roger demanded with her and his wife. Sometime during the night of September 28, she made her move. Cheri rose from the bed she shared with Mr. and Mrs. Pomarleau and went to the kitchen. There, she found a butcher knife, and walked back to the dimly lit bedroom. According to Cheri, an argument followed.

When the "argument" was over, Roger Pomarleau lay naked on his back on the plush carpet of his bedroom. He was dead, covered with blood from sixteen stab wounds. Two of them had punctured his heart. His young wife ran screaming to the neighbors for help. She also had sixteen stab wounds, but they were not to vital organs, and she eventually recovered.

Cheri Schak suffered cuts to her hands and legs, but was able to flag down a passing truck driver. She was about to leave the scene when a neighbor pulled her out of the truck cab and held her for police.

Charged with second-degree murder and first-degree assault, Cheri's story in court was bolstered by the testimony of a rather unlikely witness: the first Mrs. Pomarleau, who said that Roger had beaten her two or three times a week when she lived with him before their marriage. "He slapped me regularly when I lived with him in 1976," she said. She testified that he had also abused her sexually and burned her with a curling iron.

"I reported him to the police," she told the jury. "And they charged him with rape and extortion, but Roger turned on the charm and promised he would go straight if I would marry him. I married him in Idaho that July, and as soon as I did, he forced me back to work as a dancer. I signed an affidavit saying that my reports to the police were false and that he never forced me to give him money, that all the sex was voluntary, and that he never burned me with the curling iron."

The ex–Mrs. Pomarleau testified that her first complaint to police had been true all along; she had suffered painful and humiliating attacks at her husband's hands. Once he had persuaded her to drop her charges against him, she realized she had been duped into signing the affidavit just so that he could avoid prosecution.

Roger Pomarleau's sudden demise left a big hole in the operation of the Exotica, but the crew pulled themselves together and the girls in the window remained a regular sight along Pike Street for a while.

Even though homicide detectives wondered whether it was really necessary for Cheri Schak to stab a man sixteen times in self-defense, and to stab his teenage wife the same number of times during the escape, her jury looked at tiny Cheri Schak and found her innocent of the charges: innocent by reason of self-defense.

With that trial over, the last sidelight on the story of Ayala's beating of Arden Lee was over. The Exotica "dance school" lasted a few years, and then quietly shut down.

There is no shortage of gullible teenagers who fall under the spell of pimps, but as high-priced condo buildings proliferated in the downtown sections of the Emerald City, Pike Street gradually ceased to be the hot spot for prostitution in Seattle. It didn't go away, however. It never goes away. In the Seattle area, sex for money moved to Aurora Avenue North and south to the highway that runs by the Seattle-Tacoma Airport — where both became a prime hunting ground for the perversely sadistic murderer known in infamy as the Green River Killer.

And with that, a whole new chapter of horror began.

IT (AIN'T) HARD OUT THERE FOR THE PIMPS

Had Arden Lee known about this man's long, long rap sheet for crimes, including sexual assault, she might never have accepted his invitation to have a drink at his house. In reality, he had no *house*, and his job as the bouncer at the Exotica "Dance Studio" didn't pay much. His confession was full of lies and cruelty. He was sentenced to forty years in prison. (SEATTLE PD PHOTO)

The victim of a savage attack had to crawl naked up these marble steps of a once-grand apartment to cry for help. Shockingly, a number of passersby ignored her pleas. (SEATTLE PD CRIME SCENE PHOTO)

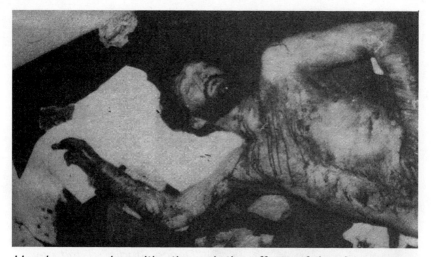

Handsome and wealthy through the efforts of the desperate women who worked for him, this man gave up the name of Arden Lee's rapist, but he had secrets of his own. When he forced one of his "dancers" to sleep between him and his teenaged bride to keep her from escaping, she grabbed a knife and stabbed him while he slept.

Sergeant Beryl Thompson had many years of experience in the Sex Crimes Unit of the Seattle Police Department, but she had never seen anyone as badly injured as the naked girl discovered near the Melrose apartments.

Seattle PD's Sex Crimes Unit detectives John Nordlund, left, and Pat Lamphere haunted the Exotica, a "dancing lesson" storefront business, and eventually tracked the suspect in Arden Lee's near-fatal sexual assault all the way to Houston before they solved the case. Their unwelcome surprise visits to the Exotica soon forced it out of business.

A good samaritan rushed to help the terribly injured rape victim, and soon the neighborhood of 1920s apartments was alive with police vehicles. Paramedics from the Seattle Fire Department's top-rated Medic One unit weren't sure, however, if they could save her life. Seattle police investigators wondered if she would ever be able to name her attacker. (SEATTLE PD CRIME SCENE PHOTO)

THE RUNAWAY AND THE SOLDIER

Teresa Sterling, who looked a great deal like actress Jodie Foster, was only sixteen when she ran away from home in Georgia to return to a more exciting life on the West Coast. She believed she was fully capable of taking care of herself, and depended on "the kindness of strangers." But then she vanished completely. (POLICE EVIDENCE PHOTO)

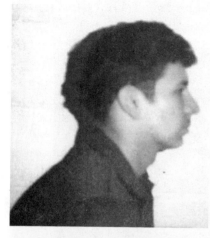

Jealousy sent this man into a rage, and tragedy ensued in the woods. He changed his life and tried to forget what he had done.

Detective Roy Gleason of the Bellevue Police Department was in charge of solving a long-undiscovered murder, identifying the victim, and finding whoever killed her. (BELLEVUE PD CRIME SCENE PHOTO)

Although the body in the woods was in skeleton form, its position showed a bizarre and grotesque sexual attack had taken place. Working under high-powered lights, a Bellevue investigator shovels very, very carefully to find any evidence that might exist. (BELLEVUE PD CRIME SCENE PHOTO)

Dr. John Eisele, left, of the King County Medical Examiner's Office, came to the site of the skeletonized body and worked by flashlight as the December sunset plunged the woods into darkness. The investigators did not know cause of death or even if the victim was male or female. (BELLEVUE PD CRIME SCENE PHOTO)

Bellevue investigators gather on a narrow road that ran close to the lonely woods where a strolling couple came across a skeleton. (BELLEVUE PD CRIME SCENE PHOTO)

THE TRAGIC ENDING OF A BANK ROBBER'S FANTASY

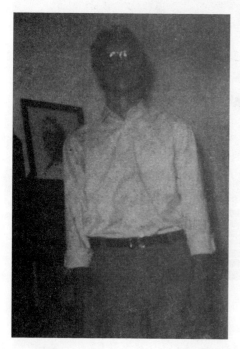

Sam Jesse was a very tall and gawky young man, intelligent, but a "preacher's kid" who sought a life of adventure and high living. His plans ended in disaster.

A hidden camera in the Prudential Bank catches the image of the tall bank robber just as Jill Mobley hands him the dye-pack of bills. He was so covered up that only a bit of his nose showed. But someone would recognize him.

(POLICE PHOTO)

A robber bought this Volkswagen "bug" with the profits from an earlier crime. He parked it far away from the bank, drove a stolen vehicle, and yet had the bad fortune to have a witness who memorized everything about it because she was a "bug fancier." (POLICE FILE COLLECTION)

Sam Jesse put the stolen bills inside concrete blocks that held up his mattress. For a tragic reason, he never did come back to get them. (POLICE FILE PHOTO)

When Seattle detectives searched Sam Jesse's
apartment, they found a plethora of physical evidence.
Here, George Marberg holds the gun that was used in
the fatal bank robbery. (SEATTLE PD CRIME SCENE PHOTO)

Sam Jesse couldn't spend the money he stole.
An orange dye-pack set to go off as he got into
his car stained every bill. Detectives found he had
put the bills on every page of a book. Perhaps he
hoped to find a way to remove the dye? (SEATTLE
PD PHOTO FILE)

Seattle Homicide Detective George Marberg followed the trail of a bank robber who thought he had planned the perfect scenario that would take away his money worries forever.

A VERY BAD CHRISTMAS

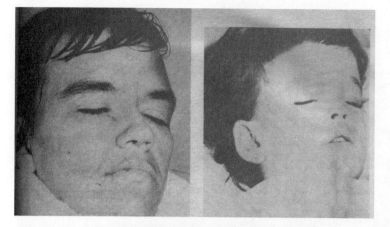

Just before Christmas, Portland, Oregon, newspapers printed these photographs. There seemed no other way to identify the young woman and the small girl who were found dead on Sauvie Island. Within a short time, two witnesses came forward after they recognized dear friends. They were even more shocked when they learned who their killer was.

Oregon State Police drag the river off Sauvie Island, looking for evidence connected to a discovery on the shore just before Christmas.

Multnomah County, Oregon, veteran Homicide Detective Darril MacNeel, who, with his long-time partner, "Blackie" Yazzolino, elicited a bizarre confession from the most unlikely suspect they had ever encountered.

To Save Their Souls

Christine Jonsen at her trial. From the judge to the jury to the gallery, and probably to the prosecutor, no one believed she should be there. But the law said differently.

. . . Or We'll Kill You

Kari Lindholm was in her twenties and working as a counselor in a crisis center when she was kidnapped by two very dangerous men. Her chances of survival were almost nil.

THE RUNAWAY
AND THE SOLDIER

Not all murders are plotted and designed in a sociopath's mind. Some killers could never have imagined that they were capable of killing another human being. And yet their victims are just as dead as those bodies left behind in the wake of a serial killer. I like to think that the vast majority of people would kill only only in self-defense. Almost any mother — animal or human — will defend her young unto death. Self-defense and the horror of war can change the conscience and sensibilities of us all.

There are other "triggers" that can evoke blind rage, and sometimes we are unaware of what they are, those secret buttons deep inside that can be pushed without warning. Fear and frustration and jealousy may be deadly triggers. Flashbacks of episodes buried in the psyche can play across the unconscious mind. A lot of murder defendants blame "blackouts," insisting that they cannot recall the moment they snapped, and are, therefore, not responsible for what they have done. In most cases, I don't buy that and neither do the vast majority of juries.

In the following case, a number of unfortunate circumstances had to have occurred in a deadly chain to set the scene for murder. Without them, it's unlikely the killer would ever have erupted into a homicidal rage. But, with the dark arrangement of circumstance, heedlessness, and the deserted crime scene, the victim's sudden death seems absolutely predestined. Indeed, the victim herself contributed to the tumbling down of safeguards that would have saved her life.

She was headstrong, and falsely confident in her own ability to make decisions. No matter how many people loved her and wanted to help her, she chose to walk away from their concern and live her own life exactly as she wanted to.

It was to be the death of her.

It is a lovely patch of woods, where the warmth of bright sunlight just above its tree-tops grows cooler as the protective branches of Douglas firs in the winter and peach trees in the spring and summer close in. It isn't that far from a well-populated area, but sound is hushed here, absorbed by a carpet of native vegetation: salal, Oregon grape, kinnikinnik, and feathery sword ferns. Woods like this are one of the inducements for home buyers to accept long commutes into Seattle, crossing over one of the two floating bridges to leave the Emerald City and move to the burgeoning suburb of Bellevue, Washington. The houses that abut these woods are mostly ramblers, huddled close to the ground, landscaped with rhododendrons and dogwoods. They are not plush, but they have grown tremendously in value over the years as suburbs to the east of Lake Washington creep steadily up into the very foothills of Snoqualmie Pass. Families who live there often walk along the meandering paths among the trees. They walk their pets there and ride horses along bridle trails, and young lovers hold hands, enjoying the hushed ambience and the feeling of privacy.

It is a peaceful sanctuary without any sense of foreboding. It is no place for violent death.

It was Friday, December 7, the anniversary of the 1941 attack on Pearl Harbor, but the young people who entered the dark woods didn't remember the event that sparked the United States to enter World War II; they hadn't even been born then. They strolled along the path shortly after noon. The girl was seventeen, her friend twenty-two. They broke off some bright red holly berry sprigs, talked about their Christmas plans, and wondered when the snowpack in Snoqualmie Pass would be deep enough for them to plan a ski trip.

As they moved deeper into the woods, the trees were so thick that it was like being in a cave made of branches. Suddenly, the young woman gasped. A skull lay directly in front of them, resting on the surface on sodden, brown leaves. It was far too big to have come from any small woods creature; it was a human skull.

Forgetting their walk, the couple ran to a nearby house and called the Bellevue Police Department. The first officer on the scene was Patrolman Bob Littlejohn. It was an irony in itself that Littlejohn should be the first lawman on the scene. Looking at the skull, he determined that it was, indeed, that of a human being. Yet he could have no way of knowing at the time that he was viewing the remains of someone he knew.

Littlejohn was joined by Patrol Lieutenant Paul Olson. As they secured the scene and notified detectives at their downtown Bellevue offices, the two officers noted that the woods and surrounding trees were part of a long-forgotten peach orchard — all that remained from the days when the development known as "Sherwood Forest" was once farmland.

Now it had become not only a favorite spot for rustic walks but also a popular dirt path for motorcyclists. Littlejohn walked carefully in an ever-widening circle radiating out from the skull. Forty feet away, he stopped and stared down at the ground.

He gazed at what first appeared to be only an abandoned Christmas tree. But as he focused his eyes, it resembled one of those drawings that change depending on how the viewer sees them: The woman's face in the mirror becomes a death's head, or black letters shift and the viewer sees that the white spaces say something different. Littlejohn suddenly became aware that this Christmas tree, its branches as bare of needles as the skull itself was denuded of flesh, covered something beneath it: bones that were the widespread legs of a skeleton. The body lay on its back, nude, and decomposition was far advanced. It had to have been here for months.

Within minutes, eight detectives and Bellevue Police Chief Don Van Blaricom arrived. Detective Roy Gleason would take over principal responsibility for the homicide probe. And detectives Gary Trent, Marvin Skeen, Jim Constantine, Mike Lambo, John Cooper, Chuck Webb, and Mike Cate would be assigned to assist in the investigation of what surely was a homicide.

As the investigators looked at the ravaged body — which from the way its hair was cut and the ragged clothes nearby was probably the remains of a female — they knew they would have to call on all their experience and expertise. Going in, this case had all the signs of a loser. The first forty-eight hours after a murder are the prime-time segment when a murder suspect will emerge, and after that the chances of finding him diminish with each passing day. The killer had a very long head start on them. They had no idea who she was, this sad victim thrown away in the woods.

"I don't think we're even going to get an identification — let alone apprehend her killer," Van Blaricom commented.

Before the crime scene search began in earnest, they cordoned the area off, and uniformed officers were stationed at key points to prevent curious passersby from entering the woods.

Although the body was naked, the investigators found several items. There was a red ski jacket, with yellow and orange stripes around the sleeves, waist, and collar. It was a mass-produced item, with a "Made in Hong Kong" label. There was a hooded, yellow cotton shirt trimmed in white with a front neck zipper and a pocket-pouch in front, also zippered. A pair of blue jeans with a twenty-seven-inch waist. White tube socks. A white bra with a J.C. Penney label. There were no panties.

It appeared to be standard attire of an average young woman, and not distinctive enough to aid in identifying the body in the woods. Still, the clothing would be carefully dried and photographed on the slight chance that someone would recognize the items.

Dr. John Eisele of the King County Medical Examiner's Office arrived to do a preliminary examination of the victim. He could give only a "ballpark figure" as to the time of death. "Two, three months ago — possibly longer."

The cause of death would be harder to determine. Much soft tissue had been lost to the elements, the burning sun of late summer and early fall, and then rain and snow in November and December. There were animals in the woods, too, mostly small. Eisele could not immediately isolate any cause of death. "I'll be able to tell more at the postmortem," he said.

Roy Gleason and his fellow detectives worked through the long, chill December afternoon, first with the rays of pale sunlight that cut through the trees, then with auxiliary lighting as the sun set. In December, that occurred well before four. They bagged and labeled the dead woman's clothing for evidence, and did the same with soil and leaf samples.

They took careful measurements, triangulating them with trees, and photographed the remains and the scene. At length, the fragile remains were removed for autopsy, and the Bellevue investigative crew cleared the scene.

The woods were now as they were before.

She had lain there for so long. There was no point in hurrying, but they were back in the woods and the adjoining neighborhood as soon as the sun rose. They canvassed the nearby homes, but their questions netted nothing helpful. Most people don't recall noises or out-of-the-ordinary incidents that happened months ago — not unless there is something on which to peg a hidden memory. Sherwood Forest residents were accustomed to a lot of foot traffic through the woods, and the less welcome roar of motorbikes and cycles.

"Who was she?" was the question that kept niggling at them. Would they ever be able to find that out from a few bagfuls of mouldering clothing? They had found some of her teeth, but they had fallen out and landed in the wet, yellowed peach leaves. It wasn't as if they had an intact jaw that a forensic odontologist might use for identification. The separate teeth had probably been knocked out in a violent struggle. There might be enough of them left in the skull for a forensic dentist to make a positive comparison — if they could locate the dental records of the dead girl. It was a vicious circle. Unless they had some inkling about her name, they wouldn't be able to locate her dental records.

Was there someone, someplace, who missed her — who would read of the discovery in the lonely orchard woods and call in? The Bellevue detectives knew that was their best hope.

Bellevue itself had no reports of women who had gone missing in the last six months, but the Seattle Police Department and the police of Lynnwood (a small town along I-5 north of Seattle) shared open files on a missing case, one that had baffled them since July 9.

Stacy Sparks, eighteen, had had no reason to run away. The recent high school graduate had a new job she liked, a ticket already purchased for a dream trip to Hawaii, and a steady boyfriend. She had lived with her mother and stepfather in the Ballard section of Seattle, apparently in complete harmony. Aware of the Sparks case, the Bellevue detectives thought first of the pretty blonde who had vanished so inexplicably on that Monday night. No one believed that Stacy had left of her own accord.

And yet, no one had seen Stacy Sparks since she left the Raintree Restaurant in Lynnwood at 9:30 P.M. on July 9. She had promised to pick up her boyfriend from his job in south Seattle, and she had been driving her prized Plymouth Arrow hatchback with the white racing stripe.

Five months now, and they had found nothing of Stacy Sparks — not even her distinctive car. The first opinion of those most familiar with her case was that this unidentified body in Sherwood Forest would prove to be Stacy's.

However, there were things that didn't fit: Stacy wore a yellow cotton shirt the night she disappeared, but hers was a T-shirt with a rose appliquéd on it — not a hooded sweatshirt. The jeans were right, but the blouse wasn't. Of course, there was always the possibility that Stacy had stopped somewhere to change her clothes before she either encountered someone dangerous or, less likely, chose to run away.

Stacy had yellow-blonde hair and the hair near the skull in Bellevue was more a "mousy" blonde, more brown than Stacy's appeared in the missing posters that still clung to fences and utility poles, faded and tattered now.

The possibility that this victim might be Stacy Sparks proved unlikely after the postmortem examination. Dr. Eisele performed the autopsy on the nameless young woman. Detectives Marv Skeen and Gary Trent attended the postmortem, and listened intently as Eisele outlined many of the facts that can be elicited from forensic pathology.

"She was very young," Eisele said. "Probably about thirteen to fourteen — possibly as young as eleven — or as old as sixteen. Caucasian. She was between five feet one and five feet, five inches tall — slender — and she had medium length light brown hair."

"Cause of death?" Trent asked.

Eisele shook his head. "There's no way to tell. I can only tell you that there's been no fracturing of her bones. No trauma to any bone, not even the skull. The internal organs have decomposed. If she was shot or stabbed, it penetrated the soft tissue — and that's gone. If she was strangled — same problem."

The dead girl could have succumbed to a bullet, a stabbing, a strangling, or suffocation, but there was no way left to say absolutely what had happened.

The motive for the killing was obvious, grotesquely apparent. Her skeleton had been found in the "classic" rape position, on its back with legs spread wide. Dr. Eisele found that a branch had been savagely shoved into the vaginal vault, effecting both a symbolic and a legal act of rape.

It's not unusual to find all manner of foreign objects in the vaginas of women who have been killed by someone in a sexual rage: bottles, umbrellas, sticks, and branches are "signatures" of impotent killers or of rapists so full of anger that they are not satisfied just to violate the bodies of their victims. They are also compelled to leave something behind to demonstrate to the person who discovers a body or to the police how powerful they are. It is an act hard for the normal mind to comprehend. In this case, any residual semen that might have been deposited during forced intercourse was, of course, gone, lost to the rain, wind, and processes of decomposition.

Following the autopsy, Roy Gleason gave information to local newspapers describing the clothing found with the victim, and her very general description. They were looking for a missing girl whose dental records might be compared with the teeth of their victim. Without the help of the public, there would be no place else to go with the case. The scant information that the detective team had managed to put together about the victim was broadcast to the thirteen western states — and then more widely — through NCIC (National Crime Information Center) computers. Bellevue police were soon inundated with responses. As there always are, there were hundreds of teenage girls missing in the United States. They received queries from as far away as New York State, as well as from California, Oregon, and other counties in Washington State.

Frantic parents whose teenage daughters had run away, or been taken away, had filed missing reports on girls who, at least on the surface, resembled the unknown victim. None of them matched Bellevue's unknown victim.

On the morning of December 10, a call came in from the mother of a teenage daughter named Nancy Dillon.* The family lived in the Bellevue area.

"I've read the article in the paper," she began, "and I think you should talk to my daughter. Nancy has a friend, a girl named Teresa Sterling. Teresa was a runaway from Georgia. We haven't seen her for a couple of months."

The Bellevue detectives were about to get a tremendous boost from some rebellious teenagers, a group who often resent the police. Roy Gleason assured Nancy that she and any of her friends who were willing to talk to him could be assured that his main — and only — concern was a homicide investigation. For the time he worked to find the answers about why a teenager had ended up dead in the woods, he would not ask witnesses about their drug or alcohol use, shoplifting, truancy, running away, or any other offenses. He had to gain the trust of his informants, or he might as well quit. And he was not about to do that. He had a feeling that the dead girl was Teresa Sterling, but he couldn't prove it by himself.

Nancy Dillon was most cooperative. She said she had been worried about Teresa Sterling after she seemingly disappeared off the face of the earth without telling anyone she was leaving.

"Tell me a little about Teresa," Gleason began. "Try to go back and fill me in on her lifestyle, her friends."

The story that came out was tragic, but not unfamiliar. Teresa Caroline Sterling had been born on December 14. As her friend described her to Gleason, he realized that in four more days, Teresa would have celebrated her sixteenth birthday.

Nancy said that Teresa had come from a large family, and that she was the youngest of five children. "She grew up in some little town outside Atlanta, Georgia. She was kind of 'country.'"

"What did she look like?" Gleason asked.

"She was a tomboy — a skinny little kid with a lot of freckles, but she was pretty, too. She looked kind of like Jodie Foster, the movie star. She wasn't very interested in school, but the only trouble she ever got into was kid stuff — just mischief."

"When did you meet Teresa?" Gleason asked.

"Well, they moved from Georgia two years ago," Nancy said. "Teresa's dad worked for some kind of freight company for an airline and he got transferred to Salt Lake City first. Then, that same year, they moved to Bellevue. That was in July. They rented a house out by Crossroads. That's when I met her."

Gleason learned that Teresa had been enrolled in the eighth grade at Odle Junior High School. Faced with two moves in one year and having to start again in two schools where she didn't know anyone, Teresa had felt lost at first. Life for teenagers in Bellevue was very different from what it was in the little town in Georgia where she had lived her whole life. Most households in Bellevue had a higher standard of living, and street drugs were plentiful. Even in junior high, a large number of students had experimented with them.

"I know Teresa tried marijuana," Nancy told Gleason. "And she probably tried other drugs, too."

Teresa was becoming a young woman during her years in Bellevue. She was caught somewhere between the winsomeness of childhood and the promise of maturity. She still wrote to teachers she'd liked back in Georgia, but she wasn't as interested in sports as she had been. Her schoolwork suffered when she began to run away from home.

"I really don't know why she ran," Nancy said. "All of her friends could see that she was getting in the habit of leaving her house, staying a few days with us or with other friends, and then she'd go home. Her parents really tried to keep her home, but no matter what they did, she would run away. Last March, her family finally moved back to Georgia. They just packed up, and they all went back to Fayetteville — everyone but Teresa's older sister."

Nancy felt that Teresa's parents had hoped to get her away from the lifestyle in the group she ran with in Bellevue, and that, once back home, she would settle down. But it was too late for Teresa. "She didn't want to live in Fayetteville any longer. She wrote to me and said she wanted to live in Bellevue, and be free to come and go when she wanted. She came back here about the middle of June," Nancy recalled. "I'm not sure just how she got here. Sometimes, she said she hitchhiked, and sometimes she said she flew or took a bus. But she just showed up here again just before the end of school."

"Where did she live?"

"With different people. She just stayed with different people."

Nancy Dillon said that she herself had gone to California on vacation during the summer, and that Teresa had planned to join her down there.

"But she never showed up. And when I came back, I didn't see her either. My mother called in about Teresa because she read that description of the cotton, hooded shirt found next to the girl's body," Nancy said with a tremble in her voice. "I gave Teresa a shirt a lot like that about a year ago. It was yellow with white trimming and it had a zippered pocket."

Gleason asked her to sketch the shirt that she had given to Teresa Sterling. When she handed the sketch to him, he saw that it was exactly like the victim's clothing. He pulled out some photos of the clothes found at the crime scene, and held them out for Nancy Dillon to look at.

She gasped. "That's the shirt — the one I gave to Teresa. I bought it in California. Does that mean that it's Teresa?"

"We'll have to check some more," Gleason told the upset youngster. "But, yes . . . it may be that it was Teresa's body found in the woods."

When Bob Littlejohn — the first patrolman at the body site — heard that they had a tentative ID on the skeletonized body, he was as shocked as Nancy Dillon was. He knew Teresa Sterling, too. He had spent a lot of time trying to counsel the Sterlings about their problems with Teresa.

The Sterlings had been afraid that Teresa was smoking marijuana, and possibly using LSD. They had been at their wits' end trying to stop her from running away. Littlejohn had talked with Teresa — to no avail — before her family moved back to Georgia.

"I remember when she ran away from Fayetteville last June 8," Littlejohn recalled. "The family asked me to do a 'locate and determine welfare' on Teresa because they thought she was headed here. They didn't have much hope of getting her to go back home. But they wanted to know that she was safe."

Littlejohn had found Teresa back in Bellevue, and he'd talked to her. Then he called her parents and said that she was all right. He'd tried to keep tabs on her, although she moved around so much that it wasn't easy. Her parents hadn't reported her as a runaway; they had just asked for information, and he had no cause to pick her up unless she broke the law. When Bob Littlejohn responded to the call about the skull in the woods, the picture of Teresa Sterling's piquant little face hadn't even crossed his mind.

The physical similarity, the identical blouse, the fact that Teresa Sterling had not been seen by her good friend for months, all pointed to the likelihood that it was her body. Littlejohn was saddened to realize now why there had been no runaway or missing report put out on her. Her parents had simply given up trying to corral her; they had tried everything, and then they had hoped and prayed that tough love might work. Short of locking her up, they hadn't been able to keep her at home, but hoped finally that maybe she would come home if she got hungry or lonely enough. Littlejohn had spent many off-duty hours trying to help Teresa, too. But no one had been able to convince her to go back to the parents who loved her.

Roy Gleason had the onerous task of notifying Teresa Sterling's stepmother that he was investigating the homicide of a young girl. "There is a possibility that the victim might be your daughter," he said gently. "We have to identify her. Would you have the names of dentists who might have cared for Teresa while you lived in the Bellevue area?"

The shocked woman said that Teresa had seen two dentists in Bellevue — one of whom had put in a gold crown. The dentist who had done the crown work gave detectives her dental records, which they carried to the medical examiner's office. The crown looked to be identical to the tooth in question. To be absolutely sure, the investigators contacted forensic odontologist Dr. Bruce Rothwell of the Mason Clinic in Seattle.

Dr. Rothwell looked at the chart and at the gold crown work. "There's no question," he said. "They are identical. Your victim is Teresa Sterling."

It was a start. Now, three days after the body's discovery, they knew the name of their victim, and something of her lifestyle. But they still had vast areas to fill in. Teresa had left Georgia alive and well on June 8, and made it safely to Bellevue. What they had to do now was to attempt to trace Teresa's movements between June 12 and December 7. Six months.

They knew that she had undoubtedly been alive for a good part of the summer, but they still could not narrow down the time period when she probably was killed. All they had to go on was the fact that she'd failed to meet Nancy Dillon in California — but that could have been simply because she'd changed her mind. She was a capricious girl who went anywhere the wind blew.

Nancy was able to help out more. She looked at her calendar and said she could isolate the few days when she had expected to see Teresa.

"Teresa had a boyfriend named Jeff,* and they promised to call me at my grandmother's house in California around July 4 — just as soon as they were close. But I didn't hear from them. I even called my mother and asked her if she knew where Teresa was — but no one had seen her. I didn't get back to Bellevue until the end of August. Teresa was still gone. I thought maybe Teresa and Jeff did make it to California, but they didn't call me. I figured they might still be still down there.

"Teresa could have stayed at my house," Nancy continued. "We offered her a place to stay when she showed up on June 12 — but she refused. She just planned to stay around with different people. She didn't like to be tied down to anyone."

Once the search for Teresa's friends began, the detectives were deluged with calls from people who wanted to help — both teenagers and their parents. Gossip moved through the teenage community as if it was being passed on by jungle drums. Most of them had kept secrets from their own parents and their friends' parents, but this was different. Teresa was dead. Murdered. That made them all feel vulnerable. They wondered if her killer was still walking among them.

Teresa had been a party girl, attending every "kegger" and beach party she heard about. During the previous summer, she had worked only one day. She had lived a kind of hand-to-mouth existence, dependent on "the kindness of strangers" and her wits. She borrowed clothes from friends, and ate her meals wherever she was at the moment.

Apparently, Teresa had stayed a very short time with her own eighteen-year-old sister and then with family friends and often with people she had just met, most of them adults. That left scores of people to be questioned. The investigators found a pair of single male adults who had taken her in for a while, but that was early in the summer. The men apparently had had nothing to do with her death.

She had dated many young men, but the name "Jeff" kept surfacing as her steady boyfriend. Sources who had known her well said that "Jeff" was eighteen-year-old Jeff Bigelow,* who lived with his parents, and who rode a motorcycle.

Police in Redmond, a city just northeast of Bellevue, were able to narrow the time of her disappearance more closely. Their department had a report that indicated one of their officers had contacted both Teresa and Jeff Bigelow around midnight in early August. "One of our patrol officers found them drinking on the beach by Lake Sammamish. We have an FIR (Field Investigation Report) on it. They were both underage," the Redmond detective said.

And then a hairdresser in Bellevue called the Bellevue detectives and said that he had done Teresa's hair on August 24. He furnished a copy of his appointment schedule for that Friday that confirmed Teresa had been in his shop. "I recognized the girl's description," he told Roy Gleason. "I knew Teresa. On August 24, she came in during the afternoon and she brought along a young guy who carried a motorcycle helmet."

Valuable tips continued to pile up. Next, the detectives got an assist from Dorcas Resnick,* an elderly woman who lived in the area where Teresa's body had been found. She called in and asked the detectives to visit her home. Roy Gleason talked to Dorcas and found she had a remarkable memory.

"I walk my dog near the peach orchard every day," she began. "If you'd like, I'll walk through the area and show you."

The woman and Gleason walked through the region, as she pointed out landmarks.

"I began to smell a very strong, foul odor," she recalled. "I know it was two weeks before the gentleman put up that split-rail fence there. There was a pair of women's panties lying near the path for about two weeks, and then they were gone. My dog kept wanting to go into the woods where the odor was so bad. I tried to stop her, but a couple of times, she did run in there. Finally, the smell was just so bad that I ended up taking a back way around the woods."

The site was exactly where Teresa's skeleton was found months later.

Gleason contacted the fence builder, and learned that the man had put up the fence on September 13. Counting back two weeks, Gleason came up with August 30. That was when Dorcas Resnick had noticed the odor; the decomposition of the body would not have begun to give off a distinctive odor immediately. Gleason conferred with his fellow detectives, and they figured that Teresa had died sometime between the night of August 24 and August 26.

She had had her hair done on the twenty-fourth — probably in preparation for a party. Had anyone seen her after that party? In the days ahead, they found no sightings after that night. It was very likely that Teresa had died on August 24.

The probers had now talked to thirty people who knew Teresa Sterling well. They learned that two of her close friends had run away from home on December 8, just as the news of the body find hit the papers. The two teenagers, Tami Wells* and Bonnie Cross,* were traced to Yakima, Washington, in the company of an adult male. They were picked up by Yakima police, and Detectives Gary Trent and Marv Skeen went over the Cascade Mountain passes to bring the girls back.

It turned out that the girls had not run away because of any guilty knowledge about Teresa's death; they had left on a whim. However, they were able to corroborate much of the information about Teresa's perambulations during her last summer. Tami verified that Teresa and Jeff had dated quite steadily all summer. "They were together all the time for about two weeks in August, and then I didn't see either one of them anymore," Tami said.

"Do you know where Teresa met Jeff?"

Gary Trent asked.

"We were walking over by Crossroads and Jeff and some guy went riding past on motorcycles, but then they stopped — and started talking to us."

"Do you know where Jeff went after you stopped seeing Teresa?"

"All I know is she kept saying they were going to California together. That's what I thought they'd done," Tami said. She had considered Teresa her very good friend, and wondered about her. "She used to call me at least once a day, and I was really surprised when she suddenly stopped calling me. She didn't even say good-bye."

Another seventeen-year-old girl volunteered an opinion. Jill Reid* told Gleason that she had known Teresa and Jeff Bigelow, although she hadn't been a close friend of either. "When we heard that Teresa had been killed, a bunch of us started talking. We kept asking each other, 'Could Jeff Bigelow have done it?'"

"Why would you feel that way?" Gleason probed.

"Well, they were together and people saw them all over, and then three months ago, they both just disappeared. Suddenly, we heard that Jeff had gone into the army, and nobody had seen Teresa at all."

No matter which angle the Bellevue detectives studied, the most rational approach kept bringing them back to eighteen-year-old Jeff Bigelow — Teresa Sterling's last boyfriend.

One of the most dissonant factors jarring the detectives was that everyone but Jeff Bigelow had called them to offer help or to ask questions. If he had been so close to Teresa, surely he would have heard by now that her body had been found. Surely he would have come forward to help in the investigation. Unless he had something to hide.

Gleason contacted military authorities and learned that Jeff Bigelow had enlisted in the army during the last few days of August, and been sent to Fort Lewis, Washington, the sprawling army base forty-five miles away. It had not been an impromptu enlistment, however; Bigelow had signed up earlier in the summer.

On December 14, Gleason and Gary Trent went to CID offices at Fort Lewis — only to learn that Bigelow had taken a four-day pass and would not be back until Tuesday, December 18. Two days later, however, Bigelow called the Bellevue Police Department. When he was told that the detectives who were looking for him were not on duty, he left his name and hung up.

On December 18, Gleason and Trent went back to Fort Lewis and met with Jeff Bigelow in the CID offices. The interview began on a casual note. He was told that they were merely seeking more information about Teresa Sterling, and Bigelow was perfectly agreeable to having the interview recorded.

Even at this point, the young soldier was not a prime suspect, but he was the one man who had evolved as being the closest to the dead girl. Trent asked him to describe their meeting, their relationship, and how often he had seen her.

The detectives were surprised by his next words. He seemed to be holding back. He was very calm as he said he had known Teresa only casually — he guessed that he might have dated her once or twice. "The last time I saw her was some time in the middle of August. It was in downtown Bellevue. I said 'Hi' and told her I was going in the army."

Trent stopped the tape. He said they knew that Bigelow's story was full of discrepancies, and that, at this point, he would be advised of his rights under Miranda. "We think you're the guy who was with Teresa at the beauty shop on August 24. All your friends

387

have told us over and over you and Teresa went to a lot of parties together."

Bigelow turned ashen and sagged a little in his chair. And he then admitted that he *was* the man with the motorcycle helmet who had been with Teresa that afternoon. "I guess I thought that was sometime earlier in August."

"We don't believe that you were only casual acquaintances," Trent said quietly. "We think you two had hooked up last summer."

"I didn't consider her my girlfriend," Bigelow argued. "I guess we did go out together, but it was only to parties and stuff."

Gleason and Trent could see that the previously calm soldier was becoming agitated. They pointed out that all their investigations indicated that Bigelow was probably the last person to see Teresa alive. Gradually, they suggested that he might have been involved in her death.

Their conversation continued for another twenty minutes or so, and then Jeff Bigelow could stand it no longer. He had a lot on his conscience, and he wanted to tell someone.

"I lost control of myself . . . and I accidentally killed her," he sighed.

Bigelow described a party the two had attended on August 24 or 25. They had both been drinking, and he guessed that they were probably pretty drunk.

"Teresa made me jealous — she was paying attention to all the other guys there, and deliberately ignoring me. It got to me."

He said he had watched her flirting and had started to seethe with envy. Just after midnight, they had left the party, riding double on his motorcycle. At that point, he said they weren't very far from where Teresa's body had been found.

"A ways down the street, I stopped," Bigelow recalled. "She kept telling me how good-looking all those dudes at the party were, and how she wanted me to take her back there. We got into an argument about it."

Bigelow said he'd heard enough of that kind of talk. He was tired of it. But Teresa kept on taunting him about how much more attractive the other guys at the party were.

He confessed that he slapped her when she argued back. Once. Twice. Teresa fought back, hitting at him with very little power. And then, Jeff Bigelow said, he grabbed her around the throat. "I lost control. I couldn't help it. She went limp, and I didn't really think she was dead — but I dragged her back into the woods."

He did not leave her there. Bigelow said he stayed beside Teresa's body for about five hours, leaving only when it started to get daylight. He had some kind of frail hope that she would open her eyes. He knew she wouldn't, but he kept hoping that what happened wasn't real.

Bigelow confided he had never had sex with Teresa, despite his attempts. "She wouldn't."

Now, with his head down so he didn't have to look at the detectives, he admitted to them that he had intercourse with her body as it lay in the woods. "I asked her if she would have sex with me while we were at the party that night, but she told me 'No,' like she always did. And kept flirting with all the other guys there."

There was one more thing that Detective Gary Trent had to get the young soldier to tell him. No one except the police, the medical examiner's office, and Teresa's killer knew about the symbolic rape with the tree limb.

As Trent asked, "Is there anything more — anything you haven't told us?" Bigelow looked away. And then, he finally admitted that he had inserted the branch into the dead girl's vagina. He didn't know why he had done that, but he had been very angry with her for teasing him the way she did.

That was the one thing that the investigators had to hear from Bigelow, the secret thing that would mark him as her murderer beyond a shadow of doubt. And now he did admit that. He gave a very detailed description of the position of the body when he left it, the foliage he'd placed over it to hide it, and the fact that he had removed Teresa's clothing and left it beside her body.

They had ridden only about five blocks from the party, where Teresa had taunted him for the last time. Bigelow said he knew the area well. Before he joined the army, he had worked as a greenskeeper on a nearby golf course. And he was just a short distance from his own home. With the first rays of dawn, he rode away from the peach orchard, leaving Teresa behind. "I cried over her body when I waited with her all night," he said. "But I never wanted to go back to the woods again."

For three months, Jeff Bigelow had gone about his army duties, comported himself well as a soldier. But throughout those months, he must have felt that someone was going to tap him on the shoulder at any moment and tell him that Teresa had been found at last.

Roy Gleason and Gary Trent arrested Bigelow on suspicion of murder and transported him back to Bellevue. Ironically, while Bigelow was in jail — before his name had been released to the media — Teresa's father called from Georgia to say, "I remember one more name of somebody that Teresa knew," he said. "It's Jeff Bigelow."

Gleason and Trent thanked him, but they could not tell him yet that they had just arrested Bigelow for the murder of his daughter.

It was almost Christmas. It had been only eleven days since Teresa's body was found, and by working double shifts, the Bellevue detectives had accomplished something of a miracle. Roy Gleason, Gary Trent, and Marv Skeen barely slept from the moment of the body discovery on December 7. They are to be commended for an excellent demonstration of precise detective work. They had gone from a skeletonized body, discovered months after a murder, a body they believed they might never identify, to the arrest of a suspect.

And that suspect had just admitted to murder.

Jeff Bigelow's parents had tried to get help for him in the past when he'd been arrested on relatively minor charges. Alarmed, they sent him to in-patient psychiatric clinics, but he had always convinced therapists that he was quite normal, and he had been released with little or no treatment. Teresa Sterling had been, in essence, still a child who didn't recognize that she was teasing and taunting the wrong person. She was heedless of the fact that she was pushing the wrong buttons and bringing up old rages in her boyfriend.

In the end, Teresa Sterling's violent murder was the culmination of two families' tragedies. Neither was a throwaway kid, and both families had tried desperately to keep their children in a solid family situation and both families had been rebuffed. It was as if each teenager had been hellbent for destruction.

On December 28, Jeffrey Bigelow pleaded guilty to a charge of murder in the second degree.

THE TRAGIC ENDING OF A BANK ROBBER'S FANTASY

There are few crimes that inspire admiration — not in the public, or among inmates in prison. Certainly not murder . . . or rape. Most convicts are not violent or bloodthirsty; those among them who are locked up for committing homicides or sexual crimes against helpless women are at the very bottom of the prison hierarchy. Prisoners in the upper echelon are popular because of their skill, dexterity, intelligence, and cunning. Clever con men evoke respect and so do the safecrackers who can hear the tumblers click into place in even the most complicated locks.

And then there are the bank robbers.

Harking back to John Dillinger and Bonnie and Clyde, there is something Robin Hood-ish about bank robbers, possessed of seeming brilliance and derring-do, which is often translated to television and movie screens. If nothing goes awry, bank robbers usually don't kill the tellers and bank officers that they rob. (Although I have talked with many bank employees after an armed robbery and most of them suffer from post-traumatic stress syndrome resulting from the terror they experienced when a bank robber held a loaded gun against their flesh. They have flashbacks that come with certain sounds and movements. Seemingly innocuous things trigger the memory of their absolute dread that they were going to die.)

The idea of thousands and thousands of dollars just sitting there in bank vaults can be as tantalizing to the working man as the possibility of winning the lottery. The idea of robbing a bank is an adventure fantasy for some young people, and it is a way out for some middle-aged and elderly people of both sexes who have been pushed to the wall by debts and unemployment. Most, of course, don't act on their imaginary plans. And the majority of those who take that avenue to instant wealth end up in jail. What works in the movies rarely works for long in the real world.

Even so, there was one young man in the Northwest who fancied himself a natural at bank robbing. It seemed to him that he had worked out every exigency in his plans to rob a bank and live a life of luxury in an island paradise. He was quite intelligent, but he was not at all realistic. He had grown tall enough to be a basketball star, but he had not matured enough to let go of the fantasy of a storybook world. His bizarre and almost childlike plotting came to tragic fruition.

It was the third week of February in Seattle. Although mornings were still cool, pussywillows, crocuses, and daffodils had popped out, and there was just a promise of spring in the way the air smelled. The business week had barely begun that Monday morning when bank teller Jill Mobley glanced out into the parking lot of the Laurelhurst branch of the Prudential Mutual Savings Bank in Seattle's North End. The small bank building was easy to access because it was located on a triangle of land bordered by three busy streets. It was some distance from freeway on-ramps, which made it less than desirable for would-be robbers who prefer to have a quick getaway.

The only personnel present in the bank at 9:37 A.M. were Jill, another female teller, and the relief manager, seventy-seven-year-old William Heggie. At an age when most men would have been long retired, Heggie had grown bored with sitting around or puttering in his garden. When he'd retired at sixty-five after twenty-five years as secretary-treasurer for the Acacia Memorial Park cemetery, he found that, as much as he loved gardening, it didn't fill his days. So he had gone to work a day or two a week as a relief bank manager for Prudential. It suited him just fine, and provided money for extras that enriched his later years. Just last year, Bill Heggie and his wife had taken a long vacation — a perfect trip to Hawaii to celebrate their golden wedding anniversary.

Jill Mobley noticed a turquoise pickup with a white canopy as it traveled all the way through a drive-in window lane and stopped in the northeast corner of the bank's parking lot. Everything seemed to be normal; she expected to see only an early customer. But then there was something about the man who emerged from the driver's door that made a prickle of concern touch the back of her neck. She looked sharply at the person near the pickup. He was a very tall man, but she really couldn't see him at all — he was completely covered by clothing. He wore a beige rain jacket with a hood, a ski mask, sunglasses, and gloves.

The weather wasn't stormy that morning, and even if it had been, this man's attire spelled only one thing to her: *bank rob-bery* . . .

She reacted quickly — before the man even entered the bank — tripping the silent alarm, which also activated a hidden camera. But she didn't have time to warn her fellow teller or Mr. Heggie. As she turned to call to them, the hooded man had already entered the bank and was walking swiftly to her window. Now she could see the black handgun with its long barrel. He held out a green cloth bag.

"Fill it," he ordered, "and don't pull the trap."

She knew this marked him as something of a pro. He obviously knew that tellers almost always have one stack of bills that will set off an automatic alarm when it is pulled from the drawer. But Jill Mobley had one more trick he seemed unaware of. Without blinking an eye, she pulled out a stack of booby-trapped ten-dollar bills. Hidden within them was a dye pack, set to release bright orange dye a minute after the person carrying them left the bank. The powdery indelible dye would instantly stain the bills themselves, and then spray the robber, anyone near him, and the immediate surroundings. He didn't notice when she slipped the dye-pack stack of bills in with the rest. She handed him the sack, hoping the booby trap would react as it was supposed to.

Satisfied, the bank robber spun around and headed for the door.

Although Jill hadn't seen him, William Heggie had silently risen from his desk ten feet away. He had seen what was going on and walked rapidly toward the bank's doors, carrying the keys in his hand. He had been trying to lock the door. The tall old man was in good shape for his age, but he was no match for the man in the hooded jacket. The women tellers watched in horror as the robber yelled, "Get out of my way!"

Heggie would give no ground. There was a scuffle at the door and then the two men tumbled out onto the sidewalk. Frozen in shock, the two women watched helplessly. Suddenly, they heard a muffled "boom!" and saw Heggie fall to the sidewalk. The gunman stepped over him, running toward his truck. He leaped into the turquoise pickup and sped away.

From the moment Jill Mobley spotted him until the shooting, no more than three minutes had passed. It had happened so rapidly that it seemed more a bad dream than reality.

Seattle Police Patrolman J. A. Nicholson, working a one-man car out of the north precinct, was only a few blocks away from the bank's location at 4500 Sand Point Way N.E. when his radio crackled with the report of a silent alarm at the Prudential Mutual Bank. A minute or so after, his radio sounded again. "Shots heard . . . man down." Nicholson raced to the bank, arriving at 9:40 A.M.

He saw the elderly man who lay unmoving on the sidewalk in front of the bank and the spreading torrent of blood that seemed to be coming from his midchest area. A young woman bent over the elderly man, attempting to administer CPR. Nicholson and Officer R. Amundson, who arrived seconds behind him, bent to assist her. A doctor from the clinic across the street came running, too, carrying his bag.

Debra Wiatrak, twenty-two, told the officers that she had been driving by and had stopped when a woman waved frantically to her. "I'm a trained EMT," she said, "and I didn't have a pulse even then."

If anyone could have saved William Heggie, he would have survived. Seattle Fire Department paramedics from Medic One — the premier emergency response program in America at the time — the doctor, his nurse, and Debra Wiatrak all tried their best.

A man standing near the bank entrance

watched sadly as medical personnel tried to get a heartbeat. "I don't think they're getting any life back," he said quietly. "He was a wonderful man. I've known him for twenty-five years and he was one of the finest people I've ever known."

And indeed he was.

If the bank robber had met Heggie forty years earlier, the denouement of their battle might well have been different. Heggie, a British Columbia native, was a robust young man who played tennis and rugby then. He had been a strong and vigorous man for all of his life. In later years, he belonged to the Shrine, the Order of Eastern Star, the Kiwanis, and a number of other service and fraternal organizations. He and his wife had raised three daughters. That he was now likely to die seemed unthinkable. After thirty minutes of fruitless effort, he was loaded onto the Medic One rig and rushed to Harborview Hospital. He was pronounced dead on arrival.

But even as medics worked over Bill Heggie, the police investigation had begun. Nicholson talked to Jill Mobley first. "I think Mr. Heggie was trying to lock the bank doors — to lock the man in," she said.

"Did you see where the truck headed when the killer left?"

She shook her head. "He went westbound — toward the University of Washington campus, but we couldn't see beyond that."

An alert was put out at once for officers to be on the lookout for the turquoise truck with the white canopy.

A phalanx of detectives and FBI agents left their downtown offices as soon as the communications scanners began broadcasting word of the bank robbery. Robbery Lieutenant Bob Holter and his detectives, Sergeant John Gray, Sergeant Chuck Schueffele, and Detectives James Lundin and Al "Beans" Lima, arrived first, followed shortly by Homicide Detectives George Marberg, Al Gerdes, Gary Fowler, and Nat Crawford. The scene at the bank was alive with fire department and police patrol personnel. Patrol Sergeants Harry Hanson and James Johnson briefed the detectives on what information they had been able to gather thus far. It wasn't much. They knew only that they were looking for a very tall person — probably a male, because of his height. But the robber had been dressed so that the tellers could not see so much as a patch of skin.

Jill Mobley told Al Lima that she could not even say for sure what race the robber was. "I'm inclined to think that he's white — but that's from his voice only," she said. "And that is just an impression . . . I could very well be mistaken."

The Seattle police detectives and the six FBI special agents divided up chores at the scene: A special agent began processing the area around the teller's window for latent prints, while pairs of detectives and agents interviewed the witnesses who had been present or nearby during the robbery. There were precious few of them; in all likelihood, the bank robber had deliberately chosen a time when the bank would probably be empty.

Jill explained that the dye pack she slipped into the robber's sack was set to explode only if it was carried through the bank door, where it would be triggered. "After a delay of some seconds, it explodes and expels red-dish-orange dye and tear gas." She thought it would have gone off just after the man got into his vehicle, but the truck was out of her sight by then.

Word came shortly after that the dye trap had done its work. A patrol officer found the turquoise pickup abandoned little more than a mile away from the bank. Detectives observed the nine-year-old Ford truck. When they glanced into the cab of the truck, they found its seat covered with bright orange powder. Certainly, the suspect would also be stained with the pervasive orange powder. If they could locate him quickly, he would still have the dye stigma marking him as a killer and a thief. It was made up of compounds that would not be easy to wash off.

They asked the radio operator to check the license number through computers and learned that the vehicle had been reported stolen over the weekend. It figured. If they had hoped to get a lead on the killer via his vehicle, they were out of luck. He'd made sure there was no connection to him. Clearly, he had dumped the truck and left this quiet residential street in some other manner.

Back at the bank, Al Gerdes and George Marberg were faced with the most frustrating kind of crime scene. Because the sea of blood left behind was so upsetting to bystanders, fire crews had hosed down the sidewalk where William Heggie died. Not only had they washed away the blood, but any possible clues that might have lain there also disappeared into the gutter drains. All the other debris had been picked up and put into trash cans. Gerdes and Marberg pawed through the trash, but found only paraphernalia left behind by the paramedics. Mr. Heggie's glasses, International Kiwanis pin, and post office key had been found on the sidewalk, carried into the bank by someone, and placed on a counter. In the aftermath of such a shocking incident, bystanders often try to "tidy up," trying to get some semblance of normalcy after disaster.

The detectives knew only that they were looking for a tall man, a man possibly bearing orange dye stains on his clothing and his person. Jill Mobley said she had given him upward of fourteen hundred dollars in ones, fives, tens, and twenties. The twenty-dollar bills bore serial numbers prerecorded by the bank. This was standard practice in a robbery — to keep marked bills handy and slip them to the thieves.

Hours went by, and the investigators felt the pressure of time passing; they wanted to get to the suspect before he could change clothes or get rid of the money. In the meantime the bulletin going out to Washington State law enforcement agencies specified that officers should be on the alert for individuals whose skin or garments bore bright-colored red or orange stains.

A Washington State Patrol officer heard the alert for the "orange man" and reported that he had just stopped someone with peculiar skin color for a traffic violation on the freeway south of Seattle. "But it wasn't a man," he said. "It was a woman — her skin was bright orange. She looked like a tangerine!"

"Was she really tall?" Marberg asked.

"I can't say that she was," the trooper said. "But she was sitting down in the car. She could have had very long legs."

He passed on the address that had come back for the woman when he did a Wants-and-Warrants search on her driver's license and registration. "She lives in Tacoma."

Tacoma was thirty miles south of the bank. Jill Mobley had been almost sure that the Prudential bank robber was male — but there was always the possibility that he had a woman waiting in his truck. If so, she, too, would have been enveloped in the cloud of orange dust. Tacoma detectives went to the "orange woman's" home to question her. She wasn't there; her roommate said she was at a doctor's office appointment.

"She has hepatitis," the friend said. "That's why her skin's that funny color. The doctor told her that's a symptom of liver trouble; your skin turns all orangey-yellow."

That eliminated the woman as a suspect; she might be a lousy driver, but she wasn't a bank robber.

A canvass of offices around the bank had produced no witnesses. No one but Jill Mobley had seen the pickup truck before the robbery, and only the two tellers had seen it speeding away.

Al Lima and Jim Lundin processed the stolen pickup with ID Technician Jeanne Ward. It was extraordinarily clean: It held few traces of the killer — nothing beyond the orange dye that stained it and a pair of sunglasses with the frame now dyed orange. Both the truck's ignition and the wires under the dashboard had been tampered with, undoubtedly when it was stolen. The ashtray was pulled out, and there was a plastic garbage bag under the dash which contained paper towels. They retained the contents of the ashtray and the garbage sack, as well as samples of the dye-stained upholstery and the driver's seat belt.

Although there had been no witnesses around the bank, Detectives Gary Fowler and Nat Crawford made a door-to-door canvass of the block where the pickup was abandoned. They had more luck; they located a man who remembered something. "Just before ten this morning," he recalled, " I heard a car with a loud engine. As it passed, I looked out the window and I saw an older Volkswagen bug. It was light blue or gray, and it was headed north on Forty-fifth N.E. It looked to me like there might have been two people inside."

The investigators figured that the person who'd abandoned the pickup had had another vehicle waiting for his getaway, and it was probably the VW bug with the noisy engine. The timing was right. He'd left the bank at about 9:40 A.M., driven the mile in the truck filled with tear gas and floating orange powder, and then changed cars. He would have been in a tearing hurry as the VW pulled away.

An even better witness on the street turned up. The young woman said she'd been on her way to classes at the University of Washington at 9:15 A.M. "I noticed an older bug parked facing northbound on the east side of Forty-fifth. I thought the people who live there had bought a different car; I noticed it especially because I also drive an old Volkswagen."

"What did it look like?" Lima asked.

"It was gray — older — maybe as old as a 1963 to 1968 model. The hood was black, as if it had been replaced, and so were two of the fenders. It was kind of beat-up, with a dent in the center of the hood. When I got home from class at a quarter to one, it was gone."

"Did you see anyone in it — or around it?"

"No. It was empty at nine-fifteen."

The information on the Volkswagen bug

411

was passed on at once to all law enforcement agencies in the thirteen western states. With every hour that passed, the killer could be another sixty or seventy miles away from Seattle.

The investigators studied films from the bank's hidden camera. They could see the bank robber at Jill Mobley's window, his left hand on the green cloth bag, and his right clutching a handgun. The only bit of skin visible was the tip of his nose. If the films were shown on TV news, they wondered if anyone might recognize something about him. Was there anything in his stance, his clothing, or his mannerisms that would trigger a memory in someone watching? The pictures were published in every paper in Seattle and the tape shown on all Northwest television news programs.

On February 26, a huge announcement appeared in the *Seattle Post-Intelligencer*. It was a message from the "Rat on a Rat" program endorsed by financial institutions in an effort to stop a rash of bank robberies:

$5,000 REWARD

For information leading to the indictment of the person who robbed the Prudential Mutual Savings Bank, 4500 Sandpoint Way N.E. at 9:40 A.M. on February 25. Description: the robber is 6' to 6'3" and wearing a tan parka, hood and ski mask. He may have red-tinted cash. He is believed to be driving a 1963 to 1968 VW Bug; blue-gray, with black hood and back fenders. During this robbery, William G. Heggie, banker, was murdered. Sometimes bank robbers take more than money.

A toll-free phone number was listed for a "no-questions-asked" tip line where an informant could call with possible leads on the bank killer's identity.

Calls began to come in from citizens who wanted to help. One woman reported seeing a blue-gray VW speeding southbound shortly after the robbery, and watched it make an illegal left turn. She hadn't been able to get the license number.

The coed witness agreed to be hypnotized to help her remember details about the VW bug she'd seen. She was an excellent subject for hypnosis by Detective Joe Nicholas, and her recall in the trance state confirmed her original description of the car. Now she was able to retrieve more details. She remembered the tires, the hubcaps, all the dents and their placement, the chrome trim — even the shape of the headlights. But she still could not visualize anyone inside the VW.

ID Tech Jeanne Ward reported that she had been unable to find any latent fingerprints in the stolen truck, and she knew why: The dashboard and console of the truck had been wiped clean. She had found glove prints which she would retain for comparison. Glove prints can be distinctive, but cloth fiber patterns are not nearly as useful as fingerprints themselves.

The owner of the Ford pickup said that his vehicle had been parked in front of his home — without the keys — Sunday night. He had discovered it was missing the next morning. He had no idea who might have taken it; he was the only one who had the key, and no one else ever drove it.

King County Medical Examiner Dr. John Eisele completed William Heggie's autopsy the morning after the deadly bank robbery. Heggie had succumbed to a single gunshot wound through the sternum near the midline of the chest. Eisele could not pinpoint the distance Heggie had stood from his killer. Surgeons in ER had cut into his chest to massage his heart in a futile attempt to save him, and any gun barrel stippling or powder burn marks were destroyed in the process. But it was clear any attempts at resuscitation would have been in vain. The elderly man's liver, right lung, and the right ventricle of his heart had been torn away by the bullet. Dr. Eisele retrieved it, and noted that it was the kind of high-impact ammunition used by Seattle police officers. It was in good condition and would be useful for ballistic comparison if detectives should ever find the shooter and his stash of bullets.

Calls from tipsters continued to come in. A Renton, Washington, bank reported that they had taken in some bills with reddish stains. But when the bills' serial numbers were checked, they did not match those missing in the Prudential robbery.

And then, George Marberg and Al Gerdes received a phone call from a police dispatcher in communications center. "A man just called in on 911 and he says his son might have some valuable information about the bank suspect. I've got a contact number for you."

This was the kind of information that every detective hopes for, especially in a case like this in which they had absolutely no idea who they were looking for — not even the race, sex, or age of a suspect.

The detective team arranged to meet the young male informant, Mark Halley,* twenty-two, in his father's downtown office. The clean-cut witness began to tell them of his suspicions about who the Prudential robber might be. What Halley had to say was riveting.

"I think it was a guy named Sam Jesse. I went to school with him; I've known him for years. . . . We graduated from high school together five years ago, and we've been close friends."

Halley said that he and Sam Jesse both lived with their mothers in Laurelhurst, which is a venerable upper-middle-class neighborhood northeast of the University of Washington. Laurelhurst was only blocks from the Prudential Bank where William Heggie was killed. They had graduated from high school in the late seventies, and had remained close friends.

"What makes you feel that this Sam would be involved in a bank robbery?" Marberg asked.

"Sam's a different kind of guy," Halley explained. "Always has been. At first you're gonna think that he's putting you on because he's always talking about stuff that doesn't seem real. But he's a 'go for it' person. He rides his motorcycle at the highest speeds, smokes a little more marijuana than anyone else, and drinks way more and gets way more blown away. It's an all-or-nothing type deal. There was always something weird about him. That's sort of what I thought was pretty cool about Sam. You just wouldn't put anything past him."

"You wouldn't put bank robbery and shooting someone past him?"

Halley shook his head. "No. Sam's always been on this bit about karma. And he's always told me that it's OK to kill people because he believes in 'survival of the fittest.' "

That still didn't explain why Halley had connected Sam Jesse to the Prudential Bank. But he hastened to explain further. "We got drunk together on New Year's Eve, and Sam was going on about how he was working eight hours a day for minimum wage. He said he had found a way around that. He was really going to go out and rob a bank. He said he was going to get enough money to live in his own apartment and buy a guitar. He wanted to start a rock band. He began to talk about things so bizarre that I found them hard to believe — even for him. But now, I'm afraid he was serious."

"Why? You didn't just think he was drunk and rambling?" Gerdes asked.

"No — because of the way he talked, and then how he acted after. Sam actually bragged to me that he'd strangled a girl once, but I didn't believe him because he once told one of our other friends that he'd knocked an old woman down to take her purse. He likes to shock people, but I began to realize that he really had worked out all the details of robbing banks, and that he was having some dark thoughts. On New Year's Eve, he asked me, 'You know what it's like to kill someone? It's like you've just been over the edge and you keep it inside you all the time.' "

Sam Jesse's father was a minister, and Halley said he had behaved like a typical "PK" (Preacher's Kid) all through school, trying to prove that he wasn't a goody-goody guy because of his father's profession. Although he was very intelligent, he had been a deliberate underachiever.

Shortly after New Year's, Sam had quit his job as a janitor. He'd told Mark Halley that he was going to start robbing banks. He explained that he had to do a small "job" first to set himself up as a bank robber. "He told me that he'd planned to rob a grocery store first. But that didn't work because he was alone in this store at night and the alarm went off. That scared him and he didn't go through with it."

But that hadn't stopped Jesse from continuing with his plan to be a master bank robber. He revealed to Halley that he intended to keep on working up to banks. "He sounded so serious that I began to watch the papers for reports of store robberies to see if Sam really meant it," Halley said, "and I saw some that I thought Sam might have pulled off. He wouldn't say 'yes' or 'no' when I asked him though.

"He told me that when you do a bank, you have to do everything right. He said that the people who get caught are the ones that just run in there — super desperate — and they don't have the whole thing thought out. He said he had a friend who'd been in jails and involved in crime before and knew a lot about it. They studied up on everything. He said it was real hard work. He'd go to the library and study up on crime statistics, how many policemen there are in certain areas, what times stores were busiest, or when people did their banking. Stuff like that. Then they'd stake out the store and watch for where the manager of the bank or store lives, and what they'd do with the money and when. Like they'd stake it out for hours at a time a week before they did it."

"Do you know who the friend was — his accomplice was?"

Halley shook his head. "I don't even know if such a guy existed. I thought maybe Sam was making that all up. It wasn't anyone I knew — I'm sure of that."

All this research had been, according to Halley, on the little jobs. It was supposedly only to get the cash they needed for the big bank jobs that lay ahead. *They* had planned to get disguises, Mace, a gun. Sam and his unknown accomplice were supposed to have planned diversionary techniques. "Sam talked about setting off a bomb near a bank they wanted to rob — or maybe have someone dressed as an old man stumble into the bank to divert attention."

"But you personally never saw anyone who was working with Sam Jesse? It was always just him who was telling you about the bank robbery plans?"

"Never saw them. But he always spoke in the plural, as if he had a partner — or even a gang."

Mark Halley's depiction of his friend, Sam Jesse, sounded pretty far-fetched; Jesse — if what Halley was saying was true — seemed to have been unduly influenced by James Bond movies, and his plans for a crime spree more like those expected from a brash young teenager than a twenty-two-year-old man. But the detectives would certainly hear this informant out. As bizarre as he sounded, Sam Jesse was the most likely suspect — the *only* real suspect they had had so far.

Asked to describe Jesse's physical appearance, Halley replied that he was very tall and skinny — well over six feet tall. "He looks younger than he is, and he's got really, really blond hair. If you saw him, you wouldn't forget him. He's kind of 'gangly.' "

"Does Sam have a gun?" Gerdes asked.

"Yeah, he went through the want ads in the Little Nickel newspaper and he found a .357 Magnum for sale up near Everett."

The bullet in William Heggie's body had been .357 ammunition.

Halley said that Sam had bought the handgun in late January or early February. "I advised him not to — I told him he didn't need a gun. The guy who sold it to him made Sam promise to register it — but he never did."

Sam Jesse had paid about $150 for the gun, and he had immediately gone to several discount stores to buy high-velocity ammunition — both regular and hollow-point. With Halley riding along, Sam had then driven to the forests along Snoqualmie Pass to try out the gun by shooting at trees.

Sam's plan for robbing banks had been very intricate, according to Mark. He would use several vehicles, some stolen. Sam said he planned to steal the vehicles by knocking their locks out, and then getting new locks. He intended to use a stolen van or truck as he drove to the banks, and after the robberies, to use yet another stolen vehicle to leave the immediate area. He would eventually end up in his own car.

"When did you have these conversations with Sam — about the bank robbery plans?" Marberg asked.

"Almost every day. I'd just get bits and pieces from him. I'd tell him about my job and he'd tell me about what he was doing. Like he was going to set off the bomb and then get in and out of the bank in ninety seconds while the police were sucked away taking care of the bomb. That was the only way they could do it and get away."

Halley said that despite all the detailed planning, he hadn't really believed that Sam was serious. Over the many years that he had known him, Sam had *always* been full of fantasy. That was his place in the group of guys who had grown up together in Laurelhurst and Windermere (an even more posh neighborhood). Sam was the chance-taker, the jokester, the one full of tall tales. He didn't seem much different at twenty-two than he had been at fourteen or fifteen. The rest of his peers matured and moved into adulthood; Sam still clung to make-believe.

Or so it seemed.

As Mark Halley spun out his reasons for suspecting that Sam Jesse was the bank killer they sought, Al Gerdes and George Marberg took page after page of notes. Too much was clicking neatly into place for Sam not to be a prime suspect. They looked at Mark and saw that he had only recently come to terms with his suspicions about the Prudential robbery. He had clearly tried to ignore what he didn't really want to believe and somehow managed to treat Sam's escalating "stories" as only that. Sam's imagination had amused his friends for years and it was easier to believe his activities were still fictional than to face the darkness creeping in. It must have been hard for Halley to go to his father with his suspicions.

The detectives noted that Mark glanced up at the clock in the Homicide Unit from time to time. When it was almost two, he looked nervous. Suddenly, Gerdes had a thought. "Where is Sam now?" he asked.

"He might be gone —"

"What do you mean?"

"I think he might be on his way to Hawaii."

Halley hadn't wanted to rat on Sam — not until he had reason to believe that the detectives agreed with his concern about his old friend. And the time had slipped by. It was ten minutes to two, and Sam Jesse had told him that he was going to board a plane for

Hawaii at two. It could be another one of Sam's big stories, but if it wasn't it was too late to stop him now.

Marberg and Gerdes were a little chagrinned, but if Sam Jesse was sitting in an airplane high over the Pacific Ocean, he wasn't going anywhere until he landed in Hawaii. If Halley's information was good, Sam could be stopped at the gate in Honolulu and held by police there. The Seattle detectives didn't feel that they had a solid enough basis yet to evaluate Halley's story and call for an emergency stop of a plane already taxiing out on the runway at SeaTac Airport.

They could, however, call Honolulu police and ask them to stand by for the next six hours. "We may need you to detain a suspect for us," George Marberg said. "We'll be in touch as soon as we have more information."

"OK," Al Gerdes said to Mark Halley. "Let's focus in on why you feel so strongly about Jesse's connection to bank robberies. Tell us specifically what changed your mind from thinking he was making things up to believing he was serious."

"OK," Halley said, drawing a deep breath. "Sam told me about a bank robbery that was going to take place on a Friday. I looked in the paper the next day and I saw an article about a bank that got robbed on that Friday. I asked Sam if it was him and he said, 'Yeah, but we hardly got anything.' I became convinced that Sam had robbed that first bank. Even though we were such close friends, it seemed like maybe Sam had crossed the line. I didn't see him very much after I went over there the day after the first robbery. He had a big, huge wad of bills and he took me to dinner one night at a real fancy place — but he said they didn't get hardly anything and they were getting ready for this big job where they would get like $250,000 and could get out of the country. He wanted to take a trip right after [the big job] . . . to Hawaii . . . maybe to Australia."

Mark said he had been upset at his own bank at the time they went out to dinner because they had bounced a check he had written and he was embarrassed. "Sam told me, 'Don't worry. I'll get back at the bank for you.' I still didn't think much of it at the time."

But Mark Halley said he had begun to avoid Sam Jesse after that because of the possibility that Sam was actually planning a big bank robbery.

Marberg and Gerdes found Halley's recall of Sam's progression as a bank robber more and more fascinating. Mark said Sam told him that he and his elusive partners were staking out a bank, watching it from a motorhome they'd stolen. Sam had told him they had to keep putting off this really big robbery until the time was ripe. This was the robbery where they were going to use some guy disguised as an old man to divert attention.

"I'm not quite sure of how that was supposed to work," Halley said. "I told him I didn't want to hear any more about it because it was getting too weird for me."

But Mark had continued to have a kind of fascination with Sam Jesse's activities, albeit from a safer distance. Two weeks later, a branch of Seattle First National Bank was robbed. Mark saw it in the paper, and then learned that Sam Jesse had rented a new apartment, bought a Volkswagen bug, and new furniture. The apartment was very nice and located on Queen Anne Hill.

Marberg asked Halley to describe Sam Jesse's newly acquired car.

"Sort of two-toned. It's got navy blue back fenders and a navy blue hood and it's sort of a grayish color. There's a small dent on the top of the hood and a spot on the side on one door."

Marberg nodded without saying anything. Halley described his feelings after reading about the robbery-murder at the Prudential Bank in Laurelhurst. "I recognized that Volkswagen description that was in the papers, and I just knew it had to be Sam."

Long before the details of the bank robbery–murder had hit the media, but only hours after it occurred, Mark had eaten lunch with Sam, unaware that he had accidentally chosen that day. Jesse had complained of feeling ill and said he'd slept very late that morning because he had a cold coming on.

"Did he call you, or did you call him?" Marberg asked.

"I called him around noon. He sounded really 'zombied-out,' like he wasn't really there. I asked him if he wanted to go get some good food at the Sunlight Café."

Sam Jesse had agreed, but urged Mark to come up to his apartment first. Sam usually wanted to drive when they ate out, but on the twenty-fifth, he wanted Mark to drive his car. They left the VW bug parked in front of Jesse's apartment and went out to lunch.

It was eight that evening before Mark read the papers, and he thought at once of Sam. The bank job sounded like Sam's "kamikaze" alternative plan that called for racing into and out of a bank. Further, the Laurelhurst branch of Prudential was an out-of-the-way bank, familiar mainly to those living in the area, and a bank that Sam had once said would be easy to "get." It was very close to the neighborhood where they had both grown up.

"Did you have any conversation with Sam that night?" Marberg asked.

"I buzzed over there at nine-fifteen. He let me in, and I went over to the paper and said, 'Did you see this?'"

Where Jesse had been eager before to discuss any and all bank robberies, he hadn't wanted to talk about the Laurelhurst incident at all.

"I said, 'Sam, you didn't do that, did you?' and he said, 'What do you think I am — crazy or something?' He totally denied the whole thing. Sam's an accomplished liar," Halley continued. "I've watched him lie to his parents for years. He can put up a wall where he shows no feelings at all. And Sam simply did not want to discuss the Prudential bank job. Finally, he told me that he had something to tell me. I expected he was going to confess about doing that bank. But he just said, 'I'm going to Hawaii, to Honolulu.' He said he was going to meet friends and stay there.

"He kept saying that they were going to travel cheap because he was poor, and hadn't gotten enough money in the last thing. He went out of his way to deny that he'd had anything to do with the Prudential Bank."

Al Gerdes held out an enlargement of the photos taken by the bank's hidden camera, and Mark Halley nodded. Even though the photo showed very little of the bank robber, Mark said he recognized the stance. "Those frozen shoulders," he said. "That's Sam. That's how he stands. I've seen him wear a down hood like that, and he's got brown work gloves, too, but I guess a lot of people do."

"So when you called Sam at noon on the twenty-fifth, did he sound like he'd just woken up?" Marberg asked, going back to the hours right after the bank robbery.

"No . . . just flat. It goes back to New Year's Eve. He was acting spooky then, and I remember his saying, 'Sometimes I feel like the devil is overtaking me.' I said, 'How can you do that? How can you endanger other people's lives?' and he said, 'It's just like I'm not even there; something else takes over.' But he also told me it was all like a big 'rush' to him."

Mark Halley admitted that he himself was no angel, and he and Sam had participated in some forbidden activities over the years.

He was frank in admitting that the two of them had indulged in psychedelic mush-rooms a few years earlier. At that time, Sam had claimed to see "spirits" floating around during the mushroom episodes.

"But he's let up on the mushrooms re-cently," Mark Halley pointed out. "Sam thinks that the world is going to end next year — with a big atomic war, and a world-wide depression. He thinks it's survival of the fittest and the world is just going to go crazy, so he's just starting a little early."

Halley's recitation was one of the most startling Marberg and Gerdes had heard in their long careers as detectives, but he was telling them things about Sam Jesse that seemed to make some kind of sense in the crazy pattern of the events at the Prudential Bank. Sam Jesse, a brilliant son of an Epis-copal minister, had seemingly been obsessed with a fantasy world in which he could rob and even kill with impunity, utterly con-sumed with the plotting and planning that appeared — at least to Sam himself — to be foolproof. If he really believed the world was coming to an end, he had apparently de-cided to arm himself with enough money and supplies to be a survivor.

Mark Halley told the two detectives that he had become more and more disturbed as he realized that Sam was probably responsible for William Heggie's death. It all added up. In the past, he and Sam had consulted a hypnotist, a kind of guru, after Sam asked Mark what he should do to find answers to his "spiritual questions."

"This guy is pretty spiritually aware," Mark explained, "and he's the one that Sam kept talking to and he was always asking him was it OK if you kill somebody? What happens to you spiritually? Is there a debt against you? This guy says, 'Only if you let it be a debt — then it's a debt.'

"That was something I just couldn't agree with."

Halley's conscience ate at him as he had wavered between going to the police and sticking by his old friend. He had clearly had his own philosophical questions about good and evil and accountability. While he tried to decide what to do, he said he had picked up a hitchhiker — a complete stranger — and run his worries about Sam by him.

"He told me the decision had to be mine, and all of a sudden, I knew what I would do. So I called my father and told him to contact you guys — to call the police."

Gerdes and Marberg believed Halley. They did a preliminary background check, and found that Sam Jesse was, indeed, the son of a minister. Until recently, he had been employed as a janitor at the Federal Office Building, a job far beneath his abilities and education. It was too late to stop him from fleeing to Hawaii. But he wouldn't get beyond the gate when he landed in Honolulu.

They asked Mark Halley to give them the most detailed description of Sam that he could.

"He's six feet, three inches tall, 180 pounds, and he has very straight blond hair, blue eyes. Sometimes he looks like he's crying because he's got this problem with his tear ducts. He wears wire-rimmed glasses."

"Any accent or speech impediment?" Marberg asked.

"No."

"Scars?"

"No."

"Mustache?"

"Not now."

Detective Sergeant Jerry Yates called the Port of Seattle Police Department and asked that a detective contact all airlines to verify that a Sam Jesse had boarded a flight to Hawaii. Port Detective Doug Sundby reported back that Samuel Henry Jesse had departed on Northwest Flight 55 from SeaTac at 2:45 P.M., and he was scheduled to land in Honolulu at 6:30 P.M. Hawaii time.

That would be 8:30 P.M. Seattle time. The Seattle detectives had a lot of work ahead of them before that plane landed.

Sundby said he would have officers from his department search the many-tiered parking garage at the airport for a gray VW bug with black hood and fenders. They quickly located a similar car on the second level of the garage. A parking ticket had been taped on the window at 8:35 A.M. Jessie must have spent the night at the airport. Detective John Nordlund, accompanied by Mark Halley, left for the airport to ID the bug left behind.

Nordlund shone his flashlight into the interior of the bug. He could make out two orange flecks on the steering wheel. The vehicle was gray-blue with a dark blue hood and right rear fender. There was damage in the front — just as the coed witness had described it. Someone had apparently tried unsuccessfully to spray-paint the dark fender with light blue paint. Nordlund photographed the bug and had it impounded.

Detective Sergeant Don Cameron, heading the night crew in Homicide, dispatched Mike Tando and John Boatman to the apartment house on Queen Anne Hill where Sam Jesse had his new apartment. They found that all the apartment mailboxes had the complete names of tenants on the slot in front. All but the mailbox for number 303. That slot read only "S.J."

No one answered the door at 303, but that didn't surprise the detectives. The tenant was reported to be thousands of miles away.

Detectives Marberg and Gerdes called the FBI and learned that the Seattle First National Bank branch at North 185th had been robbed on February 13, 1980, at 2:23 P.M.

It was now 6:00 P.M., two and a half hours before Sam was scheduled to land in Honolulu. Judge William Lewis issued an arrest warrant for Samuel Henry Jesse after taking the information telephonically, and Marberg and Gerdes picked it up. The warrant said that Jesse was to be arrested on suspicion of first-degree robbery of the Prudential Bank. A search warrant for his apartment was obtained at the same time.

Sam Jesse's plane had passed the point of no return over the ocean; he would deplane in Honolulu in a little more than two hours. FBI special agents in Hawaii were made aware of the arrest warrant and would meet his plane.

Armed with their search warrant, George Marberg and Al Gerdes went to Jesse's apartment house. From outside, they could see a light burning in number 303, and they gained access from the balcony outside an unlocked bedroom window. Just in case, Cameron, Tando, and Boatman waited in the hallway outside the front door to Sam's apartment. But Sam wasn't there. The apartment was empty.

It was a small, one-bedroom apartment. If Jesse had ever planned to cover his tracks in case he decided to return to Seattle, he had apparently given that idea up. He probably had been panicked by Mark Halley's questions. His apartment was rife with physical evidence that would connect him to both the bank robbery and the murder. The investigators located a blue nylon knapsack containing a Smith & Wesson .357 Magnum handgun with a four-inch barrel in a black leather holster. The gun's grips were stained orange. Further down in the bag, they found an algebra textbook. When the detectives opened the book, they found a profusion of twenty-dollar bills stuck between its pages. The edge of every bill was bright orange.

They found three ignition sets — all Ford products — in the knapsack. They were standard replacement ignitions which could be used to bypass a vehicle's ignition when it was unplugged. Sam had been fully prepared to steal the vehicles he needed to help disguise his identity when he drove to his target banks.

The bed in the neat apartment was just a box spring and mattress set atop four concrete blocks. When the mattress and springs were removed, Marberg and Gerdes saw that the spaces in one block were filled with twenty-five twenty-dollar bills.

There was a length of nylon rope in the closet, stained with orange powder.

In the kitchen cabinet, they found more bills — ones and fives — in a cereal bowl. They also found a bill of sale for the VW bug, purchased for $840 on February 15, just two days after the Seattle First National Bank robbery. The apartment rental agreement showed that Sam Jesse had rented it on February 17 for $225 a month. He had spent his first bank money as his friend Mark suspected, setting himself up in an apartment and buying a car.

And now they found a picture of the missing Sam Jesse: The tall, big-boned youth smiled into the camera self-consciously. He held a newspaper in one hand, but it was impossible to read the headline. He didn't look like either a killer or a bank robber. He looked like a teenager whose muscles had yet to catch up with his height. The length of his limbs and his awkwardness suggested that he might be suffering from Marfan's Disease, the illness that Abe Lincoln was diagnosed as having. Sam was broad-shouldered, and he had huge hands. He appeared to be about sixteen or seventeen, much younger than he really was, a kid posing shyly for a friend's camera.

Detectives outside the apartment searched the Dumpster and found a handwritten bill of sale for a Smith & Wesson .357 Magnum. The buyer was listed as J. T. Jay, and the date was January 28. The "J" was written to look like a "G" — the same peculiarity in handwriting present in Sam Jesse's signature on the rental agreement.

On the rental agreement, Jesse had listed his employer as Metro Transit, Seattle's bus system, and noted that he worked nights. He did not, of course, work for the transit company; he didn't have a job at all.

The investigators gathered up their bags of evidence, and double-locked the apartment. Back at the Homicide Unit, detectives got word that Sam Jesse had been taken into custody in Hawaii as he left the plane. He had told FBI agents that he knew nothing of a bank robbery or shooting in Seattle.

Sergeant Don Cameron drove to the home of Jesse's mother and explained as gently as he could about her son's arrest for bank robbery. The shocked woman said she had seen Sam last on Sunday afternoon, the day before the Prudential Bank robbery. He had told her then that he might be going away with friends for a week, but gave no details beyond that.

His mother had come to understand Sam's need to get away occasionally. It was his pattern, she said, to go into the hills a few times a year, and he told her he had been cutting wood for spending money. He'd told her that he worked for Metro Transit until six months before. She didn't mention the janitorial job. Sam was quite intelligent, she said, and he had completed several semesters of college at Bellevue Community College where he'd been principally focused on mathematics. When Cameron asked her about Sam's personality and if he was ever violent, she shook her head in surprise. On the contrary, she said, he was always easygoing and mild around his family.

When detectives counted the money they'd recovered from Sam's apartment, it totaled $1,416. The serial numbers matched the list of marked bills the teller at the Prudential Bank had handed over on February 25. These were probably the bills in the dye pack. Some of them were wet — as if he had attempted to wash the orange stain from them. If Sam had used stolen money to buy his plane ticket to Hawaii, it had not been from the dye pack. For some reason, he'd left most of the stolen money behind — even the unstained bills.

Maybe he'd been haunted by the memory of the old man he shot.

Sam Jesse never got to see Hawaii, nothing beyond the FBI offices in Honolulu. He continued to deny any culpability in the Prudential Bank robbery for a long time, even after he was informed that Seattle detectives had found the gun and the stolen money in his apartment. He insisted the agents had "the wrong man."

Back on the mainland, however, the evidence continued to pile up. The bullet retrieved at William Heggie's autopsy proved to have been fired from the barrel of the .357 Magnum recovered in Sam Jesse's apartment. The orange stains on the VW bug matched the bank's orange dye microscopically.

At length, Jesse agreed to give a verbal statement to FBI agents in Hawaii, although he refused to sign any written statement. He said he had driven his VW bug around the area near his apartment on Queen Anne Hill until he located the truck he wanted to steal for the bank robbery. He parked his VW at his apartment, and walked the four blocks to the turquoise pickup. He quickly changed the ignition and stole it. He'd then driven it to the Laurelhurst area and parked it within blocks of the Prudential Bank. That accomplished, he'd taken a cab back to his apartment.

The next morning, which was the Monday of the robbery, Sam said, he'd driven his VW bug to the block where witnesses had spotted it. He'd used the stolen pickup to get to the bank. At that point, everything was going just as he had planned.

But not for long. All of his careful choreography had evaporated as he turned to exit the bank with his bounty. Even so, his voice was relatively calm as he described his struggle with the old man and having to shoot him — something he had never envisioned. Then there was the "WHOOSH!" as the dye trap exploded in the cab of the truck.

He'd dumped the pickup, retrieved his VW bug, and returned to his apartment. Working feverishly, he'd pulled off his stained clothing and fished out some of the bills with the darkest dye color and placed them in a plastic garbage bag. He threw the bag off the Aurora Bridge at the deepest part of the Lake Washington ship canal.

At two o'clock on Tuesday morning, he'd bought some blue spray at a 7-Eleven store and attempted to paint over the rear fender of the bug, but it was raining so hard that the paint kept running, and the results weren't what he hoped for. Jesse also said that his suitcase, the one federal agents had seized as he landed in Honolulu, contained a thousand dollars, some of the few unstained proceeds from the Prudential Bank robbery, as well as some cash from "a previous one."

Asked what ammunition he used in the .357, he said he'd used Remington hollow-point, semijacketed, 158-grain ammunition. It was quickly apparent that Sam Jesse had felt far more comfortable talking about his plans for the bank robbery, and the way it had gone down, than he did talking about the death of William Heggie.

He told the FBI agents that he had never intended to kill anyone. He hadn't noticed the old man in the bank until he was robbing the teller. Out of the corner of his eye, he'd seen the man trying to put a key into the bank's door. The agitated bank manager made three attempts to lock the door without success, and Sam said he'd decided he had to get out of the bank quickly. He grabbed the money bag and headed for the door, bumping into the elderly man.

"When I got to my truck, I saw that the guy had followed me," Jesse said. "I only

441

meant to scare him when I pointed the gun right at him. But instead of backing off, he just reached out and grabbed the gun with both his hands, and he started trying to wrestle it away from me.

"I was wearing gloves, trying to pull the gun back. I heard the gun hammer cock, and there was an explosion. The old man said something like, 'Oh, my God,' and he fell down. I just panicked and drove off. I guess I was about one hundred yards from the bank when the dye pack detonated."

Sam Jesse admitted he had no partner, and no gang. He waived extradition and was flown back to Seattle, charged now with first-degree murder and first-degree robbery, his bail set at a quarter of a million dollars. It was an ignominious end for a young man who had fantasized a life of leisure, the fruits of a masterminded plan to rob banks. He had never envisioned jail. Jail was what happened to dummies who didn't plan things out carefully.

Anyone who looked at the case saw the uselessness of it all. Bill Heggie was dead, even though it was quite possible that Sam Jesse never meant for it to happen. Each of them had reacted irrationally, but a loaded gun is a loaded gun. Anyone who carries one has to be aware that it has the potential to fire. For all intents and purposes both Heggie's and Jesse's lives ended in that terrible split-second when the hammer on the .357 slipped into the cocked position, even though the weapon had been intended just to frighten a bank teller into handing over money without question.

Nothing had turned out the way Sam planned on New Year's Eve. Instead of living it up in Honolulu, he was locked up with hundreds of other prisoners, packed into the antique King County Jail. He was devastated, pacing like a caged animal. More than most men, he simply could not accept a life behind bars. That was the one contingency that had never occurred to him.

Sam Jesse never went to trial. On the evening of March 16, he told his cellmates he wasn't hungry and they went off to eat supper without him. When they returned, they found Sam hanging from a pipe on the ceiling of their cell. Using his height and agility, he had twisted and knotted his bunk sheets, cinched a loop around his neck, and thrown the material over the top of the pipe.

Medic One paramedics could not bring him back any more than they had been able to bring back his victim, William Heggie, only three weeks earlier.

There may well have been more involved than Sam Jesse's horror at being locked up. He had once asked the psychic he considered his mentor, "Is it OK if you kill somebody? What happens to you spiritually? Is there a debt against you?" and the answer had been, "Only if you let it be a debt."

Sam Jesse may have figured that he owed a debt.

None of it worked out the way he planned. He believed in survival of the fittest, and it must have been a terrible realization for him to find that he was not among the most fit. He had said the world would end in a very short time.

For Sam Jesse, it did.

A Very Bad Christmas

Sometimes I wonder why I have written about so many homicide cases that either happen during the Christmas holidays or come to the end stage of a trial just when the streets outside the courthouse are lined with brightly colored holiday lights. Inadvertently, I happened to select cases for this collection that had Christmas connections, even though I chose them for entirely different reasons and didn't even notice the season. Maybe there are more homicides during the holidays; someday I'll check that out. Emotions tend to run too high at Christmas. I think some of us use the holiday as a watershed point to come to decisions: "If my marriage doesn't get any better by Christmas, I'm going to file for divorce," or "I just have to have a job by Christmas or I'll give up."

Too often, we expect to relive the same wonderful Christmases we had as children, or, conversely, the memories of a miserable

445

childhood may come rushing back to over-whelm us. There are myriad "triggers" that force us to face recollections of dark things we have successfully buried for years: songs and special food, weather and fragrances, relatives we never see except on holidays (and sometimes wish we didn't have to), ex-pectations and disappointments. They can all stack up to place an overwhelming bur-den on our psyches, and we may tend to be-lieve we are the only ones who feel sadness when we should be glorying in joy and cele-bration.

Maybe it's not even that complicated. It might be that we simply remember violent tragedies that happen on Christmas because they don't fit into the holiday spirit, and the glaring headlines become ghastly counter-points to stories about human kindness, joy-ous reunions, and happy times.

The case that follows is one of the most "unholiday" stories I ever came across, as gruesome as a Grimm's fairy tale. I doubt that anyone who lived near Portland, Ore-gon, the year it happened will ever forget it either.

Sauvie Island, the largest island in the mighty Columbia River, appears to drift in the river about ten miles west-northwest of Portland, Oregon. Its northern tip juts into Columbia County, but most of it lies within Multnomah County. The large part of Sauvie Island is either farmland or devoted to wildlife refuge, and only about a thousand people live there year-round. There are riverside beaches there, some for family picnics and even some that are "clothing optional." The island also has miles and miles of flat road for bicyclists. Until a bridge was built in 1950, a small ferry served Sauvie, and even today it is an out-of-the-way spot, virtually unknown to anyone but Oregon residents. In the summer, Sauvie Island is alive with activity, but the shorter days of winter and relentless rain shutter it down as the holidays approach.

Two days before Christmas, the island was

bleak and cold, its brown beach grass and leafless trees grating and rattling in the winter wind. Most people stayed inside by their fireplaces, or, if they had to go out, hurried about their errands with their heads bent against the stormy weather.

It was the job of two tugboat operators for the State Log Patrol to venture out on the Columbia River and search for logs and driftwood that might foul the engines of boats. That day, as they edged their craft along the east boundary of the island, one of them suddenly pointed toward the shoreline and cried out, "Oh, my God! Look! Look over there!"

What looked like a large doll or a small child lay face-down on the beach near the river as it lapped against the beach. As they drew closer, they realized with sinking hearts that it was a little girl. She was fully clothed, and it looked as if she had drowned, as unlikely as it was that she could have wandered so far out on this lonely shore. And she certainly wasn't dressed suitably to be on a boat's deck, but she must have somehow fallen overboard.

The tugboat men radioed the St. Helens office of the Oregon State Police to tell troopers there about their sad discovery. Corporal H. D. Watson and Lieutenant Benninghoff were dispatched at once to the scene. The child still rested where the witnesses had found her, her face in the shallow water. Drowned. But when the state police investigators rolled her over, they saw a large jagged cut in the middle of her forehead. There was blood in the sand where her head had rested. Eighty-one feet south of the child, Watson and Benninghoff observed a large, pink, oblong bundle near the water's edge. The condition of the child and the shape of the bundle were ominous enough for them to put in an immediate call to the State Police Crime Lab for assistance before they proceeded further. Evidence that might be there could easily wash away in the river water if they weren't extremely careful to preserve it.

At 4:38 P.M., Lieutenant Robert Pinnick and his crew of criminalists arrived at the desolate spot. The sun was a pale shadow in the western sky as it set, and they carried auxiliary lights to help them explore the windswept beach.

Bob Pinnick unwrapped the large bundle on the sand only enough to see what was inside. And it was what all the men there suspected. The blankets were a shroud hiding the nude body of an adult female. As unlikely as it might seem, the child might have drowned accidentally, but the discovery of the woman's body meant they were now working a homicide.

Oregon State Medical Examiner Dr. William Brady joined the first investigators on the beach, and knelt to pull the blanket further apart to view the woman. Then he looked up at the circle of investigators and said rather quietly, "She's been decapitated."

Within a matter of minutes, it was completely dark. Only two days had elapsed since the shortest day of the whole year, and the murky shoreline was probably one of the more difficult crime scenes the officers would ever be called upon to process. However, they set to work, using their powerful floodlights to illuminate the grim job before them.

They found no identification papers at all near the two bodies, but they felt confident that they would eventually be able to identify them. The child's clothing was apparently intact, and her garments bore some manufacturers' labels. Although the woman was naked, her body was wrapped in sheets and blankets with distinctive patterns that could probably be traced. In addition, they found a white towel near the woman's body and a pink plastic necklace on the sand near the little girl.

After they had spent many hours in the frigid December air gleaning every bit of physical evidence they could, the investigators released the bodies to be taken to the Multnomah County Morgue in Portland to await autopsy.

It was now early in the morning of Christmas Eve. The gruesome task before the detectives was completely incongruous with the spirit of the season. Who could have taken the lives of the young woman and the little girl and then tossed their bodies away so heedlessly? Whoever it was, he (or they — or perhaps even her) had left precious little behind of himself. There seemed to be no question about the criminal intent on the part of the person who had disposed of the bodies. While it was possible that the child had drowned accidentally and that her head wounds had come from the rocks along the shore, there was no plausible explanation for the woman's body being in the state it was — other than homicide.

At the Medical Examiner's Office, forensic pathologists estimated that the woman had been between seventeen and thirty years old. She was probably in her twenties. She had been between five feet two, and five feet, four inches tall and had weighed about 125 pounds. Clearly, her killer had wanted to delay any identification of her body — which seemed to suggest that she had some connection to him. The severing of her head from her body had been accomplished neatly, so neatly that it was possible that the killer had had some special knowledge of anatomy. Her legs were bent at the knees and her feet pulled up behind her buttocks and tied around her hips with a one-half-inch cotton rope. Her left ring finger had been removed at the third joint — probably to remove any rings, which would have led to her identity. The only pertinent scar on the headless body was an old three-inch surgical scar just over the tail bone. She had given birth to at least one child.

Her body had been wrapped in six bedsheets and two blankets, the bedding tied with half-inch cotton rope identical to that around her legs.

This information was sent out on teletype wires at the Oregon State Police station in Milwaukie, Oregon. The clues to the child's identity followed: "White female child, approximately four to six years old, forty-three inches tall, forty-five pounds, brown eyes, brown armpit length hair in one small ponytail tied with red rubber band. Wearing reversible ski-type jacket, lime green on one side, other side yellow and pink flowers with no brand on jacket. Jacket had hood and pull string. 'Zipper Sim Co.' brand. Light blue dress with green and white rickrack in color, six green buttons and rickrack tie with lace in bodice. No brand. White all cotton slip size four with three ruffles around skirt, label marked 'exclusive of decoration.' Also shows 3100 R and Manufacturers number 3139. White undershirt with safety pin ties, the type used on smaller youngsters. No brand. White underpants size six, Eiderdown brand, almost new. Has four wounds on head but cause of death unknown at this time."

Although the wording of the notification to the thirteen western states had no emotion in it — just the pure facts — the investigators didn't feel that way. This was a little girl who should have been waiting for Santa Claus to come, but somehow she had become entangled in an adult situation that had ended in horror. Some of the detectives brushed away tears as they read the description of the little dress with the green and white rickrack; it might have been her Christmas dress.

There had to be someone along the route of the teletyped alert who would recognize the description of the dead toddler and woman who'd been found on the lonely beach. They had not been dead long, probably no more than a day. If they were expected someplace for Christmas Eve, someone would be worried. Someone would call a police agency somewhere and give a description.

Multnomah County Detectives Tom Sawyer, Orlando "Blackie" Yazzolino, and Darril MacNeel, along with Portland Police detectives, watched the development of the case closely. Although the northern tip of Sauvie Island where the bodies were found is in Columbia County, there was no evidence to indicate that the murder of the victims had occurred on the island itself. It was quite possible that they had been killed in Multnomah County or even within the city limits of Portland.

Dr. Brady, one of the outstanding forensic pathologists in the Northwest, performed the postmortem exams on the nameless victims at 8:30 A.M. on Christmas Eve. It was impossible to pinpoint cause of death in the woman. Of course, decapitation itself would have been fatal, but Brady felt that had occurred after death, even though that was impossible for him to ascertain. He found some abrasions and bruises on her neck, but any bludgeoning, cutting, or other wounds delivered to the woman's head were, of course, missing.

454

The little girl had succumbed to head wounds. While the adult woman (her mother?) had not eaten for many hours before her death, the child had partially digested food in her stomach — which appeared to be cookies, candy, and french fries.

Was it possible that the dead woman and her child had been attempting to hitchhike into the Portland area for Christmas and were picked up by a maniac? Had he decided to rape the mother and ended up killing her, only to realize he had to get rid of her child, too? A possible theory, but why would a killer have felt compelled to destroy all vestiges of identification if the victims had been strangers to him? No. Detectives were convinced that the pitiful victims were somehow linked to their killer. He (or she) did not want their identity known because that might send police to his door asking questions.

Further, although the woman had been found nude, vaginal smears failed to indicate the presence of semen or seminal fluid. Although such evidence could very well have dissipated after the body's immersion in water, there were no other signs of scratches or contusions on the inner thighs which usually accompany forcible rape.

Multnomah County Chief Deputy District

Attorney Des Connell assigned a photographer from the Department of Public Safety to take pictures of the dead child for identification purposes and for possible press releases. Robert Zion from the Scientific Investigation Unit did his best to make the photographs something that would be suitable to appear in the media. The child's wounds were covered with makeup and the resulting photos showed only a pretty little girl who appeared to be asleep.

Shortly after two that afternoon, Zion was summoned again to the ME's office. Search parties on Sauvie Island had made another grisly discovery. Deputy Ernie Thompson of Columbia County, who had spent much of the morning rowing back and forth through the chill waters of the Columbia, had hooked onto a white pillowcase with an object inside. It was a woman's head. It was brought to Dr. Brady's office, and there was no question that this head belonged to the body found the night before. Zion waited while the head was prepared and made up for photographs.

The woman appeared to be between twenty-five and twenty-seven. She had dark brown hair which was short and curved around her ears, with bangs. Her complexion was slightly rough as if she had suffered acne as a teenager. Still, in life, she had probably been attractive. Now, a large, reddened contusion on the left temple area extended back into her hairline. Someone had dealt her a powerful blow to the head, fracturing her skull.

The head had been wrapped in six pillow-cases slipped one inside the other to make a relatively thick bag. The white case with a purple and green trim which actually encased the head was heavily soaked with blood.

The decapitated head was not the only item retrieved from the river. A thermal undershirt, large beach towel, white terry cloth bathrobe, pink and white striped blanket, two bags of costume jewelry, and a green and blue checked dress (cut up the back and through each sleeve) were also marked and tagged for evidence. It was beginning to look as if the killer, whoever he was, had used almost the entire contents of an average family's linen closet to cover up his bloody crime. Why had he thrown away the costume jewelry? Perhaps he feared it would haunt him, and he never wanted to see the pieces again.

Christmas Eve came and still no police agencies had reports of missing persons whose descriptions matched the dead woman and child. Portland papers and television stations cooperated with police by showing the photographs of the victims. Headlines cried out: "Do You Know This Woman and Little Girl?" It was not a happy Christmas feature, not the kind of heartwarming news that city editors seek on the most sentimental holiday of the year, but it had to be done.

Detectives felt sure that somewhere there was a Christmas tree waiting for the small girl whose body had washed up on the island. Yet they received no calls regarding the published pictures. They could only assume that the victims had come from some distance away from Portland, outside the normal circulation of city newspapers and TV stations. Or perhaps there was a father somewhere, and he, too, might have been a victim of murder — one not yet discovered.

Finally the publication of the pictures struck a nerve with someone. A young woman who lived with her parents in a suburb southeast of Portland was stunned when she opened her paper. Judy King stared at the face of the Jane Doe, whose hair had been combed neatly, whose eyes were closed, but who was no longer alive. Judy didn't want to acknowledge the similarities to one of her closest friends and to the friend's small daughter. She even tried to tell herself she was being influenced by the power of suggestion. But she knew better. She recognized her friend Carol Ann Hamilton and her daughter, Judith Ann Hamilton. Filled with horror, she stared at the two photographs in the *Oregonian.*

Judy King was twenty. Her mother, Gladys King, had befriended Carol Hamilton and her husband, Richard, many years before. At that time the couple were not yet married; they were students attending the Warner Bible School in Portland. Both Carol and Richard had come from out of state and they had no relatives in Oregon. Mrs. King had "sort of adopted" them into her family. Although Carol was a few years older than Judy, the teenagers had become good friends. When Dick and Carol were married, Judy was thrilled to be the maid of honor at their wedding.

When their first baby, a girl, was born, she was named "Judy" in honor of Judy King. Two years later, they had a baby boy, Robert Lee. Both Judy and her mother had been babysitters for the youngsters and grown even closer to the family. When Carol Hamilton found steady work at the post office, she hired a full-time sitter, but she still visited with the Kings often.

Dick Hamilton still attended the Bible college and also worked as a part-time medical technician. With Carol working and Dick's part-time job, they were able to buy their own home on S.E. 157th. Judy had always seen them as the ideal family. That was why she and her folks had been shocked on the previous Sunday evening when they received a visit from Dick Hamilton. What he told them left them thoroughly confused. When he showed up at their home unexpectedly, Dick was disheveled and upset. He had obvious scratches on his face. With great difficulty, he told Judy and her mother that Carol had left him for another man.

Dick was so distraught over the thought of losing his wife to a lover that he said he'd walked for miles on Saturday night trying to sort things out in his mind. At one point, he said, he had fallen, hurting his hand and scratching his face.

Mrs. King could not imagine Carol Hamilton being involved with another man. She felt she knew the young mother as well as anyone. Carol was a devoted mother, a faithful churchgoer, and a hard worker. Was it possible that she had been carrying on an affair so torrid that she would take her children and walk out on her husband less than a week before Christmas? Mrs. King could not believe it.

After Dick left, she and Judy had stared at one another, dumbfounded. Neither of them could picture Carol Hamilton cheating on Dick. She had always adored him, and they had never seen her with any other man.

Now the two women studied the faces in the newspaper. There was no mistake; that was Carol and little Judy. But where was the little boy — Bobby Lee? Had Dick been right after all? Had Carol run off with a man, a man who'd killed her and Judy, and abducted Bobby?

"We have to call Dick," Mrs. King said grimly. "Better we tell him than have him read it in the paper."

But she was too late; Dick Hamilton already knew. It was a quarter to five on the afternoon of Christmas Eve when Multnomah County Detective Tom Sawyer received a call from the Portland Police Department's major crime unit. Hamilton had called the Portland police to say that he believed the unidentified bodies found on Sauvie Island were his wife and daughter. The Portland detectives told him to remain at his home; someone from the sheriff's office would contact him right away.

Tom Sawyer phoned Hamilton, who

seemed to be doing a good job of keeping his emotions in check. He said he had seen the picture of his daughter in the paper and read the clothing description. He was positive it was his little girl. "The last time I saw Judy — last Saturday, the twenty-first — she was wearing her blue dress and her parka jacket."

Sawyer asked Hamilton if he felt able to come to the morgue to make a positive identification, and he said he could. Less than an hour later, the slender, twenty-five-year-old Bible college student appeared at Sawyer's eighth-floor office. Judy King had driven him down, and she told the detectives that her family was trying to support him in his hour of grief. Hamilton identified his daughter's photo.

Sawyer, along with Phil Todd and Phil Jackson of the Portland Police Department, talked with Hamilton. They advised him of his rights under Miranda, explaining that he seemed to be the last person to see his family. Hamilton nodded politely as if he understood.

Jackson asked quietly, "Does your wife have any scars on her back?"

"Yes," Hamilton said. "One at the end of her tailbone — where she had a cyst taken off."

Jackson looked at Sawyer over Hamilton's

bent head and shook his head. He then showed Hamilton the picture of Carol Hamilton that Bob Zion had taken.

Hamilton swallowed hard and then he nodded sadly. "That's her . . . that's my wife."

The detective trio asked no more questions. Instead, they asked Hamilton to wait for a few moments and contacted Detectives Yazzolino and MacNeel, who had been assigned to work the case. The two were legendary in the Homicide Unit in Multnomah County, having worked some of the most infamous cases in Portland's criminal history.

Blackie was garrulous and usually had a grin on his face; he was known all over Portland. MacNeel was more reserved. Together, they were perfect detective partners. Now the veteran investigators headed for downtown Portland, driving along glistening black pavement where Christmas lights on trees along the curb cast colored haloes through the rain. It wasn't the first Christmas they'd been called out, not by a long shot, but the case that awaited them would flash back on their conscious minds for every Christmas that lay ahead.

Richard Hamilton, still maintaining a rigid control of his emotions, listened once again as they read him his rights. Again he nodded that he understood. He was quite willing to talk to them, seemingly anxious to get the weight of the world off his shoulders. Sighing, he told Yazzolino and MacNeel about the upheaval in his formerly happy home.

"It all happened in the past few weeks, and I had no idea what was coming," he said.

"I never expected that she would betray me like that."

The two detectives waited for him to go on. Hamilton said he had asked to be let off early from his job at the medical laboratory on Saturday afternoon, December 21. "I usually work Saturdays from seven in the morning until five-thirty. But I told my supervisor that I had 'babysitting' problems at home. I told him my wife had to work at the post office because of the Christmas rush. So I left work around three-thirty."

But Hamilton told Detectives Yazzolino and MacNeel that the real reason he wanted to go home early on Saturday was that he believed his wife had been seeing a man in their home, having an affair in their own bedroom. "I planned to surprise them. I've found evidence around the house before, and always on a Saturday.

"I saw a man's T-shirt lying under the bed in our bedroom once," he said. "When I pulled it out, I saw it was not a brand I wore

— and it was much too large for me. I guess I was in shock. I pushed it back under the bed. Later, it was gone, and my wife never mentioned it."

There were other things that made him suspicious. "I found hair on one of the pillows of our bed. It was light-colored and it was very greasy. I don't use hair gel," Hamilton said. "I also found indentations on the pillows, and I knew I didn't make them."

Hamilton said the final blow was when he found a partially burned note in an ashtray. "It was addressed to someone named 'Ron,' and it was in my wife's handwriting. It said she would be back soon."

"Did you ever confront your wife with your suspicions?" Yazzolino asked.

Hamilton shook his head.

"So what happened when you came home last Saturday?" MacNeel asked.

Hamilton said that he'd arrived home shortly before four. When he entered his house, he'd seen a man sitting in the living room while his wife was in the kitchen. His children had both been playing inside. "The man was about twenty-five," he said. "I'd never seen him before. He was husky, with light brown hair, and he was wearing gray fabric gloves."

"They didn't hear you come in?"

"Not at first. I was prepared to deal with them, though. I had typed out a confession for Carol to sign. I confronted them and told them what I suspected. I gave them the note of confession. It was an admission of Carol's infidelity and she signed it."

"Just like that?" MacNeel asked. "She didn't object or try to explain anything?"

"No."

"Then what?" Yazzolino said, never changing expression.

"I told her she'd have to leave and that I would help her move her things from the house."

Hamilton said that Carol had hurriedly packed her clothing, sheets, and blankets. "Everything. She put it all in her car that was parked in the driveway. It's a red Ford. That was the last I saw of her or my children."

Dick Hamilton said that he had been completely overwhelmed by her faithlessness, so much so that he'd simply turned on his heel and walked away from his home, headed west toward the Gresham area. "I just wanted to leave all of it behind."

He had not yet mentioned his small son. That seemed a blazing red flag to the two detectives. They had waited for Hamilton to ask about him, but he didn't. Yazzolino and MacNeel looked at each other. They each had more than two decades on the force, and a long time working as partners. They no longer had to speak their feelings aloud to each other, but they were totally in accord at this point. They had seen and heard some mighty peculiar examples of human behavior in their day, and now, with just the slightest flick of an eye, they signaled each other that something was hinky.

Sure, it was possible that a sweet, churchgoing little wife could become smitten with another man and forget her marriage vows. They'd seen that happen in other cases. It was even possible that Carol Hamilton's best friends might have had no idea of what was going on. Judy King, who sat quietly by while Hamilton answered questions, looked totally bewildered by the story he was telling, but she appeared to be a naive woman who might have missed signs of Carol's infidelity.

Stretching possibility even further, the two detectives supposed a woman could even have run off with her lover, had a violent fight with him a few hours later, and ended up dead before the affair ever got off the ground.

It was possible, but not likely. Something didn't wash. The man before them showed so little emotion, evinced no outward signs of grief — not even when he had just seen pictures of his wife and small daughter, pictures taken after death. Shock could account for that flatness of emotion, but a man in shock would hardly be able to point out so many details and tell them such a complete story. And he still hadn't mentioned his son. Most fathers would be frantic by now, hoping against hope that the last member of his family might have survived.

Hamilton seemed oblivious to that glaring exception to expected behavior. Instead, he agreed to go through his recollection of the previous Saturday once more. In the second telling, his story changed somewhat. This time, he recalled that when his wife and children were leaving their home, they were in a different car. Not a red Ford at all. "It was a Hillman automobile," Hamilton said, "and it had Washington plates. Ron was driving."

"But didn't you say that you last saw your wife loading her things into her red Ford?" Yazzolino asked.

Hamilton seemed perplexed as he realized he'd made a mistep in his story. "I guess I'm a little confused," he muttered. "I'm kind of in shock."

Yazzolino suggested that it might be easier to sort things out if he took a polygraph test. But Dick Hamilton said "No" at once. He didn't want to take a lie-detector test. That wasn't necessary. He thought it might be best to stop the interview, until he could talk to his minister.

Darril MacNeel called the Hamiltons' pastor, who said he would leave at once for the homicide offices. Gladys King accompanied him. Both she and her daughter felt so sorry for Dick that they were doing their best to stand by him.

An hour later, Mrs. King and the pastor arrived at the Multnomah County sheriff's offices. The minister spoke privately with Hamilton for twenty minutes. Gladys and Judy King told Yazzolino and MacNeel that they had known Dick for a long time, and they could not even imagine that he might have guilty knowledge of the tragedy that had occurred.

And now their minister walked from the interview room, his face a study of deep distress. He beckoned to the two detectives. "I'm convinced that Dick had nothing to do with what happened to Carol," he said. "I've talked to him and I feel he's innocent of any wrongdoing."

Detectives Yazzolino and MacNeel felt sorry for the preacher. The man before them was a good man and a good Christian, but he was as naive as the two women. Patiently, they outlined the discrepancies in Hamilton's story for him, and he listened intently. Finally they suggested that he be present in the interview room while they talked with Hamilton. Both the suspect and his pastor agreed to this. The four of them met behind closed doors while Judy and Gladys King waited outside.

Yazzolino again asked Dick Hamilton if he would submit to a lie-detector test.

"I don't believe in such tests," Hamilton said.

"Richard," his pastor said. "If you have nothing to hide, it could do you nothing but good to take a polygraph. It will clear your name."

The small room grew quiet except for the sound of a ticking clock. Hamilton stared down at his hands, which were folded on the tabletop. Finally he blurted out, "I'm ready to tell you what really happened now. But I want to write it down . . ."

Although Yazzolino and MacNeel were convinced that Dick Hamilton was somehow involved in the disappearance of his family, even they were not prepared for the statement which Hamilton wrote out painstakingly in his own hand. Many of the words in the scrawled document were misspelled. Even so, his confession was, in its own

470

grotesque way, a classic statement. It is still used today in many Northwest law schools as a prime example of a confession that demonstrates intent, premeditation, and the suspect's cognizance of right and wrong at the time of the actual crime.

It is shocking and difficult to read:

I don't know when I first planed [sic] to kill my wife. I starting planning about 3 or 4 weeks ago. First I thought I would hide the bodies in the Columbia up by the Sandy River. At first I planded to dismember the bodies this way mabey [sic] they would never be found.

On the day it first snowed I went out there and found that I wouldn't be able to get over to the river because of a deep stream that crossed the way. I went on to work and told my boss that I had stopped to help some people out of the snow. At one time I asked one of the janitors for some plastic bags so I would be able to carry the bodies without a lot of blood.

On Friday night I called (a friend) and asked her if she would type a paper for me. She said she would the (next) day. On Saturday about noon she did type my paper as I asked her to.

I went home at 3:30 Saturday afternoon. When I got home, Carol let me in. Sometime later — I don't just (know) how long, I asked Carol to sign the paper. I had it covered with another sheet. I told her it was part of her Christmas present. Then I asked her to come into the bedroom and take her glasses off. I asked her to turn around, I think she sensed something as she acted nervoise. I tried to break her neck quickly but I couldn't. She screamed some and I tried to quiet her and choke her. Then Robert tried to open the door and come in. I pushed the door closed with my head and told him to go back to his room. In the fight Carol scratched me and a lot of the furniture was kicked around the room. At last I got all the way on top and hit her head on the floor. When I stoped she was still breathing so (I got) my hunting knife and cut her throat.

The incredibly evil confession continued as Hamilton wrote about washing up. One of Carol's friends from work had stopped by to give her a ride, but he said he had gone to the door and told her that his wife was "sick" and wouldn't be going to work.

He wrote of fixing the children's supper.

Then he had settled them in front of the television while he returned to the bedroom. He cleaned up and carried his wife's body into the bathroom.

"I cut her head off and her ring finger off but just couldn't cut anymore. After trying to eat some boiled eggs, I wraped [sic] Carol up."

Hamilton wrote that he had then driven to a drugstore to get "some pills" for himself. He sent his children to their room while he placed Carol Hamilton's body in the trunk of her car. He threw her clothes and other possessions into the trunk, too. His children sat near the decorated tree as he made several trips in and out. And then he had put their coats on and taken them to the car.

> We left about 9 or 9:30, I think. First I went to several Goodwill and Salvation Army boxes and left everything. Then I got myself a milkshake and some frenchfries for the kids. Then I drove out to the Sauvie Island turnoff, but thought I should go further on. I paused 2 or 3 times and even drove part way down to the river. I findly made up my mind to start back and at the latest do it at Sauvie Island. When I got there the kids were still asleep and I carried Carol's body

down to the water put it in. Then I carried Robert down and put him into the water and hit him 2 or 3 times with a rock on the head. When I got Judy she was crying and I felt horrible but I couldn't stop. I hit her on the head 2 times with a rock and ran back to the car. I drove so fast trying to get off the island I nearly had several wrecks.

Page by page, Hamilton handed his confession over to the investigators. And, still, he continued his chilling narrative. He wrote of how he had parked his wife's red Ford in a parking lot before he threw his knife and his own bloody clothes off a bridge. He left the car, and he walked aimlessly for a while. But he got cold and tired, and decided to call a cab. He didn't give his exact address to the driver but asked to be let off in the general vicinity of his home.

He had destroyed his entire family and left them floating off the beach on Sauvie Island. Once home, he wrote, he had hidden his bloodied, sandy shoes in the attic. "Then I took two sleeping pills and went to bed."

There had been no clandestine lover for poor Carol Hamilton. There had only been a husband who wanted out of his marriage. He was tired of being tied down by the responsibility of supporting two small children. With all of the options Dick Hamilton had — separation, divorce, counseling, or just disappearing himself — he had chosen the most horrible way imaginable to rid himself of his wife, Carol, and his children, Judy and Bobby Lee.

Leaving Hamilton's stunned friends to deal with his dark confession, Blackie Yazzolino and Darril MacNeel took the confessed killer to the old Rocky Butte Jail. There, an ID tech took black and white and color photographs of Hamilton's scratched cheek and jaw, his lacerated right hand, and a bruised area on his left chest. It was obvious that Carol Hamilton had fought desperately for her life and the lives of her children. Hamilton was booked into Rocky Butte, charged with three counts of first-degree murder.

There would be no bail.

Judge Carl Etling signed a search warrant that allowed Chief Deputy District Attorney of Multnomah County Des Connell, Portland Detective Sergeant Hank Kaczenski, and Lieutenant Robert Pinnick of the State Police, and Detectives Sawyer, MacNeel, Yazzolino, Barst, Phil Jackson, and Hugh Swaney from the Multnomah County Sheriff's Office to enter the Hamilton residence. It was now after one in the morning on

Christmas Day. But there was no Christmas spirit now. As with all search warrants, there were specific items listed: one human finger; a wedding ring belonging to Carol Hamilton; white cotton rope approximately one-half inch in diameter (similar to that used to tie bedclothes around the body); bedclothes to compare with those found with the body and head; women's clothing of the same size as that found near the decapitated body; children's clothing to test for size and laundry marks; a sharp cutting instrument to test for bloodstains; bloodstains about the premises or on items in the premises; insurance policies on the life of Carol Hamilton and/or Judy Hamilton.

The Hamiltons' house was a neat three-bedroom rambler, indistinguishable at first glance from thousands of similar homes in Portland. But it wasn't the same at all. "The first thing we noticed," Yazzolino recalled, "was the floors. They were hardwood floors, but someone had sloshed so much water over them in an attempt to clean them, that they were warped all out of shape."

The walls *looked* clean, but on closer observation, the investigators saw what appeared to be dried droplets of blood. These were principally in the area of the southeast bedroom and the bathroom. Bob Pinnick took scrapings of these stains after they were photographed. The outside surface of the garage door was smeared with a dark red dried substance. A shower curtain rested in a laundry basket inside the garage, its lower edges stained with dark brown.

Oddly, there were no women's clothes in the master bedroom — or in any other room. Hamilton must have wanted to rid himself of every vestige of Carol. An envelope lay in an open bureau drawer in the northwest bedroom. There was no address on it. When it was opened, the following statement was found inside:

I, Carol Ann Hamilton, do admit that I did commit adultery with Ron Wilson [the name was written in after the paper had been typed] on the Saturday afternoons of November 16, November 23, and December 21. I also admit seeing this person often since the first of August.

On agreement made verbly [sic] at this time (December 21), I will not oppose a divorce prepared by my husband on any grounds he wants. December 21, 1968.

Carol A. Hamilton [written in]

This was the statement that Dick Hamilton had prepared and asked Carol to sign without reading, because it was "part of her Christmas present."

Now the investigators' attention wandered unbidden to the Christmas tree, even though they had tried to ignore it. It was too sad to think of. But they had to look. There were carefully wrapped presents there with Judy's and Bobby's names on them. Yazzolino noticed that a few presents had been unwrapped; they were the packages with Dick Hamilton's name on them. A box that had held an electric shaver still rested on a crumpled bed of wrapping paper and bore a tag, "To Dick, from Carol."

"He's already opened it," Yazzolino said. "He's been using the razor she meant to give him on Christmas."

Detective Hugh Swaney located a trapdoor that led to a crawl space beneath the house. It was in a bedroom closet. He opened it and saw a small pile of freshly dug dirt directly under the opening. The pile measured approximately two feet in diameter. The thought uppermost on everyone's mind was Bobby Lee. The two-year-old boy was still missing. Swaney photographed the small hill of dirt and then tediously removed the soil with a serving spoon. There was no hole beneath the dirt; it had to have come from somewhere else under the house. He held his breath as he saw the pair of small black mittens that lay near the edge of the pile of dirt. There was a cigarette filter there, too. Swaney lowered himself down into the crawl space, which measured between eighteen inches and two feet in height. It was not an assignment for anyone with even a trace of claustrophobia. He clutched a flashlight and crawled on his belly over the entire square footage of the crawl space. Twenty feet from the trapdoor, Swaney found a freshly dug hole four feet by eighteen inches. The dirt in the hole was removed with the serving spoon. There was nothing in the hole.

(Later, Hamilton would say that he had considered burying some member of his family down there but had discarded the idea as impractical.)

After the sun rose on Christmas Day, Swaney went back to the quiet neighborhood in southeast Portland. Accompanied by uniformed officers Milligan and La Follette, he carried the pictures of Carol and Judy and began a door-to-door canvass of the Hamiltons' neighbors. The family immediately north of the Hamilton home had just watched a television broadcast about the bodies that had been found on Sauvie Island. They had thought the dead child pictured looked familiar. But they hadn't realized the child was Judy. Now, looking at the photo, the wife cried, "Oh my God, it is her! It's Judy!" She put her head down on the chair and began to sob. It was grief that would sweep the blocks that surrounded the Hamiltons' small house. None of their neighbors could recall any dissension in the family. They had seemed quiet, religious, and devoted to each other. No one had ever seen a strange man entering the Hamilton home while Dick Hamilton was away.

Patrol officers located Carol Hamilton's red Ford behind a Safeway store located on Hayden Island. Yazzolino and MacNeel ordered it towed to a garage where Bob Pinnick oversaw it as it was processed for evidence. Pinnick removed a number of items and sealed and tagged them: two blankets; two stuffed animals; one nylon stocking; one cardboard box with magazines and newspapers; one white rag; a brown paper bag with potato chips and cookies; a red and white plastic flashlight; jack, a jack-handle and lug wrench; one spare tire and wheel; one axe; one hunting knife; vacuum sweepings of entire vehicle; a black sock; dirt from under front fenders; radio knobs (for latent prints); a piece of plastic and plastic bags.

At eight-thirty on the morning after Christmas, MacNeel and Yazzolino arrived on Sauvie Island to assist Oregon State Police in their dragging operations for Bobby Lee's body. Hamilton had said his tiny son was wearing a red blazer jacket, dark pants, and brown shoes. Working with River Patrol deputies F. Hanna and F. Pearce, the men rowed back and forth for six hours, looking for some trace of the little boy in the twelve-foot-deep river. The OSP crew had already dragged the river for three days, and they had found a number of items connected with the case, but they hadn't found Bobby Lee.

They never found Bobby Lee's body. He was lost in the mighty Columbia River, perhaps even carried out to the Pacific Ocean.

On December 30, Dick Hamilton talked again to his minister — who advised Yazzolino and MacNeel that there had never been a "Ron Wilson." They were not surprised at all; the veteran detectives figured Hamilton had simply made him up out of whole cloth. He was someone to blame for the slaughter of Carol, Judy, and Bobby Lee.

The obvious question, not so easily answered, was "Why? Why had Hamilton wanted his family dead?" It had haunted the detectives as they carried out their investigation of the triple murder. There was no lover. There never had been. So Hamilton could not have been jealous of Carol. Her friends and coworkers could not recall that she had ever spoken of problems in her marriage. She was a private woman, yes, but they felt sure she would have said something or made some slip if she was hiding such a huge secret. Adultery was against her morals and her religion. Besides, she loved Dick.

Gladys and Judy King said that Dick had been the strong disciplinarian in his family, while Carol tended to be more permissive. "We think they might have argued over that," Judy said, "but I never thought that Dick would be violent."

Still, as they pushed their search for a motive further, Blackie Yazzolino and Darril MacNeel discovered hidden dimensions of Hamilton's personality. They found he had fancied himself something of a ladies' man — or at least he believed he had great potential in that area. Several young women at his job said that he had made attempts to date them. And they had turned him down. The bonds of marriage and fatherhood had begun to chafe. He had married too young. He wanted out, but he didn't want to be burdened with alimony payments and child support payments. He wanted to be as free as he had been before he met Carol. But the detective partners didn't find any women who had actually agreed to date Hamilton.

Richard Duane Hamilton went on trial on three counts of murder in the first degree. His plea of temporary insanity was rejected by the jury when they saw the voluminous physical evidence, listened to witnesses, and then read his gruesome and almost matter-of-fact confession.

He was found guilty on all three counts and sentenced to three consecutive life sentences in the Oregon State Penitentiary at Salem. Each life sentence carried a twenty-five-year minimum of hard time before he could be considered for parole

No one will ever really know what went on behind the closed doors of Dick and Carol Hamilton's home. If Carol had reason to be afraid, she never told anyone. She trusted in the Bible, in her church, and in her husband.

TO SAVE THEIR SOULS

I remember almost every case I've written over the last twenty-five years very clearly. Yes, I falter occasionally on names, but the events stay in my brain even when I'd prefer to forget them. This story of Christine Jonsen* is one that I've tried to forget. Few authors would want to write it, and it's a case that will be difficult to read, but I think it illustrates one of the most difficult dilemmas in the criminal justice system. Was a confessed murderer sane or insane at the time of the crime? How many times have I heard someone say: "Well, he had to be crazy to do that!" More than I can count. Still, with some eleven hundred true-crime stories behind me, only a handful have gone to court with a "Not Guilty by Reason of Insanity" plea. Often suspects will initially attempt to appear psychotic, but even their own attorneys quickly detect the falseness there and talk them out of making such a plea.

"Temporary insanity" is a handy catch-all that works in the movies and on television — but rarely in real life. Christine Jonsen's story is one of the few I have covered where I felt that a murder defendant was actually innocent by reason of insanity. She was, I believe, a woman driven to carry out one of the saddest crimes I have ever written about. I have no sympathy for the cold-blooded killer who plans his — or her — murder meticulously and then talks about a sudden "blackout" or fakes mental illness. These defendants are despicable.

But for this desperate woman, it was a far different story. Afterward, she did have agonizing regrets, but she still believed she had done what she had to do to save the very souls of those she loved most in all the world.

Christine was most assuredly not a Diane Downs or a Susan Smith. She wanted nothing for herself; she had no lover waiting for her, no better life to run to. Indeed, this case reminds me of poor, deranged Andrea Yates, who on one tragic morning in Texas methodically destroyed her four children. In her second trial, in July 2006, Andrea Yates *was* found innocent by reason of insanity.

When stories like this flood the media, I wonder why nobody saw the danger, or if they did, why no one saw fit to step forward and get involved. Not all cries for help are loud and piercing screams — some are subtle: curtains drawn against the sunshine, children kept indoors rather than being let out to play, or a vacant look in a mother's eyes.

I sat in the trial that ended this case and felt nothing but compassion for the accused. Perhaps you will see it in the same way. And if you ever feel the need to intervene in a situation that seems somehow wrong, please do.

I promise you: You will have no regrets.

I have had to deal with all manner of brutality, tragedy, sorrow, and pain, but I can recall no other story I have researched that had the sheer gut-wrenching impact of the Christine Jonsen case.

Beyond the news headlines, there were questions raised and differing legal philosophies that had to be dealt with. Few of my readers choose to read about murder cases for their sensationalism, and if they do, they will be disappointed. I believe they want to understand the motivations behind the killings and to learn how detectives approach each case and combine modern forensic science techniques with old-fashioned hunches and years of experience. In this light, in this case, it's important to explore the ramifications of the most widely accepted standard used to weigh insanity and murder in America: the M'Naughton Rule.

This premise originated in England in 1843 at the trial of a man named M'Naughton. In essence, it is a very simple rule: If the accused recognized the difference between right and wrong at the time he committed the crime, he was legally sane. Further, the rule decreed that if he knew what he was doing was wrong and made an attempt to escape detection by covering up his crime, most juries would find him guilty. However, if he should be found sitting next to his victim babbling incoherently, making no excuses, and with no comprehension of what he has done, he will be far more likely to be deemed insane. But it is a judgment almost impossible to assess. Unless the jury members were there at the crime scene — which they cannot have been — they cannot know what the mental acuity of the perpetrator was at that precise moment. A defendant may have been seen before the crime, and he may have been seen after the crime. But who can say that his mind is the same mind it was at the time of the murder?

Some forty-five years ago, the American Law Institute, objecting to the "right or wrong concept" of M'Naughton, suggested a substitute ruling to test insanity. This modified test would ask, "Did the defendant have the substantial capacity to conform his conduct to the requirements of the law?"

That is, the defendant might have known that what he was doing was wrong — but, if insane, would not have had the ability to stop. In 1971, the Washington State Supreme Court upheld the M'Naughton Rule in a murder conviction and threw out the proposed substitute.

This is all fairly technical, but in viewing Christine Jonsen's case, it is necessary in order to understand and evaluate what she did on an icy night along the Columbia River in eastern Washington.

Before I attended Christine's trial, I wrote about three other cases in which I doubted the sanity of the defendants.

- A brilliant and wealthy young man had been under psychiatric care since his mother committed suicide a few years before. He himself had attempted suicide three times. He knew that his mind was not tracking well, and he went to Western Washington State Hospital and begged to be admitted. He told doctors there that he was afraid he would hurt someone, but they gave him tranquilizers and sent him away. The next day he beat two elderly neighbors to death with a hammer he had just borrowed from them. That, of course, seemed to be the act of an insane person. But he took pains to wash his own bloodied clothing — allegedly to escape detection. Under M'Naughton, he was found guilty of first-degree murder and sent into the general population of the Washington State Penitentiary.

- A fifteen-year-old boy whose father had been diagnosed as insane saw his parents literally "shoot it out" in a gun battle when he was three years old. He was close enough to be drenched by their blood as he crouched, screaming in terror. He had shown signs of profound mental illness for years before he finally raped three women and killed two more. But he, too, made efforts to cover up his crimes. He was convicted as an adult of first-degree murder and sent to prison under the M'Naughton Rule.

- A young man, also highly intelligent, who had fled to Turkey to avoid the "CIA," who were "trying to assassinate me," hid in his mother's home, terrified of "them." Voices told him to kill his mother, the mother who had tried vainly to have him admitted to a mental institution. He did kill her, and then returned to the blood-washed home where the crime occurred. He cleaned up all signs of her murder and gave detectives a strange alibi. He, too, was convicted under the M'Naughton Rule.

None of these frankly psychotic defendants had anything at all to gain from their crimes. They were caught in the grip of tortured, fragmented minds, and although they had cried out for help, no help came. Each made vague efforts to cover up their crimes, and these efforts made them guilty under the M'Naughton Rule. They should not have been loose in society, yet one wonders what possible good came from throwing them into a prison where there was only token treatment for mental illness.

Those who kill for lust, financial gain, jealousy, pure meanness, or in the commission of another felony deserve what they get — every bit of it. But what of the truly lost souls?

Christine Jonsen was lost. She was a delicately pretty and very shy young woman with haunted dark eyes. She was born in Yugoslavia, but her father left soon after her birth and her mother died when she was only five. Apparently there was no one in Yugoslavia who was able to take the little girl in. She was shipped off, alone, to America, where a cousin who lived in southwest Washington had agreed to adopt her. And so, she grew up in that rainy, often economically depressed corner of the state where most people make their living catering to tourists, or from logging and commercial fishing.

Christine tried very hard to be perfect, perhaps because she was an orphan, taken in by kind relatives. She wanted them to be proud of her, and she never wanted to be a burden. She won citizenship awards in high school, made the honor roll, and was named a princess in a local logging festival. Yet she always needed to belong, to have someone to call her own.

After graduation from high school, Christine went to Grays Harbor Community College. During her college years, she and her roommate became involved in the Mormon Church and transferred to Brigham Young University in Provo, Utah. The Church would become a powerful influence in Christine's life, and she lived, always, by its tenets. Or, rather, by the way she interpreted them.

A few years later, Christine met the man who would become her husband when they both worked for a company selling camp-ground sites. He was thirteen years older than she was, but that seemed a good thing to her; he made her feel safe and protected. They dated for two years before they married. When Christine's husband got a job as a salesman in eastern Washington, they moved far away from Grays Harbor County and her relatives.

Richland-Pasco-Kennewick, Washington, called the "Tri-Cities," are relatively new cities that sprouted up from the brown earth along the Columbia River in the forties and fifties with the advent of atomic power. It was as different from the Pacific Coast towns that Christine had grown up in as if she had moved to the middle of the desert in Arizona. But she was happy; she had what she'd always wanted and needed: a man she loved to whom she would devote her entire life. She had no ambitions for herself beyond being a good wife, and a mother.

Christine was thrilled when her first son, Ryan, was born eighteen months later. He was a lovely baby, husky, smiling, cheerful. Her friends recall her as a most devoted mother. A year and a half later, she gave birth to a second son, Christopher. He, too, was a handsome little boy, and their mother loved both sons fiercely. She hoped to give them all the things she never had and vowed to keep them safe always.

She took the toddlers to church every Sunday, and the only time she ever left them was when she went to work as a waitress at a restaurant to help the family finances. Often her husband didn't make the sales commissions he expected. The restaurant was one of a chain that paid barely minimum wage. Waitresses there had to depend on tips to make a living wage. A company rule decreed that, even with burning hot plates of food to carry, waitresses could not use oven mitts. It was a stupid rule, and many nights, Christine went home with blisters up and down her arms. But she never complained. She considered herself lucky to have her husband, her babies, and her church.

In the Mormon Church, marriage is ideally meant to be for life. Christine believed serenely that she and her husband had married with the hope of being together forever — in both life and the Celestial Kingdom beyond. She never looked at another man; it didn't even occur to her to do that.

And then, during the Thanksgiving holiday, Christine's whole world collapsed: She learned that her husband was involved with another woman. She was shocked, but typically, for her, she didn't blame him; she blamed herself — for being a failure as a wife. She had tried very hard to be the perfect mate, and she had failed.

Her husband moved out, leaving Christine to support her little boys on her small salary. They moved into a tiny mobile home, and as Christmas neared, she didn't have enough money for her rent. Her car broke down, and she couldn't afford to fix it. And she was running out of groceries. Her church was known for taking care of its own, and it maintained warehouses full of food to help members in financial distress. But, as always, Christine was too proud to ask.

She had been a good worker at the restaurant, but it soon became clear to her fellow waitresses that she just couldn't handle it anymore. One friend recalled later, "Her hurt was so obvious — you could almost touch it."

Now that her husband was gone, Christine had no one to look after the little boys while she worked. Her bosses noted that she couldn't keep up with her diners' orders, and that she wasn't smiling or joking enough with the customers. Her job was the next thing to go. She was fired just before Christmas. Her phone was disconnected. She stayed inside the trailer, hiding from the world that had suddenly slapped her in the face. And still she cuddled her baby sons and saw that they prayed before each meal — however meager the meal was.

She tried to give Ryan and Christopher a Christmas. She had no money for a Christmas tree, but she had an idea. A police officer saw her collecting discarded pine boughs from a tree lot. She planned to take them home and wire them together to make them look like a real tree. When she saw the officer watching her, she offered to put them back. He assured her that would not be necessary.

Alone in their trailer as the bitter winter winds buffeted it, Christine kept going over the sudden ending of her marriage. She took all the blame when it would have been so much better if she had been able to get angry at the man who deserted her. And, slowly, she went from regret to depression and then descended into insanity. She might have been Ophelia twisting blossoms in her hair, insane because she thought Hamlet had deserted her. Christine was just as frail, just as abandoned.

But dangerous.

As her thought processes were revealed later in court, she began to believe that she must be very evil indeed to have failed as a wife. Soon she built on her delusions and thought that her husband was also terribly evil. Her disturbed conclusions got all tangled up with what she believed were Mormon beliefs, beliefs never taught by the Church that had been her guide for so long. Unable to distinguish between what the Church truly said and her own bizarre imaginings, Christine decided that she was what the Mormons called a "son of perdition." Perdition was synonymous with Satan, and a son or daughter of perdition was an anti-Christ figure closely associated with the devil.

Christine felt that all hope was gone; she would be cast into "outer darkness" and "go away into a lake of fire and brimstone with the devil and his angels."

The Church bishop who talked to the distraught young mother described a "son of perdition" as a person who has gone "beyond faith into absolute knowledge. They have to throw away that knowledge and actually fight Christ — deny that knowledge — become an enemy of Christ and deny that he exists. Judas was a son of perdition."

He did not realize how fragmented Christine's mind had become.

Christine, spinning deeper and deeper into psychosis, was terrified that her "evil" would become apparent to the Church elders and that they would come and take her children away from her. And yet, she somehow realized that it might be better if her children were removed from her for a while. Again, failing to recognize the danger in her, the bishop assured her that her children needed to be with her.

In early January, a home teacher of the Mormon Church went to the trailer home and talked with Christine. He was gravely concerned when he saw that her whole personality had changed. He found her on the verge of "being completely crazy and suicidal." He took her to his home and called the bishop. The two men spent the evening trying to counsel Christine, but she was too distraught to listen to them.

The men from her church set up two appointments with psychiatrists for Christine, but when they went to pick her up to drive her to the doctors' office, she would not answer the door.

It was far too late. Christine Jonsen was consumed with a terrible guilt that her "evil" and her estranged husband's "evil" would somehow contaminate the children she loved so much.

She had tried everything she knew how to try. She had begged the bishop to find a home where someone kind could take her boys for a few months. She would work two jobs, and she would get out of her terrible financial dilemma. But he had advised her gently that the boys needed her. Their father's desertion was enough of a trauma for them to cope with. They could not have their mother go away, too.

The church offered to find a babysitter so that she could work afternoons, but Christine knew she couldn't make enough money that way. They would all starve.

At a certain point, starving no longer mattered. Christine became worried about her babies' immortal souls.

In her mental state, she felt that she would only become more evil, that the devil himself would drive her further and further from God. As a Mormon, she believed that if her babies died before their eighth birthday, they would be assured of a place in the Celestial Kingdom. Children could not be baptized in the Mormon Church until they reached the age of accountability, but if they died before they were eight, they would go to Heaven because they were without sin.

Christine agonized over what she should do. What if she became increasingly a daughter of perdition — to the point where she would no longer be concerned with her sons' salvation? She couldn't keep them from the cold and hunger now, and every day things got worse.

On February 4, the snow was deep and crusted with ice in the Tri-Cities area. Christine had heard that freezing to death wasn't painful. She planned to join the boys as they went peacefully to sleep and froze. Holding them close, she sat in the snow outside the trailer home, waiting for death to overtake them. But Christopher began to cry and she realized that this plan would not be painless, and she could not bear to have them suffer — even for an instant — as she helped to free them from the wickedness that pervaded her life.

She took the youngsters back inside the trailer house and dressed them warmly, and then she carried them to her car. They drove around the Tri-Cities area all day while she tried to come up with a plan. Periodically, she stopped and parked so that she could think. Several times, she stopped to buy food for the little boys.

Now Christine knew what she had to do. She had decided that she must drown her two precious babies. But it was so hard to do.

The Pasco-Kennewick Bridge is suspended by cables forty feet above the Columbia River that roars beneath. In February, the river was as icy as death itself. Back and forth, back and forth, she drove. It was midnight, and then 2:00 A.M. If she waited until daylight, it would be too late. Sometimes, there were too many cars on the bridge; sometimes there were cars just behind her. And then, finally, there was no one — no one except the desperate mother and her two sleeping sons.

"By then," she would say later, "I knew it had to be done. I did it."

Christopher, the baby, was first. She carried the still-sleeping child to the center of the bridge and dropped him into the frigid water, hearing a splash far below — and then . . . nothing. Tears streaming down her face, Christine walked back to the car and got Ryan. He, too, disappeared under the black water below. And then she stood alone on the empty bridge, the wind tearing at her clothing. She had made the ultimate sacrifice.

They were gone from her, but they were entering the Celestial Kingdom.

Several hours later, a disheveled Christine Jonsen walked into the Pasco Police Department and asked to talk to someone. She had killed her children, and she wanted to turn herself in.

Detective Archie Pittman, horrified and

disbelieving, interviewed Christine. He taped his interview with her as she described what she had done in a flat, emotionless voice. "I had to do it," she said. "I dropped my babies into the water. I heard two 'ker-plunks' a long way down."

"Why?" Pittman asked in a strangled voice. "Why did you do this?"

She looked at him as if he could not understand, even though it was so clear in her mind. "You can't know why I did it unless you look at my whole life. He [her estranged husband] is partner to this . . . This is how evil we are. Each of us have used people in our lives. We're not pure at heart. Not loving people, but using them.

"I was lazy and rebellious and I fought against everything that's good and I had degenerated, rather than grown. The only change was that I lied about it. I would always lie to myself."

To the detective, the soft-faced woman before him looked like anything but a degenerate sinner. She looked as if life itself had risen up and crushed her. Pittman said a silent prayer that what she was telling him was not the truth, only the ramblings of a broken mind.

It might be impossible to prove what she was telling him. If the children were in the river, there was a good chance they would never be found. The Columbia was so deep as it passed through the city and its current so powerful that two tiny bodies would quickly disappear.

Pasco police detectives, all of them hoping this was only a nightmare from a psychotic mind, found the little trailer cold and empty. There were children's clothes and toys there, teddy bears left behind — but no sign of Christopher and Ryan. They looked in the cupboards and found little food. There were only stacks of unpaid bills, and an almost palpable air of despair in the small mobile home.

Christine Jonsen was arrested, and she seemed relieved. She had asked to be taken into custody, saying that she was fully prepared to be hanged for what she had done. Long months of psychiatric evaluation lay ahead. Now there were so many "if onlys" spoken by her neighbors and the members of her church. If only they had known. But hindsight could not save either the little boys or Christine herself.

If Christine's sons were to be found so that there could be a funeral or a memorial service, it would take some kind of a miracle.

Since the majority of detectives think in terms of hard evidence and things that can be seen, touched, smelled, and proven to a jury absolutely, they are rarely impressed by psychics. Three thousand miles away from the Tri-Cities area, a detective in Nutley, New Jersey, had overcome his own doubts about the positive results that could come from clairvoyance. Salvatore Luberpazzi, of the Nutley Police Department, was highly resistant when he first met a fifty-four-year-old grandmother named Dorothy Allison. Dorothy was a typical middle-aged woman in the Italian community, but there were many people who had turned to her in desperation when all other methods to find their missing loved one had failed. She was neither highly educated nor extremely brilliant, but Dorothy Allison had a remarkable gift, one that sometimes haunted her so much that she wished it would just go away. She could see where the bodies of lost people rested. She was especially psychic when she was asked to find children, particularly children who were under water.

Luberpazzi had very reluctantly agreed to let her work on some of his cold cases. "It's a very strange feeling to go up to this woman and tell her what I'm looking for and she describes an area that's miles and miles away." He shook his head in wonderment as he said: "In the past eleven years, she has found twenty missing or deceased persons for us."

Dorothy Allison had no axe to grind. Unlike many well-known psychics, she certainly wasn't into clairvoyance for the money; she asked only for reimbursement for the cost of transportation and lodging when she had to travel far from her home. She had a family and would have preferred to be with them, but she accepted that she had been blessed — or cursed — with her ability to "see" what was hidden to everyone else. By the time Christine's boys vanished beneath the river's surface, Dorothy had long since overcome police skepticism about her ability to locate those she called "my babies . . . my angels." Although the earthly remains of missing children might be only decomposed skeletons, they were smiling, innocent children to her, and she was compelled by the visions that came to her.

Dorothy Allison's involvement in the search for missing children began in 1968 when she woke from a nightmare. She had seen the image of a little boy stuck in a pipe. For a month, she tried to put it out of her mind, and then she went to the Nutley police. When she told the desk sergeant what she had dreamed, she described his reaction: "The officer jumped off his chair like a maniac and told me a little boy with that description was missing and believed drowned."

The police followed Dorothy's instructions, and she led them to that small boy. Michael Kurcsics, five years old, was found caught in a drainage pipe, and became the first picture in Mrs. Allison's "book of angels."

She had seen that Michael's rubber boots were on the wrong feet, and down to that small detail, she was correct.

Soon, Dorothy pictured the body of fourteen-year-old Susan Jacobson and led Staten Island police to an oil drum where her killer had secreted her body. He was caught and convicted. She "saw" the grave of eighteen-year-old Debbie Kline of Waynesboro, Pennsylvania, and gave police a composite sketch of the man who had killed her. It was uncannily accurate, almost as if the prime suspect had posed for it.

Asked if she might be able to receive images from the other side of the country, Dorothy agreed to try. When she was alone and in a meditative mood, images rushed into her mind. Although Dorothy Allison had never been in Washington State, the pictures in her head sounded familiar to the Pasco police investigators. She told them that she could see Ryan and Christopher

Jonsen in a wide river. For some reason, she kept getting a sense of "doubles — everything is double." Even she didn't know what that meant.

Dorothy said she saw the bodies near a bridge, and she could make out the numbers seven and eight. She also saw the number four and thought that that might mean the bodies would be found in the fourth month. "And there are cars," she added. "Many cars parked nearby."

Dorothy's visions were published in an article in a local paper on March 21, and John Waibel, a retired man who lived in Wallulah Junction, some twenty miles south of the Tri-Cities, decided to see if he could locate an area similar to what she had described. He drove to a spot near Sacajawea Park, which was three miles downstream from the Pasco-Kennewick Bridge where Christine Jonsen said she'd thrown her children into the icy Columbia.

He stepped out of his truck, and his breath caught in his throat as he looked around. Right in front of him, he saw two huge electrical towers, two railroad bridges, two looming holding tanks. Two Rivers Park was just across the river. The park had a large parking lot filled with cars. And on one of the electrical transmission towers he read the number

"78." A nearby buoy bobbing in the river had "44" painted on it. Doubles. Doubles. *Doubles.*

Waibel began his eerie search, hoping that he wouldn't find what he was looking for. But he did. The body of two-year-old Ryan Jonsen, clad only in a diaper, rested face up where his body was caught on the rocks. Well preserved in the freezing water, he appeared to be only asleep.

Dorothy Allison had been tragically accurate.

And then, eleven days later, it was again doubles. It was now the first day of the fourth month, April 1, when a pair of seventeen-year-old twins from Hermiston, Oregon, were fishing in the Columbia River. The twins found Christopher's body. It, too, was lodged among the rocks of the river.

There were two more "angels" whose pictures would be placed in Mrs. Allison's pathetic scrapbook.

There was probably no one in the Tri-Cities area who could read who did not know the details of Christine Jonsen's "crime," so a change of venue was granted at the defense's request. Her trial began on October 3, in Seattle, with Benton-Franklin County Superior Court Judge Albert Yencopal presiding.

Franklin County Deputy Prosecutors Stan Moore and Michael Kinnie would argue that, although they agreed that Christine was emotionally disturbed, she was not legally insane under M'Naughton, the guideline in the State of Washington. Moore would insist in his opening statements that the young mother had prepared for her crime, and sought to avoid detection until she confessed, and that she had a purpose in what she was doing. These elements, he stressed, would block the defense claim that she did not know right from wrong at the time of her crime.

The state would not, however, seek the death penalty — a penalty that Christine herself was fully prepared to accept. She *wanted* to die so she could be with her children.

As the trial progressed, the six-man, six-woman jury were not immune from the overwhelming sense of grief that gripped the courtroom. There were many, many tears there. Christine wept quietly as her defense lawyers, J. D. Evans and Greg Lawless, described what her life had been like since her husband had walked out on her the prior Thanksgiving.

"She just broke," Evans said. "She thought she was evil and her husband was evil. She thought the children had no chance in life other than to go to hell."

Christine's plea — innocent by reason of insanity — seemed the most cogent plea ever heard in a courtroom. "It's our position," Evans said, "that no mother in her right mind, who loves her children, could take them to a bridge in the middle of winter and drop them into the water. There's a motive for every crime. The only reason or motive for what she did is insanity."

Christine, her soft, dark hair parted in the middle and her face virtually expressionless beyond a consuming sadness, had only one dress, a dress she wore each day to the long trial. Clothes mattered nothing to her; indeed, life itself seemed to mean nothing to her. Whatever the verdict, it was patently clear to observers that she herself had "died" on that windswept bridge in February, all hope and dreams gone for her as surely as they were for the smiling little boys she had adored.

Friends came forward to testify in her behalf, waitresses who had worked with her, women with little money themselves who had given up two days' work and paid their own fares to travel across the Cascade Mountains. They told of Christine's metamorphosis from a happy young wife to a desperate woman who had been deserted. They had watched her disintegrate as she was left penniless and stunned when her world evaporated. Neighbors from the trailer park took the witness stand and told of a Christine who had hugged baby Ryan two days before he died and crooned, "I love you." No one had ever seen her hurt her children, or even raise her voice to them.

Dr. Thomas Corlew, a psychiatrist from Eastern Washington State Hospital, testified that when he examined Christine in June, he had found her "the most profoundly depressed person I have ever seen." Corlew felt that she met both tests of legal insanity: In his opinion, she was unable to tell right from wrong on the night she killed her babies, and she was unable to perceive the nature and quality of her actions.

"The day after she killed her children, she seemed to be under the severe influence of an outside force [something] that seemed to be controlling her."

"Did she say what that influence was?" Evans asked.

"She said it was Satan."

Even the husband who had left her testified for the defense. He had left Christine, yes, but he had always found her to be a loving mother whose one concern was to see

513

that their sons were happy and healthy. His eyes, too, were haunted. He had to be thinking that if he hadn't left his family the tragedy would never have happened.

The Mormon leaders testified, castigating themselves for not realizing how profound Christine's mental aberration was.

Dr. Claude McCoy, a Seattle psychiatrist, testified for the prosecution. McCoy, who agreed with the defense lawyers when they pointed out that he had never personally examined Christine, said his diagnosis that she was legally sane at the time of her crime was based on his conclusions after reading police reports and medical documents. "People who have a mental illness usually know what they are doing," he said somewhat obscurely. "I believe Christine Jonsen is no exception."

The defense asked Dr. McCoy if he had *ever* concluded in court that a defendant was criminally insane.

"No, I have not," he admitted.

The tape of Christine Jonsen's confession to Detective Pittman played in the hushed courtroom. For twenty-five minutes, we heard the quavering voice of a mother who had killed her babies — to save them from hell. Several jurors wiped tears from their eyes as she relived the moments on the bridge, relived hearing the "kerplunk" as the children hit the water. Then she told how she had driven around for a while before going to City Hall. She thought that that was where the police station was located. She was then directed to the correct location, where she approached Detective Pittman.

In an attempt to console her, Pittman had murmured, "Things will work out. They always do."

"No," she had replied without hope. "They won't work out."

And now, "the best mother in the world," according to her friends, would have her fate decided by a jury. The prosecution claimed she was a woman who had planned her crime, however "mentally ill, mentally diseased, mentally defective." The defense scorned the state's psychiatric witness who had never even examined her, and deemed the taped confession only further proof of legal insanity.

Attorney Greg Lawless said, "You heard it — the way she talked . . . the flat voice . . . it gave me the chills."

The Christine Jonsen case was on the lips of everyone this writer talked to during the weekend of October 13–14. And the consensus of opinion was that she was, indeed, medically and legally insane, that she fit within the narrow parameters of M'Naughton.

All of us who waited for a verdict were reluctant to leave the marble corridor outside the courtroom. We expected the jury to return within a few hours. But time yawned, and to our surprise they deliberated more than fifteen hours. When they filed back in, the strain of their ordeal was apparent. Several seemed near tears, and their heads were bowed.

They did not even glance at Christine, and that was a very bad sign.

The jury foreman handed the verdict to the court clerk. They had found Christine guilty of first-degree murder on two counts.

Christine Jonsen showed no emotion at all. No tears. She had expected it, and she still believed that she was too unworthy to be forgiven. The verdict was only further proof that she needed to be punished: punished for being a bad wife, a bad mother, "a daughter of perdition." She had believed that the police would draw their guns and shoot her on that bleak February morning when she'd gone to tell them what she had done. And then she expected to be hanged. Now she expected to be sentenced to the gallows.

When her lawyers tried to comfort her, she could not speak to them.

If there was emotion in that courtroom, it was from the jurors. Immediately after

516

Christine was convicted, the jury foreman, Baxter Zilbauer, bitterly denounced the M'Naughton Rule, and the instructions to the jury that had left them no way to return with anything but a guilty verdict.

"We the members of the jury find the M'Naughton Rule morally objectionable. I speak for every member of the jury when I say this."

The other jurors nodded. One spoke up. "We had to find her guilty under this rule whether we wanted to or not."

The prosecution took no joy in the verdict. When a member of the courtroom gallery came up to congratulate Deputy Prosecutor Stan Moore on winning, he said curtly, "You don't understand. I don't want congratulations."

But the jury had been convinced that, as the law was interpreted, Christine Jonsen had known right from wrong. And that was the criterion they had to base their judgment on. Had they had the option to consider whether she had the substantial capacity to conform her conduct to the requirements of the law, the jury would not have convicted her.

Christine faced the possibility of two life sentences in prison, which would mean that she would be behind bars for at least thirteen years and four months, twice that if her two sentences were to be served consecutively. If she should go to prison, few informed people believed she would survive. She had already been harassed and tormented by female prisoners in county jails. At the time, one long-time probation worker commented bluntly, "If she goes to Purdy [the Washington State Women's Prison], they will kill her. Some morning, the guards will find her dead."

A Seattle homicide detective, not actively involved in the case, lamented the problem. "I've seen several cases where killers were frankly psychotic. The blame is on society. We simply have nowhere to send them, and our laws stop us from forcing them to obtain treatment before they become so sick that they do kill someone. Then, when they do, what do you do with them? Warehouse them? It's a problem the people are going to have to face up to — and change the laws before it's too late."

Christine did not go to prison, at least not in the immediate aftermath of her trial. She went, instead, to a state mental hospital to undergo more tests. It was conceivable that Judge Yencopal could place her on probation. Oddly, she simply disappeared from the headlines, and as the years have passed, I have been unable to find her. I wish I could say whether Christine is alive or dead, or if she ever managed to pick up the frayed threads of her life.

One thing I know — Christine Jonsen's dreams will never be free of what happened on the edge of the Columbia River. She threw her life away, too — as surely as if she had leaped after the children.

Perhaps she wishes she had.

... Or We'll Kill You

If any one of us were to be totally candid, I think all women would admit to moments of fear that we might encounter a rapist or some other violent man intent on taking us away from all the people and places that make us feel safe. We know statistics are on our side, and that the chance of meeting up with someone infinitely dangerous are slim. And yet there are always times when the sun goes down and we are alone. Although we didn't expect to be walking or driving down a shadowy street, sometimes circumstances work out that way. Or we are alone in our own homes, listening to every creaking floorboard or the wind riffling bushes so that they scrape noisily against the house.

We wonder, "What would I do if I had to fight for my life? Would I panic or would I be able to use my head and make rational choices to save myself?"

Some of us have taken self-defense

courses, while others hide their heads in the sand and try to ignore the possibility that something bad might happen. How many of us carry Mace or even a gun? Some women always carry a pair of athletic shoes in their cars so that they can slip out of high-heeled shoes after work, and feel somehow safer that they can run if they have to.

I can't even count the number of women I've written about who did *not* survive encounters with total strangers or with someone they had trusted. I can't tally up the stories told to me by women who lived to tell about what happened to them.

The story that follows was told to me by one of my readers, just a sketchy overview in an email at first, and then shared in minute detail when I asked her to tell me more. I found Kari Lindholm's* story totally compelling and an experience that should be shared with other women. With Kari's permission, the tale of her hours of chilling terror follows. By all rights, she probably should not have survived — but, somehow, she did.

As you read this, think about what *you* would have done. More important, plan what you will do if you should ever encounter someone like the suspects in Kari's case. Every self-defense expert I have ever talked to has told me that the women who live through an attack like this are those who have some kind of plan already programmed into their brains.

"The women who don't make it are the ones who freeze with terror — the ones who say, 'This can't be happening to me — it's a bad dream.'" An expert on self-defense at a Nashville, Tennessee, conference told a roomful of detectives and postrape counselors: "The ones who survive are ready. They tap into a plan they have — just in case. They don't lose those vital first seconds they can use to get away."

Kari Lindholm was happy with her life. At twenty-seven, she was a pretty, healthy young woman. She had a good marriage, and a job she loved. She and her husband, Ben,* were hoping to start a family. If there was any sadness at all in her life, it was that she had failed to conceive despite several months of trying.

Because she was normally so upbeat, it was odd that on the night of September 20, 1980, Kari woke up from a terrible nightmare. "I dreamed that I'd been kidnapped," she remembers. "But I was using some of the techniques I'd learned in my training as a counselor to help me get away."

In a sense, it was a familiar dream. Kari worked as a counselor at the Solano County Crisis Intervention Office in Fairfield, California. It was a twenty-four-hour facility, commonly referred to as "Sancho Panza," named for Don Quixote's right-hand man in

Cervantes' sixteenth-century novel. The effete Quixote, a member of the lowest rank of Spanish nobility, was a little nuts — but well-intentioned — and believed his quest was to save the poor, the orphaned, and the oppressed. Sancho Panza, a stocky commoner, was his partner, his "Tonto," the one who had the common sense in the duo. Still, he eventually came to believe in Don Quixote's cause — even as Quixote challenged windmills and a flock of sheep, thinking them giants and invading armies.

So Sancho Panza was an apt name for a crisis center that was an island of calm and compassion in the midst of the craziness that often came to them via phone calls, drop-in visits from people on the edges of society, or lawmen who brought in disturbed patients.

Kari Lindholm was used to the chaos in the county-funded facility on Ohio Street. The staff served all manner of people with problems. "We had a telephone hotline, some group therapy sessions, and we were there to help people. Sometimes it was abused women who had run away from domestic violence; occasionally, we counseled rape victims. Basically, anybody in crisis could call or come to Sancho Panza."

It wasn't unusual to have sheriff's deputies bring clients in, so the counselors had the sense that they had armed backup nearby when they needed help. Lots of people with large and small problems simply walked into Sancho Panza on their own. "Clients" who were admitted as in-patients were often emotionally disturbed, but not so much that they were considered dangerous.

The center was located in a big old house, just around the corner from a halfway house where a few residents with criminal convictions who weren't deemed dangerous enough to go to prison were housed. Staff there were also available to the counselors at the crisis center. Security wasn't a problem, or at least it didn't seem to be until the night of September 20.

Sancho Panza had eight beds, a huge kitchen space, a waiting room with old but comfortable couches and chairs, and offices in the back of the house. Two counselors at a time — preferably a male and female duo — were always available. Kari Lindholm routinely worked the "graveyard shift" with a male partner. Her husband, Ben, worried about her but she assured him that she was perfectly safe.

And then on Saturday night, September 20, Kari's regular male coworker called in sick, and Shelly Corelli[*] agreed to fill in. Shelly and Kari fielded the calls and the people who were brought in or dropped in. It was the first day of autumn, and the moon was full. Anyone who has ever worked in law enforcement, hospital delivery rooms, crisis centers, or other facilities that deal with emergencies knows full well that it is not just folklore that says the fullness of the moon and the surging of tides that come with it have a great deal to do with "craziness" and the unexpected in human behavior.

It was a deceptively lovely night: Eucalyptus trees filled the air with their pungent odor and the heat of the Napa Valley day cooled rapidly. Summer was over.

The two women overseeing Sancho Panza on the graveyard shift were constantly busy, running between the phones and the counter as they dealt with humans in distress. Cops came and went, the resident clients were uneasy, and Kari and Shelly had no breaks. As soon as they handled one situation, another seemed to pop up.

It was three-thirty in the morning when two men walked in. They said they had been on their way to Reno 120 miles east, but they had run out of gas. "We decided to wait here," one of them said, "until it gets daylight and the gas stations open."

Both men looked to be in their midthirties. One of them was very small, not more than five feet, seven inches tall, and he couldn't have weighed more than 125 pounds. He had straight black hair that he'd slicked back. Kari noticed that his teeth needed attention from a dentist: They were dirty and crooked. He didn't say much.

The other man also had black hair, but his had been cut professionally. He was nearly six feet tall. Kari noticed that he had numerous tattoos, but the only one she recognized at first was a teardrop beneath his left eye. He told them that his name was John and his friend's name was Mike.

John mentioned the name of one of their counselors, and seemed familiar with Sancho Panza. Kari didn't recognize his name or his face, but assumed that he had probably worked with someone on the day shift. He was quite talkative, seemingly at ease. Shelly thought John looked familiar, and vaguely recalled that he had been an outpatient at Sancho Panza. When she looked at him more closely, she realized that he had been in on prior occasions to talk with some of the counselors. She didn't know what his background was, but he was an "alumnus" and she wasn't at all uneasy about letting him wait there.

They routinely saw people from all walks of life come through Sancho Panza's door, and the two men didn't ring any alarm bells in their minds.

"We were so busy that neither Shelly nor I had time to talk to them very much," Kari recalls. "They sipped coffee and smoked out in the living room part of the house where people can wait. I remember that one of them came back once and asked if he could make more coffee. It was the one named John."

About four-fifteen that morning, one of the female residents of the crisis center became very agitated and threatened suicide. Kari and Shelly were used to such psychotic breaks among their residents, and Kari quickly called the Solano County Sheriff's Office, while Shelly enlisted the two strangers to help her in restraining the out-of-control resident. They quickly stepped forward to help her.

Despite their skinny bodies, John and Mike proved to be strong enough to hold on to the hysterical patient. Kari and Shelly were grateful that they were there — since they had no male employees to help them. Within a few minutes, two sheriff's cars arrived. Solano County deputies Jim Bridewell, Paul King, and Steve Begley evaluated the situation and called an ambulance. Then they helped load the patient into the rig to be transported to Napa State Hospital.

The excitement was over within minutes.

"John and Mike went back to the living room and sat down again," Kari said. "And Shelly and I got back to filling out our paperwork."

It was quiet for the first time that night, save for a clock ticking and the occasional wails from an ambulance or a police unit far away. Smoke rose in clouds from the living room area as the men chain-smoked. Soon it was five-thirty in the morning — not too long until daylight. The full moon would blur in the sky as the sun rose, and the long, difficult night would be over.

Kari looked forward to going home to a hot shower and several hours of sleep. Maybe her husband, Ben, would be able to join her for breakfast. They hardly saw each other when she was working nights and he was on a day shift, working for the county. Bent over the log she was working on, Kari was only peripherally aware that one of the strangers was asking Shelly a question.

And then something completely unexpected happened.

As Kari concentrated on filling out the required report of the suicidal incident, she felt someone behind her. Before she could turn around, a man's strong arm snaked around her upper body and held her fast. She had no warning. Suddenly she was helpless, pinned to her chair from behind.

"He was holding me tight above my chest with his left arm," she said later. "In his right hand, he held a knife, and he was pressing it against my neck."

She could smell his acrid sweat and feel the tenseness in his body. Mostly, she was in shock. She hadn't even realized the men were in the room until one of them grabbed her. The knife was cold against the skin of her neck.

"He told me the knife was razor sharp, and then he said, 'I will slit your throat open unless you do exactly what I say.' "

Kari didn't struggle; she forced herself to stay as calm as possible. She had managed to turn around just long enough to see that it was the man she knew as John — the taller one of the duo who had been waiting for sunrise.

"We have been running drugs and we are fucked up, desperate men," he rasped. "Just take it easy, and be careful."

Kari waited to see what they wanted. She couldn't see what Shelly was doing, and didn't dare look at her.

Shelly stared at the smaller man. He was carrying an electric cord he'd cut from a lamp and a tieback from the drapes. "Okay," the taller man — John — said. "This is what we're going to do. We don't want to hurt you. We just want to tie you up."

He ordered Shelly onto the floor on her stomach, and the one called Mike quickly tied her wrists together behind her back, and then looped the cords around one of her ankles, drawing her leg up so that she was hog-tied.

"It's too tight," she cried, struggling to get free.

Mike spoke for the first time. *"Don't,"* he said. There was something about his tone that was chilling, and, frightened, Shelly stopped protesting.

"We want all your money," John said, "and one of those cars out front. Who owns the silver car?"

"It's mine," Kari said.

Gradually, John's arm, still holding her against the chair, relaxed, but John continued to bark out orders. "Close the drapes."

She tensed. What were the men going to do to them once no one outside could see what was going on? She and Shelly couldn't hope for help if no one knew they were in trouble. She knew that the Sheriff's Department were about to come to the end of their shift; chances were they were filling out paperwork, too, and probably weren't out on the road. That meant they wouldn't be bringing anyone into Sancho Panza soon.

Kari got up slowly and went to the front windows where she pulled the drapery cords. Shut inside now with two armed men, Kari and Shelly felt even more foreboding.

"Now," John said to Kari, "I want you to tear the last pages out of your log — anything that mentions we were here. And don't move too quickly or your throat will be cut."

She did as he said, handing the pages to him. He stuffed them in his pocket. She could see that the other man — Mike — had Shelly on the floor, tied up.

She wondered if they were both about to be killed.

No. John was asking for money. "Tell me where your purses are."

Kari told him, and he ordered her to get them from the closet. "And your car keys, too," he added.

Despite her training, Kari began to cry. She had dealt with a lot of tense situations, but this was beyond anything she had imagined — except for her dream the night before. She wondered now if she had dreamed that because she was going to die soon — if it was some kind of warning. *Why* hadn't she paid more attention?

"I'll get the purses," she said, "but please don't hurt me."

"I won't hesitate to kill you if you cry or get hysterical," John answered in a voice as cold as ice.

Again, Kari begged the men not to hurt her. "You can have the keys to my car, anything — just don't hurt us."

"I've never hurt anyone in my life," John said in a steely voice, "and I don't want to hurt you. We're just going to take you out to a field and let you go."

She didn't believe him, but at that point, Kari pulled herself together. She knew he was right on the edge, and that she had to stay strong or she would set him off. She had no doubt at all that he would just as soon kill them. By sheer force of will she stopped herself from crying.

"OK," she said. "I will do whatever you say."

That was, apparently, the right answer — and Kari could see John breathe easier.

"Go get your purses out of the closet and your car keys," he ordered. "I want you to take the keys out of your purse for me." Kari moved to the closet, grabbed her purse and Shelly's, and dropped them on the floor. John picked them up.

"You," he said, pointing at Kari, "you are going with us."

At least she and Shelly weren't going to be killed right here. But they were going to be separated. Shelly couldn't move, hog-tied as she was. And John still held the knife point against the skin of Kari's neck.

John turned to Shelly, "What time is the next shift coming in?"

"Seven."

"You'd better be right. If you value your friend's life, don't call the sheriff, police, or anyone."

"Shelly," Kari pleaded, "*please* don't call anyone."

"I won't," Shelly said. "I promise."

"I don't want you to call anybody, or answer the phone, or wake anyone up until after seven o'clock," John said again, more forcefully this time. *"Or Kari will be dead. I'll kill her for sure!"*

And then the two men and Kari were gone, and Shelly was alone in the silent office, tied up so tightly that it felt as if her hands and feet were going numb. Her attempts at getting free only sent her muscles into spasms.

Outside, Kari unlocked her four-year-old Ford Granada with shaking hands. John forced her into the backseat, and then crawled in beside her. Mike got behind the wheel of her car.

"You know we're going to kill you," John said flatly. "But first, we need three hundred dollars."

Kari believed him. She was more frightened than she had ever been in her life. But she saw that her captors were extremely nervous, too, and suspected they were under the influence of some kind of drug. She had to go along with them while she figured out a way to survive.

Now John asked her more questions about the shift changes and residents at Sancho Panza. "How many residents live there? What time do they get up? Are your conversations in the office automatically recorded? When does the morning shift come to work?"

She told him the truth — that there were five residents and they didn't usually wake up until after eight. The day shift counselor, Gracie,* came to work at 7:00 A.M.

"And the recorder in the office?" John pushed.

"There is no recorder in the office," she said. "That would be illegal, don't you think?"

Kari sensed that her best approach would

be to let John think she was on his side, or at least that she was treating him with respect. If anything, Mike was more nervous than John. Or maybe he was just a lousy driver. He swerved, driving so erratically that they either were going to end up in a ditch or, blessedly, would attract the eye of a cop in a squad car.

John told her that they wanted to head for Reno, by way of Sacramento. "What's the quickest way to get on the freeway?"

For the life of her, Kari couldn't visualize the roads nearby. She was still so frightened. They had turned left on West Texas from Ohio Street, and then right on Beck Avenue at her suggestion. But she'd made a mistake, and they couldn't find an eastbound freeway entrance.

"You'd better think quick," John warned her again, "or you are dead."

Kari was too scared to think, her mind frozen with fear, and they got on the wrong side of the freeway — onto the lanes heading west toward Vallejo and San Francisco, *away* from Sacramento. Finally, Mike said he was going to get off the freeway and take surface roads. At least they would be heading east again toward Reno. Their trip was a comedy of errors, or would have been if it weren't so menacing.

Kari's job and training demanded that she be competent about assessing people in a short time. Gradually, she found herself moving into her social-worker mode, still a victim certainly, but a woman who knew that her own survival depended on reading John and Mike correctly.

"I quickly assessed John as emotionally unpredictable, emotionally unstable, and insecure about his own masculinity," she says. She knew she had to avoid startling or frightening him, and, above all, should do nothing to undercut his tenuous grasp of his masculinity. That was easy in group therapy sessions — but infinitely more difficult when she herself was his captive.

As they hurtled, willy-nilly, along the dark, almost deserted freeway, Kari tried to think. If they got her to a field, she was pretty sure they weren't going to just let her out there. Alive, she would be a danger to them and their freedom.

Back at Sancho Panza, Shelly Corelli worked desperately to get out of the twists and turns of the lamp cord and the drape sash that bound her. By wiggling and twisting, she managed to slip one wrist out, and then was able to use that hand to pull the cord off her foot. Kari and the men had been gone for about twenty minutes, and Shelly wasn't sure where they were. For all she knew, they might still be out in front of Sancho Panza. She didn't dare risk going out that way. And she didn't want to stay around to use the phone. Instead, she crawled along the floor toward the rear of the building. She exited through a patio door and crept toward the fence. She pulled enough boards out so she could slide through. One of the counselors lived nearby, and Shelly ran to pound on Jack Owens's[*] door.

Woken from a sound sleep, Owens opened his door to see Shelly standing there, disheveled from crawling through the fence, the severed electric cord still hanging from one wrist.

"They've got Kari," she said. "We've got to call the sheriff!"

Owens ran back to Sancho Panza and called the Solano County sheriff and Fairfield Police Department's emergency lines.

Along with Fairfield officer Fred Jones, the same trio of officers who had responded to the call for help with the suicidal resident only about an hour earlier were back. They had the advantage of having seen the men who had abducted Kari. But there was no sign of them or of Kari or her car now.

An all-points bulletin was issued for the

Ford Granada and its occupants. They all hoped that there were still *three* people in the car.

The taller man — John Martin — *was* familiar to some of the counseling staff at Sancho Panza, and police learned that he had walked away from the Delancey Street facility in San Francisco without authorization only the night before. A look at his rap sheet was not encouraging: John Martin had a number of aliases, including "Butch Martin" and "Leroi Martin." He had previously been arrested for rape, grand theft, and some lesser crimes. Martin had been charged under California statute 261.3 P.C. — "Rape by Force." Deemed a candidate for rehabilitation, he had been placed in the Delancey Street offenders' program in lieu of state prison.

The investigators also called Ben Lindholm,★ Kari's husband, and told him that his wife was missing — missing under highly disturbing circumstances. He threw on his clothes and drove to Sancho Panza. He made up his mind that he would not tell Kari's mother — who lived hundreds of miles away, just north of Los Angeles — that her daughter had been kidnapped. If they could find Kari quickly, her mother might never have to know. Why put her through the anxiety if he didn't have to?

If the news wasn't good, Kari's mother would have to know soon enough.

Sergeant Jim Bridewell went into the living room to gather up whatever evidence the kidnappers might have left. He carefully bagged their coffee cups into evidence, along with the cord from around Shelly's wrist and a pile of cigarette butts. Then he asked that an ID technician be dispatched to the abduction scene to dust for fingerprints.

The counselor due to come on duty for the morning shift, Gracie Phelps,* was notified, and she came to work early so that, if Kari somehow managed to call, she could be told that everything was normal and the police had not been called. Moreover, *someone* had to be on duty at Sancho Panza to oversee the residents and the clients who would be coming in for counseling.

Kari was still alive. It was probably lucky that she didn't know about John Martin's criminal background, and yet she dreaded the possibility that either he or the man behind the wheel might have more than kidnapping in mind.

Unfortunately, she was right. Once they appeared to be heading in the right direction, John turned toward Kari and applied more pressure with the knife that he continued to hold against the skin of her throat, stopping just short of drawing blood. He traced an invisible pattern in her flesh, enjoying the way she involuntarily cringed.

"Take off your pants," he ordered, adding, "I'm sure you knew this was going to happen."

Kari had made up her mind to do whatever she had to do to live, and she had known all along that a sexual attack was a very real danger. She had to disassociate her body from her mind. If she fought John, as unstable as he seemed to be, it might well set him off. She had no hope of escape at this point. She had to do what he ordered.

"I took off my shoes first, and then my pants. John said, 'Keep going,' so I took off my nylons, which left me completely exposed from the waist down . . ."

"Lay down [sic]," John directed. "No — lay down on top of me." He didn't remove his trousers but unzipped his fly as he rested on his back in the backseat. Kari obeyed his order and moved on top of him.

"He then started kissing me, thrusting his tongue in my mouth. He started rubbing his penis mechanically against my pubic area until he started to get an erection. John also put his finger up my vagina and began to probe, hurtfully."

She tried not to think about his body odor, or what sexually transmitted diseases he might have. She knew how insecure he was, and that showing distaste or revulsion toward him would surely make him angry.

"I didn't fight or struggle or protest while John was raping me," she recalls. "I had decided that my best bet was to go along with him. The knife was ever present. He told me to get on the bottom. I was so frightened that when he was through — if he was *ever* through — that would be when he would kill me, and dump me off on some deserted road. If he didn't have an orgasm, he would be so angry that he would probably kill me."

It seemed to Kari that, either way, she didn't have much of a chance.

"John thrust his penis up my vagina so violently that it hurt and he started pumping. I thought he was going to knock the wind out of me," she remembers. "After what seemed like an eternity, he had what *seemed* like an orgasm. His body sort of 'tremored' and he seemed to lose his erection. He got off me, and told me to get my clothes back on."

Kari dressed, all but her shoes. Satiated, John appeared to feel some regret for raping her.

"I'm not proud of what I just did," he said, "but I'm a sicko person, and I haven't had a woman in a long time."

Kari would never remember just when they had finally gotten on the freeway headed toward Reno. Her captors had a plan of sorts. Their main concern was to get as far from Fairfield and Sancho Panza as they could before 7 A.M. when the day shift showed up for work. They would find Shelly tied up on the floor of the office, and would surely call the police and report her kidnapping. They planned to ditch Kari's car before then, and obtain a rental car. They had expected to find enough money in the two women's purses to pay for the rental car, but they still needed three hundred dollars — whatever that was for.

John now pawed through the two purses, looking for cash and credit cards. But Shelly had only fifteen dollars in hers, and Kari had nothing but change.

"I have my paycheck," Kari offered. "It's for $306.50. I can probably cash it at an Albertson's store because I have a check guarantee card with them."

"We're not going back to Fairfield," John argued.

"No — no," Kari soothed. "There are

some Albertson's stores in Sacramento. I think they'll honor my guarantee card."

Although she had convinced John and Mike that they needed her alive in order to get cash, she was very careful not to say much to either of them. "They were very jumpy, nervous, and seemed like they could blow it at any moment."

As they hurtled east on the freeway, John told Kari that the two of them had been planning to assault her and Shelly as they sat in the living room of Sancho Panza. "At first, we were going to kill both of you, steal your purses, and take one of your cars," he said, as easily as if he were talking about the weather.

It chilled her blood to think that the two men had been sitting near them for hours, calmly planning their murders when, all the while, she and Shelly had been completely unaware of the danger.

"For some reason," Kari remembers, "they didn't kill us. It might have been because we had to call the sheriff for the resident and the deputies arrived so quickly. Maybe they figured it would be too risky to hang around there."

John kept telling Kari that they were "totally desperate men. We don't have a goddammed thing going for us. We don't give a fuck what happens."

And then, with what seemed to be flawed reasoning, John explained that it would be better for them when they were captured to be facing murder charges as well as kidnapping, auto theft, and any other charges. He said that would get them fewer years in the penitentiary. Kari didn't dare ask them how it could possibly work out that way. Murder charges certainly didn't add any stars to felons' crowns.

But she didn't argue with them. Any criticism on her part would, she knew, be like waving a red flag in front of a bull.

The two men spoke of how they had never had a chance in their miserable lives. "Nobody never gave us no breaks," Mike whined.

Kari realized now that John must have been treated at Sancho Panza, because he knew the names of several counselors who worked there. While he and Mike bemoaned their unhappy past, Kari also detected anger, hostility, and fear.

"This hostility was precariously maintained and controlled," she says. "They needed constant reassurance that we weren't being followed by the California Highway Patrol or the Solano County sheriff's deputies. I kept telling them that Shelly

547

wouldn't call the police, and that she was tied up, anyway, so she *couldn't* call anyone. Mike, John, and I agreed that I should call Sancho Panza right at 7:00 A.M. so I could catch Gracie before *she* called anyone."

Even though Kari was cooperating with her kidnappers and subtly giving them the sense that the three of them were in this dilemma together and they seemed to trust her, she still believed that they intended to kill her.

"I just didn't know when . . ."

If she had any chance of escape, Kari knew that she had to get to a place where there were other people around. She didn't want anyone else to get hurt, but she hoped she could let someone know where she was. She thought about how she might alert a clerk or manager at an Albertson's store. But if John caught her signaling, she had no doubt he would dispose of her as soon as possible.

Now, as they entered the outskirts of Sacramento, they exited the freeway at the Jefferson off-ramp. Kari had thought that would take them into the historic Old Town section of the California state capital, but once again, she was lost. Mike was getting antsy. He wanted to dump her car before 7:00 A.M. when an alarm might go out from the day crew at Sancho Panza. He was trying to find a deserted area along the Sacramento River where her car wouldn't be noticeable, but they couldn't even find the river itself.

"I'm goin' back on the freeway," Mike muttered.

Now they were headed south toward Los Angeles. But Mike jumped from freeway to freeway, and ended up on the one that led back to San Francisco.

"Mike seemed to know where he was going," Kari remembered, "and I saw a sign that said, 'Airport Boating Recreation,' and he got off there. Both of them were really nervous because it was almost seven. They were frantic to find a deserted phone booth where I could call Sancho Panza and tell the day shift people not to call the police . . ."

They came to a small café on a narrow road that ran parallel to the Sacramento River, and John pulled Kari out of the car, warning her, "You better pray that nobody at Sancho Panza has called the sheriff. Your life depends on that."

He kept the knife pressed into her flesh as he walked her to the phone booth.

"I placed a collect phone call," Kari said, "and Gracie answered the phone in the office."

Kari's voice sounded odd even to her as she said, "Gracie — please tell me that you have not called the sheriff, the police, or anyone — otherwise I'm dead." She had to be very careful what she said, because John had his head pressed to hers so he could listen to the other end of the conversation.

"I haven't called anyone, Kari," Gracie lied. "And I won't call anyone. I promise."

John grabbed the phone from Kari's hand, and said, "Shelly, your friend's life depends on this. If we see a sheriff, we *will* kill her. We have nothing to lose — we're going to the pen. If nobody comes after us, she can phone after two. If everything goes right, we will leave her in a designated area, locked in her car." It wasn't Shelly on the end of the line; it was Gracie, but he had forgotten that. "And Shelly," he said, using the wrong name again, "we're going to party awhile before we let her go."

Kari wondered how Shelly was doing and if they had untied her yet, but she didn't dare ask. "Gracie," Kari said, cutting her off before she could blurt out something that might trigger John into another spate of paranoia. "I *will* call you at two o'clock —"

John placed his finger on the phone lever, and the phone went dead.

Unfortunately, the phone call had been too

short for the investigators to trace the location Kari had called from. Her coworkers prayed that the "partying" John Martin had referred to didn't mean that Kari was headed for a hellish experience.

And then they were in Kari's car again, hurtling along back roads until Mike turned at a sign that pointed toward the airport. The kidnappers decided it would be best to get a rental car, one that wouldn't be so easy to spot by police — just in case the people back at Sancho Panza were lying and had already reported Kari's abduction.

Kari herself didn't know if they had or not. Gracie had been amazingly cool, and she wondered if that meant there was already a dragnet out looking for her car.

She devoutly hoped so.

Her kidnappers told her they would need the three hundred dollars in cash just as soon as they had the rental car. She had a leaden feeling that she was not going to survive this crazy crisscrossing of the city of Sacramento; something would surely go wrong again. John continually reminded her that she was going to be killed, but then he would reverse himself and say he might let her live if she did everything they told her to do. He was far too volatile to read.

They parked at the airport and John led

Kari toward the Hertz rental counter. He warned her again not to "pull anything" because he still had the knife. "It's right here under my sweater," he repeated. "You stay cool, and you pretend you're my wife, and tell them we need the car for two days because we're going to Reno."

It wasn't 8:00 A.M. yet and Kari's heart sank as she saw the Hertz desk wasn't technically open for business. But the woman behind the glass spotted them, smiled, and opened the window.

The clerk noted that the couple appeared quite nervous, but the man kept talking to her — explaining that they were headed for Reno. He jingled change in his pocket as he said they were going "gambling."

Kari said what John had told her to say: that her brother-in-law had dropped them off outside the airport.

"I thought they were having an affair," the Hertz clerk said later, "and that was why they seemed so anxious."

The woman showed her a credit card in the name of Ben Lindholm (which the clerk noted did not match the name "John" that the man had given her).

The woman began to write a personal check for the car, saying, "It's OK — he knows about this."

That made the Hertz representative believe even more that these two were sneaking away for a stolen weekend. "John" was being absolutely charming and charismatic, babbling on about how he and "the wife" were going to have a fabulous holiday in Reno. Still, when Kari handed her check over, the clerk told her she couldn't accept the check. She had to have something with Kari's name on it.

Kari glanced at John, and he seemed perfectly at ease, playing his role as her husband. Kari had her Chevron Travelers' Card, and the woman behind the counter said that would do. Kari knew it was out of date, and she hoped the clerk would notice that and at least call her manager or *someone*. Any other time she would have, but this time, she was distracted by John's rapid-fire conversation. The clerk didn't care who they were or what their relationship was — as long as their credit was good.

Although Kari darted her eyes around the rental car area, she didn't see anyone she could run to for help; at this time of day, it was virtually deserted. If she screamed, she would only endanger the Hertz clerk. The two women would have no chance of overpowering John, not with his knife just beneath his sweater. As far as finding a place to hide in, there was nothing, no stairwell or cubbyhole or door she could rush through and shut behind her. The moment John realized she was trying to escape, she would be as good as dead.

She gave up for the moment. Maybe she would get another chance at their next stop.

Soon, they were out of the airport and headed toward the red and white Thunderbird that John had selected. Once more, Kari wondered about his common sense; it wasn't an inconspicuous car. It was a dumb choice for someone who wanted to avoid the police.

"You drive," John ordered. "I don't have a driver's license. Mike will follow us in your car until we find a place to ditch it."

She almost laughed. John had already broken a number of laws that were far more serious than driving without a valid license. But she didn't argue; she climbed behind the wheel and put a shaky foot on the accelerator.

"We headed back toward the river," Kari remembers. "It was about ten miles away from the airport, and we were on the road that ran beside the river again. John told me to take a road off to the right, but I missed it, and had to turn around. We were in a farming area and he finally told me to pull the car off the dirt road next to some kind of abandoned structure, with a lot of trees around. I knew that they were probably going to kill me at that point and stuff my body in the trunk of my car.

"John told me to get my belongings out of my car. There was no one around, not a person, not a car, for miles."

She wondered if this was to be the "field" where they would "drop her off." Or if they were going to lock her in her car trunk. In California in September, under a hot sun, she would suffocate in there before anyone found her.

And then, just as Kari accepted she was about to die, she was surprised to hear John order her into the rental car. She sat in the middle of the front seat between Mike and John — who had changed his mind about the dangers of not having a license and was now driving.

The men seemed to have relaxed a bit, now that they had another car, and, seemingly, a new identity. But Kari was still full of dread. "My life depended on my getting that three hundred dollars for them."

Kari had homed in on their predictable behavior, but that didn't make her feel much safer. Their pattern of response was up and down, and back and forth. But she figured they needed her at *least* until she got the money for them. They were leery of going in to cash a check without her. As she tried to lull John and Mike into believing they could trust her, Kari found herself employing the same arguments and sentences that she had used in her dream only last night.

It was eerie that her dream was keeping her alive — at least for the moment.

Even now, the California Highway Patrol troopers and sheriff's deputies from several counties were spreading out looking for the Ford Granada. But they weren't likely to find it; it was tucked away back in the brush near the broken-down farmhouse near the Sacramento River. Kari and her captors were in the sporty Thunderbird heading east once more — toward Reno.

Kari's husband knew that the last time she was seen, she was captive, driving off with two strange and violent men, a knife held against her neck. Ben Lindholm knew that *anything* might have happened to his wife in the hours since 5:30 A.M. She could be hundreds of miles away, she could be injured, or — and he tried not to think about it — she could be dead. Ben called a close friend, a man who worked at the Solano County Probation Office, and asked him to check for any prior arrests of the man who had given his name as John Martin when he came into Sancho Panza. Ben now knew that Kari was with a sexual predator. Shelly had heard John threaten to kill Kari several times before they drove off with her.

As the morning passed with no word of Kari, it was very difficult to keep hoping for a happy outcome. Ben Lindholm could only sit by his phone waiting for it to ring. He had faith in Kari's ability to handle emergencies, but this was one in which she was outnumbered and outweighed.

Detective Ray Van Eck of Solano County told him that the entire California police network was now alerted to watch for the Lindholms' car and for Kari and her abductors. That only reminded Ben of how far away Kari might be by now.

"I knew I had to find some money for them," Kari said. "John kept asking if there was a highway patrolman behind us. I had to do a considerable amount of reassuring with them, and tell them that, 'No, there aren't any highway patrolmen behind us, and we're not going to see any. We're in a whole different car now — we look just like anybody else on the freeway.'

"That seemed to relax them, and that was exactly what I was aiming for. I knew if I

557

could get them to feel relaxed around me — and trust me — that I could make my escape when they least expected it."

Kari planned her words very carefully, determined to make her captors believe that she was very much like them. She created a life story for herself as someone who had also had a rough childhood who was just trying to get by in an uncaring world.

"I had to make them think that I came from a background similar to theirs in order to develop bonds of trust. It made them nervous when I got upset, so I tried to display a positive air — assuring them that I would find a way to get them their three hundred dollars."

Clearly, Mike and John didn't draw much strength from one another. Kari realized she was succeeding in bolstering their egos. She could at least put temporary Band-Aids on them by telling them how she had risen above her miserable childhood.

"If I can do it," she said, "you can, too!"

She wanted to seem very strong to them and still maintain her image as someone who had suffered, too.

She didn't feel strong. It hadn't yet been three hours since they left Sancho Panza, but it seemed like days had passed. Every nerve in her body was standing on end; she had believed she was on the edge of death many times as they stumbled around Sacramento, and that wasn't a feeling that went away easily.

It was close to 9:00 A.M., and the thick commuter traffic was beginning to slack off. Now they planned to get off the freeway at Elkhorn Drive in the North Highlands section. She knew where there was an Albertson's store, but she pointed out a Safeway, the first supermarket they came to. Once more, John, his knife tucked into his sleeve, walked Kari into a building. This time, she tried to cash her paycheck.

The clerk shook her head. They could not cash checks for any more than the amount of purchases. John turned on the charm while Kari darted her eyes around, looking for someplace she might run, but again, she found no shelter nearby. It would be foolhardy of her to try to run.

Finally, John picked up a twelve-pack of beer and some cigarettes. The clerk, responding to his compliments, grudgingly allowed Kari to write a check for twenty dollars over the amount on the sales slip.

Kari had her role down pat. No matter how frightened she was, she managed to smile and even laugh at John's jokes so that he would think she was calm and had no intention of bailing on them. But this didn't give her a chance to signal anyone with her eyes, and she had no way to write a note to leave behind.

They hurried back to the Thunderbird, and drove on the surface street until they came to the Albertson's store. Once again, the clerk shook her head. Kari's check-cashing card was for the Fairfield-area stores, and there was no manager on duty to OK handing out over three hundred dollars. Kari nodded and kept her face calm, but she wondered how she could be having so much bad luck. Inside, she felt like screaming.

"So," John said when they were back in the Thunderbird, "what's your next plan for getting our money?"

Kari thought fast. "I have some friends who live in North Highlands — not far from here. They keep money in a safe in their house. They might cash my check."

"Let's go," John said. "Maybe we should drive by their house and see if they're home."

There was a car in the driveway, but John said he wanted to be cautious. "We'll go to a pay phone," he said. "You call them up, and tell them you have car trouble and you need some cash to pay for the repair job."

Kari did as she was told, but she felt completely hopeless as her friends' phone rang a dozen or more times and no one answered. It seemed as if the whole world was turning its back on her.

Only yesterday, Kari Lindholm had been happy and secure. She and Ben had their problems, of course — all couples did. Both of them were bitterly disappointed that she hadn't become pregnant yet. They wanted a baby so much. They didn't have a lot of money — but neither did anyone else in their social circle. That wasn't a top priority on their list of where happiness lay.

Mike and John were swigging down the beer she had paid for at the Safeway store, and getting more unstable with every bottle. They hadn't made a lot of sense when they were sober, and now Kari wondered if their inhibitions would disappear and all her efforts to reason with them wouldn't count for anything.

She should have been home by now. Surely, her husband would have called Sancho Panza to see why she was late. She prayed that someone was looking for her. And then she felt a new kind of panic. What if they did encounter the deputies or the highway patrol? Would there be a car chase — bullets fired into the car she was in? She knew John and Mike wouldn't hesitate to push her out of a moving car if they had to save themselves.

It seemed as if whatever was going to happen, she might not see the end of this day.

The "getaway" was proving to be one of the most inefficient escapes in California's criminal history. With all their turns, returns, missed freeways, and stops, in four hours they had logged less than fifty miles toward Reno. Mike had now decided to head to Auburn, northeast of Sacramento on U.S. 80. Both men were growing more insistent that Kari get them their three hundred dollars — or else.

Kari knew there was one last person she could ask for money. Her mother. She told her captors that she would ask her mother to wire three hundred dollars to the Western Union Office in Auburn.

"We can just pick it up there," she promised. "Within fifteen minutes of when she sends it."

Kari knew her mother would be able to hear tension in her voice, but she couldn't think of any way to tell her what was really happening. She would have to think of some code phrase that might work. John and his knife would be right there next to her, and he was likely to listen in to the conversation.

They pulled in beside an outside pay telephone booth in the North Highlands area of Sacramento. John walked Kari into the booth, holding his sleeved arm against her back. She felt the unyielding surface of the long knife blade there as it pressed against her. If she made a mistake, she could be dead within a few minutes, her life's blood gushing from her lungs or heart.

She tried to keep her voice steady as her mother answered her phone. She wondered what Kari was doing — knowing that at this time of morning, shortly after nine, she was usually sleeping after working all night.

"I'm on the road, Mom," Kari said. "And my car broke down. Could you wire me three hundred dollars?"

"Well . . . yes, I think so. What's wrong with your car?"

"I don't know for sure — but it will take three hundred dollars, and I don't have the right credit cards with me —"

"Are you OK? You sound kind of funny —"

"I'm fine, just tired."

"Where's Ben?"

"He's at work."

"And you're by yourself?"

"Sort of — Can you wire me the money?"

There was a long pause, and then Kari's

mother asked, "How do I send it?"

"Just call Western Union, and you can put it on your credit card. I'll pick it up in Auburn at their office there. Send it to *Kari Rowe* . . ."

"Your *maiden* name? Why?"

"No reason."

"But — what are you doing in Auburn?"

"I've gotta go now."

John had been about to grab the phone away from her, and Kari didn't want him asking her why she'd told her mother a different name. Kari hoped against hope that her mother would put two and two together, and know that her using her maiden name — when she never did — was a code. At least her mother knew now the general area where she was. It sounded as though her kidnapping *still* hadn't been reported. Her mother certainly didn't know about it.

Where was everybody? Were they really just waiting around for her to call back at two? She desperately needed them to call the police. At this point, Kari was willing to risk a police chase, and even a shoot-out. John and Mike were getting drunker and drunker.

Ben Lindholm's phone rang, and it was his mother-in-law. She had immediately picked up that something was wrong, but she'd come to the wrong conclusion. She thought that he and Kari had had an argument or something.

"Kari just called me from a phone booth someplace, and her car's broken down," Mary Rowe said. "Are you two having trouble? Did you break up? What is going on?"

Ben tried to convince her that everything was fine, but she grew more concerned, convinced that something was very wrong.

"Kari sounded breathless and nervous," Mary Rowe said. "And she talked so fast. I *know* that something's wrong and I want you to tell me. She asked me to wire her three hundred dollars. Why didn't she call you?"

Ben Lindholm sighed. Now he had to tell Mary the truth — that her daughter was missing. "Kari's been kidnapped," he said. Mary drew her breath in sharply.

"What can I do?" she asked.

"Send the money," he said. "If she's going to be in Auburn, I'll alert the police there. I'll have the detective in charge call you. At least we know where she is. And that she's alive."

Ray Van Eck called Kari's mother and explained what had happened, trying to reassure her that there were dozens of police officers looking for Kari.

"We know where she's headed now, and

we'll find her. If she calls back, just go along with whatever she says."

"Why — ?"

"We think that one of the men with her is listening in on her calls."

It was a terrible thing for a mother to hear, and all the assurances in the world didn't make Mary Rowe feel better. Van Eck promised to call her the moment they had any news at all. In the meantime, he asked her to wire the money to Kari.

Now Ray Van Eck had an alert sent out notifying CHP officers and city and county patrol officers to surveil Interstate 80 from south of Auburn to Reno, and Highway 50 from Sacramento to Lake Tahoe as well as Highways 49 and 89. In addition to California law enforcement officers, Douglas and Washoe counties in Nevada were placed on alert for Kari and the men who had her. Van Eck also arranged to work with Douglas County, Nevada, and the Casino Security network.

"Kari Lindholm has her paycheck with her and she may attempt to cash it," Van Eck said. "The most likely place to have that much money on hand would probably be a casino. And the suspects talked repeatedly about 'going gambling' so we expect them to show up at one of the casinos."

566

Van Eck called the Western Union Office in Auburn, and the phone rang until an answering machine came on and said it was closed. Next, he talked with detectives in the Auburn Police Department and asked them to locate the owner or operator so that the facility would be open as soon as possible. "We want the money drop to be completed under controlled circumstances," Van Eck said.

Ray Van Eck talked to the counselors at Sancho Panza, trying to get more of a handle on what kind of men they were dealing with. He spoke with the social worker named Matteo[*] who John Martin had specifically asked for.

"I know him," Matteo said. "He often came to Sancho Panza as a drop-in client or just to visit so he could talk with me. I established some rapport with him while he was a residential patient."

"Do you know who the other man with him might be?"

"No, I'm afraid I don't. I left Sancho Panza last May to help run the Horizon House in Vallejo. I haven't seen John since that time."

John Martin's file held the names of many people he had allegedly been associated with, but most of them turned out to be fictitious. The only "real" people in his file were his mother and an ex-girlfriend. Otherwise, he had either made up people or concocted fake names for those who came up in his therapy. He had served time in prison at Vacaville, and been arrested for rape since his parole. Counselors who had worked with him noted the rape he was arrested for during the previous May. They said he respected his mother but hated his father, who he claimed had brutalized him. He was totally unpredictable, but clever and charismatic when he wanted to be.

Kari had certainly seen that. Now, in her fifth hour of captivity, she could see that both John and Mike were on the verge of being intoxicated. They vacillated between telling her that they weren't going to hurt her to hinting darkly about how close she had come. "If you had been hysterical and tried to fight us," John said, "we probably would have killed you.

"We still might."

Still, they were headed toward Auburn and she felt she was very close to freedom. Something had to happen at Western Union. John and Mike, their tongues loosened by alcohol, appeared to have another change of heart. Now they apologized to Kari for kidnapping her, for the rape, and for scaring her.

"Maybe we should go back to Fairfield," John offered. "We can drive you back and surrender."

"Let's go," Kari said. "Let's do it now."

John smirked slyly. "No. I'm not that stupid. I'm not going back."

John had been playing head games. Kari made up her mind that she would seize the first possible chance to escape. She couldn't trust him at all. But he and Mike were growing sloppy and careless. The more they trusted her, the more lax they would become. She would pick her place to run. She felt she had nothing to lose.

They were driving into Auburn, but they made no effort to stop at Western Union, and kept right on going.

Kari's stomach flipped over.

John said he had to go to the bathroom and Kari said she did, too. They pulled into a Shell station, and John warned her, "Don't you try to split," as he went into the men's side. She had every intention of doing just that, but she could find no way out of the women's restroom other than the door, and one of the men stood outside all the time.

Police were already stationed all around the Western Union Office, watching for a car with two men and a woman in it.

Now Mike came up with another crazy

plan. His grip on reality had weakened as he drank beer after beer. He wanted to go to the North San Juan area to find his mother. "She put a hex on me," he told Kari. "If I take you to see her and tell her that you're my wife, she'll just *die* to see I'm married and that will take the hex off me."

"We'll make it a picnic," John said cheerfully.

Kari almost gave up. Instead of heading toward Reno, they were turning north toward Grass Valley. The area was sparsely populated, and she knew she would have less chance to escape with every mile.

"She lives in North San Juan," Mike said. "We'll go there and surprise her, and then we can go back and get the money in Auburn."

They stopped at the S&C Market in the little town to buy bread and bologna and more beer. John went to the bathroom again, and Mike stayed with Kari.

But Mike didn't have any money to pay for the groceries and he looked angry. John had kept it all in *his* pocket. They had to wait until he came back. Mike got fidgety whenever John was out of sight.

Kari didn't try to run. There was only one woman behind the counter, and she didn't look strong enough to be any protection. Mike drove up Highway 49, and slowed down to study the mailboxes alongside a dirt road. Kari saw he was looking at one that said something like "Hostead" on it.

"If we show up and she just looks at us, she'll fall down dead," Mike said grimly. "She'll see you and fall down dead . . ."

Kari hoped that he didn't mean that literally.

But his mother wasn't home. "We'll come back after we eat," Mike said.

They went a few miles farther and pulled into the Oregon Creek Campground just beyond the Nevada County/Yuba County line. They parked in an almost deserted part of the campground near the Yuba River, and Kari made sandwiches for them.

She had been with them for almost eight hours on a meandering, aimless journey. Before long it would be 2:00 P.M., and she didn't think she would be calling to let her husband and her coworkers back in Fairfield know that she was safe at that deadline. She wasn't safe — not at all.

The beer was getting to the men, and they could not walk a straight line. John turned to Kari and said, "Walk down the river with me."

She had no choice but to obey.

"Take off your stockings," he said. "So you can go wading."

Kari felt stark terror. She didn't want to do that, fearing that he was preparing to rape her again. She made excuses and managed to coax him back to where Mike was drinking beer.

"I kept handing them cans of beer," she recalls. "Trying to get them drunker."

John said he had to go to the bathroom again, and Kari said she wanted to go, too. They had quite a long walk to the rustic restrooms.

Without being obvious, Kari looked out of the corners of her eyes to see who else might be in the campground.

This was her last chance. She knew it in her heart.

While deputies and CHP officers were stationed outside the Western Union or patrolling the very roads over which they'd traveled, none of them had spotted Kari Lindholm and her captors. They didn't know that her Ford Granada had been dumped hours ago, or that they should be on the alert for a red and white Thunderbird.

Now John waited outside the women's restroom for a while, apparently wondering if he could trust Kari. She watched him through a window inside. She could see that he stumbled as he moved to lean against a wall. Neither of them had had any sleep the night before, but *she* wasn't drunk, and every synapse of her brain was working well.

She went over to one of the stalls and slammed the door loudly — but she didn't go in. When she moved silently back to the window, she saw John entering the men's side.

Looking beyond him, Kari saw several men dressed in hunting clothes who were sitting at a picnic table. They had guns beside them. After all the stops they had made where there were only women clerks, finally, there was someone who could protect her. John had a knife — but he didn't have a gun — and he wasn't close enough to stab her.

Kari made up her mind.

She walked out of the restroom without looking back and headed toward the picnic table where the hunters sat. Her back prickled with fear and she picked up speed, running toward the strangers. John still had the knife, and he was very drunk. Would he be so angry and frustrated that he might throw it at her? Adrenaline coursed through her body. The men who might rescue her seemed a long way away, but they were really quite close.

"I've been kidnapped," she cried. "Please help me!"

The startled men stared at her, their mouths dropping open. For a second, Kari wondered if they were going to turn away. She heard John slamming the restroom door, and she whirled. He walked toward them, and she saw that familiar look on his face — the "charmer," the man who believed he could talk his way out of anything. He must have his knife tucked up his sleeve.

"That's one of them," she said to the men. "Please. Please — I don't want to go with him."

Would they believe her? She knew that often strangers didn't want to get involved. They might think she was crazy — or that she'd been drinking.

And then one of the hunters — a middle-aged man — stood up, and he cradled his rifle in his hands, letting John see that he was armed.

"I don't believe the lady wants to go with you. I think you'd better leave," he said, standing between Kari and John.

John paused for a moment, stared at Kari, and then shook his head. He turned and walked back hurriedly to where Mike waited with the Ford Thunderbird.

Richard Bessey, his son, John Bessey,

eighteen, and Alan Kramar — all from La Mirada — quickly surrounded Kari and led her to their vehicle. They didn't know the circumstances, but she looked exhausted and as if she was in shock. She wore no shoes, and her clothing was wrinkled. They might be interfering in a domestic situation, a family fight, but they had seen the terror in the young woman's eyes, and they weren't going to leave her there.

As they headed out of the campground, Bessey saw that the suspects' car was right behind them. Both vehicles headed toward Highway 49, but the men in the Ford didn't try to stop Bessey's truck. When they reached the road, Bessey turned left toward North San Juan, and the red and white Thunderbird turned right and headed northbound on 49 — toward Downieville.

It was close to one in the afternoon when Kari and her rescuers walked into the S&C Market. The same woman was behind the counter, and she pointed toward a phone on the wall when they said they had to call the sheriff. When they reached the dispatcher at the Nevada County Sheriff's Office, Deputy Mike McPeters was dispatched to meet them at the North San Juan store.

McPeters asked Kari what had happened

575

to her, and if she was hurt. She told him she had been kidnapped and raped. And, yes, she could describe the men who abducted her and she was ready to give a statement. She didn't quite believe that she had survived her time with two dangerous, drunk, half-delusional men. But she had. She looked at the clock behind the counter. It was 1:37 P.M. on Sunday.

"Please let my husband and my mother know," she said to McPeters. "And tell my friends at Sancho Panza that I'm okay. Tell them I made the 2:00 P.M. call, with some time to spare."

Although Kari tried to hold herself together, McPeters could see that the disheveled woman was extremely upset, and she trembled as she tried to give him a preliminary statement.

Kari was in shock, and she had trouble remembering the order of the events that had begun the night before. Her captors had rambled here and there, retracing their travels, threatening to kill her if she didn't get money for them. The weird visit to Mike's mother's house out in the countryside was her most recent memory, and she had had a sense of doom about that. Mike so clearly hated his mother that she wondered if it would have been enough for him to introduce Kari as his wife? Or would he have ended up hurting both her and his mother? She had a better fix on John; she had even begun to predict what would set him off — but Mike had been somehow more frightening. His silence and the way he had spoken to Shelly when he was tying her up was more chilling than John's open threats.

"The knife might have been a Buck knife," Kari told Deputy McPeters. "It was long when it was open — probably eight or nine inches long. He always had it in his shirt sleeve — or his jacket sleeve."

A mile the other side of the Indian Valley Restaurant, a woman was driving at the speed limit when a red car came up behind her so fast that she thought it was going to rear-end her car. She sped up to stay ahead of it, but the other driver just went faster. She knew the road well, and worried about the many sharp curves ahead. If they met another car, they would all be dead. She looked for a wide spot where she could get over to the shoulder and let them pass. She found one just in time as they were trying to edge her off. The two men in the car waved to her in thanks as they sped past.

She saw someone in the car ahead throw a bag out of the window, and then the Thunderbird disappeared.

Now she saw a CHP officer heading toward her, and a few miles up the road she saw a sheriff's car making a U-turn, and heading in the direction of the speeding car. Several miles farther on, she saw the deputy had pulled the Thunderbird over, and that he had two men leaning over the back of it. He was attempting to hold them and radio for backup at the same time.

"One of the men got back in the car and tried to escape," she later told the sheriff's detectives. "But they stopped him."

Nevada County Deputy Albert Johnson and Sierra County Deputy David Marshall arrested Mike Hutson, thirty-five, and John Martin, thirty-four, less than a half hour after Kari Lindholm ran to freedom.

Their rented Thunderbird was a treasure trove of evidence. Kari Lindholm's and Shelly Corelli's credit and ID cards were all there, solid physical links between the kidnappers and the victims. There were fifteen empty twelve-ounce beer cans, and the remains of the "picnic" — a loaf of Rainbow wholewheat bread and a pack of lunch meat. The beer was Olympia and Miller High Life, and John and Mike had been even more eclectic in their choice of cigarette brands: Pall Malls, Marlboros, and Kool Lights.

Kari's nylons were on the floor of the backseat, and her Nordstrom's sweater, turned
inside out.

John Martin and Mike Hutson were taken
first to the Sierra County Jail in Downieville,
and later transferred back to Solano County
to be booked into jail there.

Whatever John's and Mike's grievances
against a cruel and uncaring world had been
before they abducted Kari, they had esca-
lated their troubles through their bumbling,
obviously unchoreographed kidnapping.
Even so, they were infinitely dangerous, the
way a vicious dog is — just because they
were so unpredictable. Had Kari Lindholm
not taken a chance and run away from John
in the campground that was far away from
where she was kidnapped, they might well
have killed her.

She would always think of what *might* have
happened if the hunters hadn't stopped for
lunch at precisely the time she and her kidnappers were at the campground. Sober,
John and Mike went back and forth about
what they would do to her. Drunk, they had
looked at her with different, colder eyes.

Deputies took Kari to the Sierra Nevada
Memorial Miner's Hospital in Grass Valley
for an examination to establish that she had

been raped, and to glean what physical evidence there might be. Doctors there brought out a rape kit, and took swabs, washings, and combings from her pubic area and her vaginal vault. They retrieved dark pubic hairs — not her own — and preserved some non-motile sperm cells. They would help to convict John of raping her.

It was hideously ironic; Kari and her husband had been trying to get pregnant for months without success. And now she was afraid she might be pregnant from the rape.

"If your next period is late," the ER doctor said, "I think you should take an early pregnancy test."

She felt sick.

There was no effective antipregnancy pill at the time, and what if she was pregnant with her husband's baby and didn't know it yet? If she should prove to have conceived, and chose to have an abortion, she might be killing the baby they had both longed for.

She also dreaded that she had contracted some sexually transmitted disease. The doctor wrote a prescription for a heavy dose of antibiotics just in case. "Keep taking them," he warned, "until they're all gone. And, of course, you'll have to be tested for a number of diseases."

The meds made her violently ill, and she

vomited often. (Long after Kari had recovered somewhat from her initial shock, she continued to have nausea from the prophylactic pills. But when she asked why her rapist couldn't be *tested* to see if he had any disease, she was told that wasn't possible because that would "rob him of his rights to privacy!")

Back in the world that had seemed safe only the day before, Kari found that everything had changed. She couldn't go back to the job she loved at Sancho Panza. She was suffering from post-traumatic stress syndrome so severe that she had to go on disability. She had really never known fear before, but being in the big old house that was Sancho Panza triggered too many memories.

Kari had not become pregnant after being raped, and that was a tremendous relief. She kept taking the meds that would fight STDs and, eventually, got a clean bill of health. John Martin was never tested — which would have saved her months of nausea from the antibiotics.

When Kari failed to conceive, she learned about a baby that might be available for adoption. "That one good thing happened, though," Kari remembers. "I wasn't pregnant and I couldn't get pregnant with my husband. One of the alumnae at Sancho Panza was about to have a baby that she could not keep. We adopted him. He had his problems; he was born with fetal alcohol syndrome because of her drinking, but we never regretted adopting him. We felt blessed to have him. He's a wonderful boy who overcame so much."

Unfortunately, Kari and Ben's good marriage gradually disintegrated, too often one of the tragic aftermaths when a wife has been raped. Some men can cope with it, and others cannot get it out of their minds. Even though they understand intellectually that a forced sexual attack is nothing their wives wanted or caused, some husbands can't deal with it emotionally. Ben and Kari Lindholm were divorced after eight years of marriage.

"My being raped was a large part of the problem," she says. "It was a difficult time and we had a tough custody fight over our adopted son — although it's all right now."

Kari eventually married again, and with her second husband concieved four children to join her beloved adopted son.

Even so, her trials weren't over. In 1998, at the age of forty-five, Kari was diagnosed with stage-three breast cancer, which had infiltrated her lymph nodes. Showing the determination and fighting spirit that she had demonstrated during her kidnapping, Kari refused to give up.

"I had three different series of chemo treatments, radiation, and a bone marrow transplant, but I'm now clear of cancer."

No longer able to work as a crisis counselor because the frightening memories tend to surge back, Kari has another career now. Living far away from the scene of the crimes against her, she still deals with people, but when John Martin and Mike Hutson abducted her, they effectively robbed others in crisis — people much like themselves — of a kind and caring counselor. Violent crime reverberates like the endless aftershocks of the earthquakes that are often felt in Solano County, California.

As for John Martin and Mike Hutson, they were sentenced to very long prison terms. Kari heard that Martin died in prison a few years after she escaped from her kidnappers. She believes Mike Hutson was eventually paroled, but his records have been swallowed up in the vast California criminal justice system.

Although it was Martin who raped Kari, she remembers being more afraid of his quiet partner in crime: "He didn't say much, and I never knew what he might do, and that was the most frightening thing of all."